Praise for *The Global Brain*

"*The Global Brain* provokes innovation practitioners with fresh conceptual and practical insights as it explores the rapidly evolving landscape of network-centric innovation that promises to achieve higher innovation productivity. A must read for global corporations seeking to differentiate themselves through innovation in a highly competitive marketplace."

—Uma Chowdhry, Senior Vice President and
Chief Science and Technology Officer, DuPont

"You can not get comfortable in today's world. You continually need to think of what is next and how you can improve upon where you are today. *The Global Brain* will not give you the answers—no book will. What this book does, backed by thorough research, is help you to open up the broad range of options and opportunities available to successfully innovate within your specific environment—this is where I see *The Global Brain* as a competitive advantage."

—Jeff Jansma, Director, New Product Commercialization,
Herman Miller

"You will find yourself referring often to *The Global Brain* as you chart your course forward on network-centric innovation approaches. A must read book on this topic."

—Vijay Govindarajan, Earl C. Daum Professor of International
Business, Tuck School, Dartmouth, Co-author,
Ten Rules for Strategic Innovators

"Innovation in the 21st century requires a fundamental shift in thinking and approach. Nambisan and Sawhney offer a systematic and incisive analysis of the diverse opportunities available to companies to tap into the Global Brain. You will come away with a clear understanding of the best options for your company, and the most effective means to pursue them. A superb book!"

—Denis Browne, Senior Vice President, Imagineering, SAP Labs

"This book provides an engaging and insightful account of a phenomenon that is of interest to practitioners and theorists alike. Innovation is no longer confined within firm boundaries and the increasingly distributed model of innovation is amply evident to most observers. Readers will find a succinct and powerful set of ideas on this novel phenomenon. A must read for managers and researchers."

—Ranjay Gulati, Michael L. Nemmers Distinguished Professor
of Strategy and Organizations, Kellogg School of Management

"Successful innovation is a difficult, often confusing, wilderness-like journey. This book gives you the map and the tools to master the challenges and forge a high speed path to innovative success."

—Toby Redshaw, Corporate Vice President, Innovation, Data Enabling
Platforms and Architecture, Motorola

"*The Global Brain* captures the mind and imagination instantly! Its focus on profitable growth, lesson on "how the mighty can stumble," insights on "Network-Centricity," and a road map for navigating the landscape for innovation, make it a very compelling book to read. Executives at middle to senior levels, who want to go beyond company walls to innovate, compete, and grow must read Nambisan and Sawhney's *The Global Brain*."

—Harit Talwar, Executive Vice President, Discover Financial Services

"The world in which we develop products and services has forever changed and *The Global Brain* is a great aid in understanding how. This book has the right combination of theory, practical examples and frameworks to help advance the way companies think about innovation. It should be required reading for managers in both large and small enterprises."

—Rod Nelson, Vice President,
Innovation and Collaboration, Schlumberger

THE
GLOBAL
BRAIN

THE
GLOBAL
BRAIN

Your Roadmap for Innovating
Faster and Smarter
in a Networked World

SATISH NAMBISAN
MOHANBIR SAWHNEY

Vice President, Publisher: Tim Moore
Associate Publisher and Director of Marketing: Amy Neidlinger
Wharton Editor: Yoram (Jerry) Wind
Acquisitions Editor: Martha Cooley
Editorial Assistant: Pamela Boland
Development Editor: Russ Hall
Digital Marketing Manager: Julie Phifer
Publicist: Amy Fandrei
Marketing Coordinator: Megan Colvin
Cover Designer: Chuti Prasertsith
Managing Editor: Gina Kanouse
Project Editor: Chelsey Marti
Copy Editor: Paula Lowell
Proofreader: Water Crest Publishing
Indexer: Angie Bess Martin
Compositor: Nonie Ratcliff
Manufacturing Buyer: Dan Uhrig

© 2008 by Pearson Education, Inc.

⦏⦐ Wharton School Publishing Publishing as Wharton School Publishing
Upper Saddle River, New Jersey 07458

Wharton School Publishing offers excellent discounts on this book when ordered in quantity for bulk purchases or special sales. For more information, please contact U.S. Corporate and Government Sales, 1-800-382-3419, corpsales@pearsontechgroup.com. For sales outside the U.S., please contact International Sales at international@pearsoned.com.

Company and product names mentioned herein are the trademarks or registered trademarks of their respective owners.

Printed in the United States of America

First Printing October 2007

ISBN-10 0-13-233951-X
ISBN-13 978-0-13-233951-3

Pearson Education LTD.
Pearson Education Australia PTY, Limited.
Pearson Education Singapore, Pte. Ltd.
Pearson Education North Asia, Ltd.
Pearson Education Canada, Ltd.
Pearson Educación de Mexico, S.A. de C.V.
Pearson Education—Japan
Pearson Education Malaysia, Pte. Ltd.

Library of Congress Cataloging-in-Publication Data

Nambisan, Satish
   The global brain : your roadmap for innovating faster and smarter in a networked world / Satish Nambisan, Mohanbir Sawhney.
      p. cm.
   ISBN 0-13-233951-X (hardback : alk. paper) 1. Technological innovations—Management.
2. Business enterprises—Technological innovations. 3. Business networks. I. Sawhney,
Mohanbir S. II. Title.
   HD45.S324 2008
   658.4'063—dc22

                                                              2007026100

To Priya and Parminder

CONTENTS

Foreword xvii

Introduction 1

Part I   From *Firm-Centric* to *Network-Centric*
          Innovation 9

          Chapter 1   The Power of Network-Centricity 11

          Chapter 2   Understanding Network-Centric Innovation 29

Part II   The Landscape of Network-Centric Innovation 49

          Chapter 3   The Four Models of Network-Centric
                       Innovation 51

          Chapter 4   Innovation Networks: The Players and
                       the Plays 67

Part III The Four Models of Network-Centric Innovation 83

          Chapter 5   The Orchestra Model 85

          Chapter 6   The Creative Bazaar Model 113

          Chapter 7   The Jam Central Model 139

          Chapter 8   The MOD ("MODification") Station Model 157

Part IV Executing Network-Centric Innovation 175

　　　　Chapter 9   Deciding Where and How to Play 177

　　　　Chapter 10   Preparing the Organization 197

Part V   Globalization and Network-Centric Innovation 217

　　　　Chapter 11   Globalizing Network-Centric Innovation:
　　　　　　　　　　The Dragon and the Tiger 219

　　　　Chapter 12   Concluding Thoughts & Actions for
　　　　　　　　　　"Monday" Morning 237

　　　　　　　　　　References 253

　　　　　　　　　　Index 267

Acknowledgments

Writing this book has been a labor of love for both of us, but it has been a labor that has been generously encouraged and supported by a large number of people who contributed their time and thoughts and to whom we acknowledge our deep gratitude.

Our interactions with Uma Chowdhry of DuPont, Irving Wladawsky-Berger and Dan McGrath of IBM, Tom Cripe of P&G, and Debra Park of Dial Corporation were instrumental in shaping our early ideas and the frameworks presented in this book. We also benefited tremendously from our conversations with the following people, each of whom generously gave their time and shared their insights on various topics: Dave Bayless, Henry Chesbrough, Steve Cugine, David Duncan, Jevin Eagle, Gary Einhaus, Robert Finnochiaro, John Funk, Harvey Gideon, Sharon Grosh, Adam Gross, Laurie Kien-Kotcher, Bill Lazaroff, Stephen Mallenbaum, Richard Marken, Stephen Maurer, Gregg McPherson, Kim Pugliese, Arti Rai, Andrej Sali, Catherine Strader, Scott Strode, Ginger Taylor, Dave Weaver, Brandon Williams, David Ylitalo, and David Yuan. There are many others—both in academia and in the industry—who critiqued our ideas and offered thoughtful comments and suggestions and to whom we are much indebted.

Several people helped us in organizing our interviews and managing our schedules related to this book. We would like to thank Jeff Horn for assisting us in our research, and we would also like to thank Gordon Evans, Jeff Leroy, Ann Schmidt, and several others who helped us in identifying the appropriate person in the various organizations and scheduling our interviews. Rahi Gurung provided valuable administrative assistance at Kellogg.

Satish would like to acknowledge his gratitude to the Kellogg School of Management and to the Center for Research in Technology & Innovation (CRTI) at Northwestern University for generously hosting his sabbatical and facilitating the initial research work that led to this book. He would like to thank Dean Dipak Jain of Kellogg for his encouragement and interest in this project. He would also like to thank Ranjay Gulati, Jim Conley, Mark Jeffrey, Rob Wolcott, and other friends and colleagues at Kellogg and CRTI for being very helpful and for making his stay both enjoyable and intellectually stimulating.

Satish also thanks Robert Baron—his friend, mentor, and colleague at Rensselaer Polytechnic Institute (RPI)—for his intellectual partnership and patience as a co-author in his other research projects during the writing of this book. He would also like to express his appreciation to President Shirley Jackson and other academic leaders at RPI for promoting research on innovation management and for bringing a vibrant, inter-disciplinary focus to this important topic.

Satish would like to express his deep gratitude to his wife Priya for her boundless enthusiasm, constant encouragement, and for believing in this book from the first day onward. She found the time—amid her own hectic schedule as a first-year assistant professor—to read the individual chapters and give comments and suggestions and to serve at various times as a sounding board, cheerleader, critic, editor, and advisor. Her unwavering love and friendship and her adventurous mind continue to be the source of joy, inspiration, and strength for Satish in his work and life.

Mohan would like to thank all the participants of the Kellogg Innovation Network who have supported our research and have served as a valuable sounding board for our ideas. He would particularly like to thank Blythe McGarvey for her incisive comments on the manuscript, Rob Wolcott for his intellectual partnership, Toby Redshaw for his intellectual provocation, and Mark Karasek for his unwavering support of the KIN. Mohan would also like to thank Dean Dipak Jain for believing in him and the Center's mission, as well as all his colleagues in the Center, including James Conley, Mark Jeffery, Rob Wolcott, and Bob Cooper.

Mohan would also like to express his profound gratitude to his new wife Parminder for being patient with him as he was working on the book while managing a long-distance relationship. Her love and support was the guiding light that kept Mohan going. And Mohan would like to thank his kids Asha and Bundev for the joy they bring to his life, and for staying out of the way while Dad worked on the book!

We would like to thank Jerry Wind of Wharton for believing in our ideas for this book and driving us to actually start writing it. We would also like to thank Tim Moore, Russ Hall, Martha Cooley, Chelsey Marti, and the rest of the Wharton School Publishing team for their commitment and enthusiastic support. Thanks are also due to Tom Stewart and Paul Hemp of *Harvard Business Review* for their support and encouragement of our ideas.

About the Authors

Satish Nambisan is a professor of technology management and strategy at the Lally School of Management, Rensselaer Polytechnic Institute in Troy, New York. He is a globally recognized researcher and thought-leader in the areas of innovation management and technology strategy, and his recent research work has focused on customer co-innovation, network-centric innovation, and IT-enabled product development. His research has been published in premier management journals such as *Harvard Business Review*, *MIT Sloan Management Review*, *Management Science*, and *Academy of Management Review*. Through his consulting work and executive lectures, Satish has helped many companies in the United States, Singapore, and India in managing innovation and product development. Prior to joining the academia, Satish held executive positions at the consumer-products giant Unilever Plc. in Mumbai, India. More details about his research and consulting are available at www.satish-nambisan.com.

Mohanbir Sawhney is the McCormick Tribune Professor of Technology and the Director of the Center for Research in Technology & Innovation at the Kellogg School of Management, Northwestern University. He is a widely published expert in the areas of innovation, marketing, and strategy. He has authored several influential articles in publications like the *Harvard Business Review* and the *MIT Sloan Management Review*. His contributions to the literature on innovation include concepts like mediated innovation, community-centric innovation, and collaborative innovation with customers in a networked world. He consults with and advises dozens of Global 2000 companies around the world. This is his fourth book.

Foreword

When Satish and Mohan asked me to write the foreword to this book, I could hardly contain my enthusiasm. Not only was I already immersed in the subject matter by virtue of my job, but I saw an opportunity to summarize some four years of acute observation and learning on a topic that is driving a new level of global, socio-economic transformation. We are in the midst of one of those rare inflection points that will forever change the way work is conducted, the way new opportunity is created, and how value is extracted from our endeavors. Of course, we are talking about the uniquely 21st century phenomena of collaborative innovation.

Certainly it is on everyone's minds. CEOs, government officials, academic and community leaders around the world are all counting on "innovation" to be the fundamental driver of economic opportunity, job creation, business competitiveness and advances in education, health care, and a vast range of other disciplines. Investing in innovation, they say, is the surest way to survive and thrive in today's complex, connected world.

But what do they really mean when they talk about innovation? Inside the information technology industry, innovation has been defined historically by the process of invention and discovery, and driven by investments in Research and Development. Bell Labs, Xerox PARC and IBM Research, along with basic research programs at the world's leading universities, epitomized the innovation engines of the 20th century.

They also operated in classic "ivory tower" mode—highly secretive and proprietary in their approaches, sharing little with others and, as a result, sometimes suffering from pain-stakingly slow paths to market for their best ideas.

But the world has changed dramatically over the past decade—and even more so, the basic nature of innovation itself. This shift first became evident earlier this decade.

Early in 2004, I had the great privilege of participating in two major initiatives to study how and why the nature of innovation is changing and the impact on business, governments, and our global society. The first was the National Innovation Initiative (NII), a special study group sponsored by the Council on Competitiveness. The NII comprised some 200 CEOs, university presidents and labor leaders whose collective mission was to help restart America's innovation engine.

Around the same time, IBM launched a unique project called the Global Innovation Outlook (GIO)—a vastly different way of identifying and acting on emerging trends, policy matters, and market opportunities, driven by input from hundreds of big thinkers in a diverse range of disciplines around the world.

We all learned a great deal from those exercises. It seems obvious now, but perhaps the most valuable finding was deep new insight into the sweeping shift in the way innovation is created, managed and delivered.

So why has the nature of innovation changed so dramatically? There are many factors, including: the dynamics of a flattening world, the march of commoditization, the rapid and global adoption of new technologies, and particularly, the open movement.

Innovation happens much faster today, and it diffuses much more rapidly into our everyday lives. It no longer is the domain of a solitary genius seeking to take the world by storm. Instead, innovation is increasingly:

Global. The widespread adoptions of networked technologies and open standards have removed barriers of geography and accessibility. Billions of people, even in the most remote regions of the world, have ready, affordable access to advanced wireless technologies and the Internet. Hitching high-speed rides on these platforms, ideas now circumnavigate the globe in a matter of minutes, if not seconds. As a result, almost anyone with a good idea can now participate in the innovation economy.

Multidisciplinary. Because the global challenges we face today are far more complex, innovation now requires a diverse mix of talent and expertise.

Consider the mapping of the human genome. Until recently, that type of research could only be conducted in wet labs, in the physical realm.

But now, incredible advances in information technology make it practical to model and process genetic information in ways never before possible.

Life Sciences just may very well be the defining science of the 21st century. At its core is the application of silicon chips, database software and powerful, lightning quick computers. To be a leader in this emerging field, you need to be as knowledgeable and facile in these domains as you are in biology and related sciences. That's a daunting and unprecedented challenge, but also a fruitful approach to unlocking new ideas and approaches to discovery that might not have otherwise emerged.

Collaborative and Open. Just about every study on innovation identifies the power of collaboration and communities as one of the major forces driving innovation in today's environment. Our first GIO exercise, for example, identified the "power of networks" as one of its top findings. Participants told us that, increasingly, their power comes largely from their ability to tap into—and sometimes transform—a larger network of people and ideas.

Similarly, more and more businesses recognize that there are a lot more capabilities for innovation in the marketplace than they could try to create on their own, no matter how big and powerful the company.

One of the key themes that emerged from a 2006 CEO study we conducted was that external collaboration is indispensable for innovation. We interviewed nearly 800 CEOs, representing a wide swath of geographic areas, a range of annual revenues, and everything from small and medium businesses to large, global enterprises. When asked which sources their companies relied on for their innovative ideas, "business partners" were right near the top of the list, just behind the general employee population.

"Customers" rounded out the top of the list, meaning that the top three significant sources of innovative ideas are predicated on open, collaborative approaches, including reaching outside the organization. In fact, CEOs said they are getting about twice as many innovation insights from customers as they are from their own sales and service organizations.

Perhaps most surprising was that "Internal R&D" was second-to-last on the list. As a career engineer and scientist-turned businessman, I would argue that those who do not see value returning from their R&D investments are not managing their portfolios to reflect the changes underway in the marketplace. In other words, they still are not collaborating externally and working directly with their customers. IBM Research is in the midst of a renaissance as a result of embracing market input. But that's probably fodder for another book entirely.

The CEOs also told us that partnering—whether crossing internal or external boundaries—is easy in principle, but very difficult in practice. This is not at all surprising. Working with different groups to achieve common objectives usually requires a change in the culture of most organizations, and cultural transformations may be the hardest of all. I am convinced that to truly embrace a culture of collaboration you must accept limitations in your ability to get things done without help.

This is particularly important for those companies, like IBM, who are addressing problems in business, government, health care, technology, and science that are very sophisticated in nature and pushing the limits of what is possible. We have learned that we cannot work on problems such as information-based medicine, integrated supply chains or advanced engineering design unless we have established a very close relationship with clients, business partners, and even other vendors who might very well be competitors.

In such an environment, to boast about being "the best" would frankly be considered crass, a sign of corporate insecurity rather than the strength of a confident leader. Instead, you want to be known as a company that helps all the various members of the team succeed in whatever problems are being addressed. Rather than claiming that you are the most innovative of companies, you want to be known as a company that helps those with whom you work become more innovative themselves.

The open movement makes all of that possible. It holds the potential to spark remarkable innovation—and also turn historical cost structures and investment models on their ears. The Linux operating system, for example, is owned by no one, yet owned by everyone at the same time.

Thousands upon thousands of programmers around the world contribute to it and make it better, creating a checks and balances system that would be impossible with proprietary, closed systems.

Historically, we know it takes about $1 billion to bring an enterprise-ready operating system to the marketplace for one computing platform. By working with the open community, we at IBM were able to get Linux across our entire product line with about one-fifth the investment we would normally make for just one platform. We did it through a combination of Linux code developed by the community, Linux code we contributed to the open community, and Linux code we developed uniquely to better support it on our products. As a result, our offerings are better tested, more robust and are market-ready more immediately.

The open movement creates a common base for infrastructure, so that the wheel never has to be re-invented. The basics are already there and agreed-upon by the global community. That enables creators to leapfrog over the mundane, and jump right to the innovative—being assured that the infrastructure is sound and secure because it has been refined and tempered by great thinkers around the world.

When more people have access to the building blocks of innovation, rich new perspectives and diverse influences are injected into the creative process. People begin to think in an interdependent, collaborative way—across disciplines, and collaborating at the intersections between them.

True innovation, then, is driven by the ecosystem; by listening to and learning from the various constituents with whom you exchange dialog and who may add value to the discussion. By embracing your ecosystem, you tear down the boundaries of culture, geography and organization to rapidly generate ideas and act on changes.

The first step is modeling your organization's own ecosystem—all the major constituency groups that are vital to your business success. I offer one approach here (see the following Figure) simply as a framework. There really is no right or wrong model, unless you choose to go it alone.

Second, you need to commit to a two-way dialogue with each of these constituencies—and also foster interaction between them, both with you and without you. You cannot control them anymore, or simply pump one-way messages and demands out to them. They will go elsewhere and collaborate with more receptive partners.

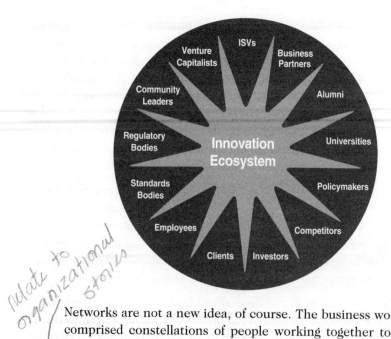

relate to organizational stories

Networks are not a new idea, of course. The business world has always comprised constellations of people working together to create value. But in the past, those relationships have generally been more limited and exclusionary in nature, bound by strictly defined legal agreements and financial understandings.

Over the past decade, however, the proliferation of communication networks has not only connected people, places and ideas in unprecedented ways, but also catalyzed the evolution of social structures. With the freedom to transcend physical and geographic borders more easily, we are more willing to partner inside and outside our traditional boundaries of organizations and countries.

Because of that shift, the 20th-century business enterprise as we know it could be history. Increasingly, the motivating force that brings people together for work is less "a business organization" and more the collective enterprise—activities driven by a common set of interests, goals or values.

The trend is accelerating, and it will have profound implications on how companies think about everything from leadership to managing and motivating global talent. It will change the way companies approach innovation itself.

As boundaries dissolve, as more fluid relationships form, as ecosystems expand, and as networks get larger, the very nature of decision-making for individuals, businesses, and the world takes on a new shape. Local actions now have global consequences, and the reverse is true as well.

To pursue open, collaborative innovation, enterprises simply must find ways to tap into the potential of the skill, talent, and creativity of people from different teams in different organizations across the globe. A company can only be as innovative as the collective capacity of the people who make up its ecosystem. And to attract and retain talented people, a company must enable those people to feel respected, as individuals, as professionals and as members of a team. The company must trust those people and encourage them to collaborate and innovate with colleagues inside and outside the business, driven as much by pride of contribution as by loyalty to the company.

These new models for collaboration offer a financial payoff as well. Studies show that companies that outperform their peer groups are much more likely to have adopted business models that focus on core expertise and collaboration with partners, rather than by strengthening their command and control posture.

Consider Bharti Tele-Ventures, the largest private telephone company in India. It recently outsourced and integrated its core functions—such as network and program management, help desk support, disaster recovery, IT, and billing—which freed it to focus exclusively on marketing and customer service strategies. As a result, Bharti tripled its subscriber base—from 6 million to 18 million subscribers—in just 20 months.

But success stories like that do not come easy. As fewer companies directly control all aspects of their operations, it becomes harder to ensure that brand experience consistently lives up to brand promise. How can a company ensure that the individuals and business partners who power its network fully understand its brand and are motivated to protect and uphold it?

During the Global Innovation Outlook sessions, several participants advanced a concept built around the term "Reputation Capital." It describes a kind of currency for building trust in a prospective worker's personal and professional qualifications. They cited examples such as Wikipedia and eBay, both of which built successful brands based on the contributions of hundreds of thousands of non-affiliated individuals.

In each case, there are standards in place enabling people to see and rate the integrity and credibility of contributors. The more a contributor consistently demonstrates a high level of accountability and quality, the more value the contributor garners. Even for businesses not built around the contributions of individuals, reputation capital has intriguing possibilities—especially for emerging global players who have only a virtual presence and no visible brand of their own.

I am convinced that the art of collaboration will be the most distinguishing leadership characteristic of the 21st century. Universities need to teach it. Government policies and regulations need to facilitate it.

For collaborative innovation to become part of our collective DNA, we must accept the notion that the surest way to make progress and solve problems is to tap into the collective knowledge of the team. Networked enterprises are the future. No individual enterprise, no matter how large and talented, can afford to go it alone in today's highly competitive, globally integrated marketplace.

Success in tapping into such a global marketplace of innovators and experts—the "Global Brain" as Satish and Mohan call it—requires companies to first develop a sound understanding of the collaborative landscape and then decide on an approach that suits them the best. One size does not fit all in this regard.

In this book, Satish and Mohan provide a rich description of the different models of networked innovation and offer a set of guidelines for companies to identify and prepare for the most promising collaborative innovation opportunities. As they emphasize, success also requires us to rethink the very nature of our relationships with innovation partners – what we need to control and what we need to let go.

I think we will find that the sacrifices, and the benefits, are well worth the journey.

Nick Donofrio

Executive Vice President for Innovation and Technology at IBM Corporation

Introduction

Innovation is critical for profitable growth. In their search for innovative ideas and technologies, companies are realizing the importance of reaching out to customers, partners, suppliers, amateur inventors, academic researchers, scientists, innovation brokers, and a host of other external entities that together constitute the Global Brain—the vast creative potential that lies beyond the boundaries of the firm. Terms such as communities of creation, innovation networks, open market innovation, and crowdsourcing are being used to refer to the future of innovation in a connected world. The promise of such *network-centric* innovation approaches is resonating in the executive suites of large corporations. A recent survey of CEOs found that the need to expand the innovation horizon by looking beyond the four walls of the company is at the top of the CEO agenda.[1] However, most executives feel that they don't know how to reach the Promised Land. Our conversations with senior executives charged with innovation initiatives suggest that they struggle with a question of singular importance, "How should we *really* go about harnessing the creative power of the Global Brain to enhance our growth and performance?"

Recent examples from companies such as P&G, IBM, Boeing, and Apple illustrate that externally focused innovation can take many forms. There are many different entities that companies can reach out to and many different types of relationships and networks they can create to harness innovative ideas. Questions abound: What are the different approaches to harnessing external networks for innovation? Which approach is best for our firm? What kinds of innovation projects lend themselves well for these approaches? What role should our firm play in our innovation network? To answer these questions, managers need a good understanding of the emerging landscape of network-centric innovation. Only with a good view of the landscape will they be able to identify the opportunities that network-centric innovation presents.

Beyond the identification of opportunities lie additional questions managers need to ask in exploiting the opportunities. What organizational capabilities do we need? How should our innovation network be designed? What benefits can we expect and how do we measure these benefits? What are the potential risks of opening up innovation? Is there a danger that we could lose control over our innovation initiatives? How should we protect our intellectual property? How should we define success?

We wrote this book to answer these two sets of questions in a practical and direct way so that companies—both large and small—can *explore* as well as *exploit* the power of the Global Brain. We hope to take you on a journey that begins with an awareness of the nature and potential of network-centric innovation to a destination where you will be able to implement a network-centric innovation strategy for your firm.

Throughout this book we will use both these terms: Global Brain to describe the diverse set of external players that constitute the innovation network for the companies; Network-centric innovation to describe the underlying principles of collaborative innovation in such a context.

HOW THIS BOOK CAME ABOUT

Both of the authors have been students of innovation for several years. Ever since the Internet gained critical mass and firms started to realize the power of networks and communities, we have been particularly interested in understanding the nature and the implications of distributed innovation, community-based innovation, and innovation networks.

Satish had studied "Virtual Customer Environments" and the role customers play in supporting and enhancing companies' innovation efforts.[2] Mohan had written about the emerging phenomenon of "Communities of Creation" in different contexts and examined their promise as a way of organizing commercial innovation initiatives.[3] Our work had also focused on new types of innovation intermediaries—or "Innomediaries" as Mohan calls them[4]—that link companies with external networks and communities.

A common theme in our research was our interest in the concept of distributed innovation—innovation initiatives that are spread across a diverse network of partners. In the summer of 2005, we participated in a research symposium on distributed innovation organized as part of the Annual Academy of Management Meeting held in Hawaii. While enjoying the sun and the beaches, we began a conversation on the growing importance of innovation networks and communities of creation. Both of us were convinced about the promise and the potential of innovation initiatives centered on such networks of individual inventors, customers, and partners. We believed, based on early evidence from the software and automotive industries, that innovation could be made far more efficient, effective, and speedy if firms could harness all the talent and ideas that lie outside their boundaries. But we suspected that, despite all the hype about the innovative power of external networks, managers had very limited guidance for implementing such network-centric innovation initiatives. We decided to explore this hunch further, to see whether we could make a contribution in this area.

Our vehicle for this exploration was the Kellogg Innovation Network (KIN)—a forum for senior innovation managers of large companies—affiliated with the Center for Research in Innovation and Technology that Mohan directs at the Kellogg School of Management. The KIN is an excellent example of the power of the Global Brain in action. It consists of senior executives from a hand-selected group of leading companies who come together in a collaborative forum to exchange ideas and best practices related to innovation. The research agenda for the KIN emerges from dialogue, discussion, and debate among the members. We initiated conversations with senior managers from KIN member companies such as Motorola, DuPont, IBM, Kraft, and Cargill. We presented our ideas on network-centric innovation in KIN seminars, and our discussions revealed that our hunch was accurate. Most managers indicated that they were very excited and enthusiastic about the opportunities posed by external innovation networks and communities, but were less convinced about their own capabilities to implement such initiatives that involve reaching out to external networks successfully. And all the media hype and buzz about open innovation, open source software, social networking, and Internet-based innovation wasn't helping. There was a lot of heat and dust, but very little enlightenment when it came to execution-related issues.

A survey of senior managers conducted by the management consulting company, Bain & Co., in 2005 supports our observation. A majority (73%) of the survey respondents agreed that companies "can dramatically boost their innovation by collaborating with outsiders," but they simultaneously expressed "deep dissatisfaction with (their) knowledge about appropriate strategies, practices, and tools" for executing such network-centric innovation.[5]

For companies to be successful in making the shift from *firm-centric* innovation to *network-centric* innovation, managers need to progress beyond a basic awareness of the potential. They need to understand the landscape of network-centric innovation. Next, they need to know the strategies and best practices that are relevant to their business context. We felt that there was a need for a book that would help managers to take these two important steps so they could harness the unbounded creative potential that lies outside their four walls.

After we decided to embark on the book project, we began with an extensive review of the academic literature as well as practitioner-oriented articles and books in the area of innovation management and networks. This review provided the background material for developing our frameworks and concepts. Next, we identified a number of companies that were leaders in externally focused innovation. These companies ranged from consumer product companies such as Dial, P&G, Staples, and Unilever to technology companies such as IBM, DuPont, Boeing, 3M, and Cisco. We decided to learn from the leaders by conducting in-depth interviews with managers leading innovation initiatives at these firms. Over a period of one year, we talked with more than 50 managers from a wide variety of firms to develop and validate our frameworks and concepts. We also talked with and analyzed the business models of boutique firms that are playing specialist intermediary roles in network-centric innovation. These companies included innovation facilitators like IgniteIP, Eureka Ranch, Evergreen IP, and InnoCentive. We also interviewed several individuals who have played leadership roles in the Open Source Software movement and other network-centric innovation contexts such as online customer communities. The diverse experiences and perspectives that we gleaned from these interviews helped us to develop the frameworks and insights related to network-centric innovation that form the core content of this book.

WHO SHOULD READ THIS BOOK

We have written this book for two primary audiences with a deep interest in innovation management.

The first audience is a CEO or senior business executive who has the primary responsibility for growth and innovation of a business unit or a major corporation. For this audience, we provide an understanding of the nature of externally focused innovation mechanisms that you can exploit for your firm, as well as your roadmap for implementing a network-centric innovation strategy.

The second audience for the book is a manager tasked with leading the innovation initiatives at a large corporation. For you, we bring clarity to the type of innovation networks you should build; the roles that your company should play within these innovation networks, and the competencies that you will need to develop at your firm to execute these roles.

What industries or markets is this book particularly relevant for? Clearly, the frameworks and concepts that we present are applicable to a broad array of industries; our book is particularly relevant for firms in the technology sector (computers, software, telecommunications, chemicals, and so on) and the consumer packaged goods sector. In addition to these sectors, the concepts we present are also relevant to other industries or fields such as health care services, medical devices, automobiles, consumer durables, and the entertainment industry, where network-centric innovation opportunities are rapidly emerging.

HOW THE BOOK IS ORGANIZED

We have organized this book, consisting of 12 chapters, into five parts. Each part addresses a set of fundamental questions related to network-centric innovation:

Part I: From *Firm-Centric* to *Network-Centric* Innovation (Chapters 1 and 2)

Part II: The Landscape of Network-Centric Innovation (Chapters 3 and 4)

Part III: The Four Models of Network-Centric Innovation (Chapters 5 to 8)

Part IV: Executing Network-Centric Innovation (Chapters 9 and 10)

Part V: Globalization and Network-Centric Innovation (Chapters 11 and 12)

We begin Part I by answering some basic questions, such as, "Why should firms 'innovate beyond boundaries'?" And, "What do you mean by adopting a 'network-centric innovation' approach?" Put more simply, "Why should I care about this?" We describe the need for companies to look outside for innovation and make the shift from firm-centric to network-centric innovation. Then, we define the concept of "network-centricity" and describe the principles of network-centric innovation. Using a number of examples, we emphasize that different "flavors" of network-centric innovation exist, and companies need to carefully map their industry and organizational context to identify the appropriate innovation approach.

In Part II, Chapters 3 and 4, we address the question, "What does the network-centric innovation landscape look like?" We present a conceptual framework to structure the emerging landscape of network-centric innovation. Our framework is based on two central dimensions of network-centric innovation—the nature of the innovation space and the structure of the network leadership. Based on these dimensions, we outline four basic models of network-centric innovation. We also identify other key elements of our conceptual framework—the different types of players in network-centric innovation (that is, a taxonomy of innovation roles) and the different types of innovation management activities and network infrastructure (for example, governance systems, IP rights management systems, and so on).

In Part III, Chapters 5 to 8, we describe in detail the four models of network-centric innovation. In each chapter, we apply the conceptual framework that we develop in Section II to analyze the nature of the innovation roles, innovation management activities, and network infrastructure that apply to that particular model. We use one "anchor" case study to ground our discussion of the important issues.

In Part IV, we address execution-related issues. We start with the question, "Where does my company fit in this landscape?" In Chapter 9, we develop a contingent framework that maps the context for innovation—industry and business environment conditions, technology and market factors, a company's innovation goals and internal resources—to alternate network-centric opportunities. This contingent framework provides guidelines for managers to evaluate the different types of opportunities and to identify the opportunities that will best align with the firm's resources, capabilities, and strategy.

In Chapter 10, we address questions such as, "Now that I know the opportunities for my firm, how exactly should I prepare my company to exploit these opportunities?" "What types of capabilities are required?" And, "What types of metrics should be used to evaluate my company's performance in these initiatives?" We describe different aspects related to preparing the organization for network-centric innovation—cultural readiness, strategic readiness, operational readiness, and so on.

In Part V, Chapters 11 and 12, we broaden our horizon and consider the implications of network-centric innovation for the emerging economies. We ask,

"What opportunities do the different types of network-centric innovation initiatives present to companies in countries such as India, China, Russia, and Brazil?" We identify some of the common trends in the emerging economies and analyze the potential for companies in these countries to plug into the global brain. We offer our final thoughts in the last chapter and leave the reader with a set of best practices and "next practices" that we have identified from our study of leaders in network-centric innovation initiatives.

Join us as we begin this journey by focusing on a question that is on the lips of every CEO: "How can we sustain profitable growth, and why is innovation so important for organic growth?"

From *Firm-Centric* to *Network-Centric* Innovation

Chapter 1   The Power of Network-Centricity   11

Chapter 2   Understanding Network-Centric
Innovation   29

1

The Power of
Network-Centricity

"The key is to be able to collaborate—across town, across countries, even to the next cube. ... Global innovation networks help make this happen."
—*Tony Affuso, UGS Chairman, CEO, and President.*[1]

Innovation used to be something companies did within their four walls. Storied organizations like AT&T's Bell Laboratories, IBM's Watson Research Center and Xerox's Palo Alto Research Center were the temples of innovation.[2] Thousands of researchers and scientists toiled deep within the bowels of large corporations to create the next big thing. Corporations viewed their innovation initiatives as proprietary and secret. And they attempted to hire the best and the brightest researchers and managers to drive basic research and new product development. In fact, any self-respecting organization was afflicted with the "Not Invented Here" (NIH) syndrome—believing that it had the best ideas and the best people, so if it did not invent a certain something, that thing wasn't worth looking at.

Then the Internet happened. With it came phenomena like the Open Source Software movement, electronic R&D marketplaces, online communities, and a whole new set of possibilities to reach out and connect with innovative ideas and talent beyond the boundaries of the corporation. Even the lexicon associated with innovation is changing, with new adjectives that describe a very different view of innovation—open, democratic, distributed, outside, external, community-led. The changes in vocabulary and metaphors suggest that the shift in the nature and the process of innovation is broad and

11

deep. Consultants, academicians, and mainstream business media have all joined the chorus to liberate innovation from organizational boundaries. Special issues and articles in business magazines with titles such as "The Power of Us," "Open Source Innovation," "and "The Innovation Economy" implore managers to reorient and amplify their innovation initiatives by tapping external networks and communities.

But, in the words of the miners in the California Gold Rush in the nineteenth century, is there real "gold in them thar hills"? Or, what exactly can such externally focused innovation deliver? To answer this question, we first need to look at the problems companies are facing in continuing to grow their revenues and profits.

THE QUEST FOR PROFITABLE GROWTH

How the mighty can stumble. Consider Dell Inc., the leading seller of personal computers and accessories. From 1995 to 2005, Dell was a paragon of profitable growth, fueled by its innovative build-to-order manufacturing and direct-to-customer sales business model. During the five-year period from 2000 to 2005, Dell's revenues grew at 16% per year and its earnings increased 21% per year. The company was widely admired for its ability to drive growth and increase its market share by executing flawlessly on its business model, and staying focused on process innovation. When other companies started imitating its business model, Dell maintained its edge by further refining its business processes to become even more efficient in its operations. However, Dell's growth engine stalled badly in 2005. In 2006, it missed investor expectations for several quarters in a row, and its stock lost almost half of its value from July 2005 to June 2006. One reason behind the downfall of Dell is that it became too much of a one-trick pony—using the same direct business model for more than two decades, and not innovating enough in terms of new products and new markets. Meanwhile, Dell's competitors, including Apple Computer and Hewlett-Packard, who placed more emphasis on innovative products and new business models, grew faster and increased their market share at the expense of Dell. Dell's growth woes are likely to persist for the foreseeable future, and its senior management will be under intense pressure to reignite the growth engine.

Dell is not the only large company facing such growth challenges. Companies such as Kraft, 3M, Sony, Ford, and IBM are all finding it difficult to drive growth. Investors closely monitor the CEOs and senior management of large public companies on their ability to grow the firms they lead. No wonder then that a majority of the CEOs consider growth to be their highest priority—even more than profits. Although growth has always been on the CEO agenda, the perennial quest for growth has become more challenging in the era of global competition and shrinking product life cycles.

In their attempt to jumpstart growth, companies often turn to inorganic growth through mergers and acquisitions (M&A). M&A deals are very appealing to senior managers—they generate an immediate boost in revenues; the hard synergies (mostly financial) are very apparent; and the internal stakeholders (that is, senior managers) have a lot to gain from making the deals. As a result, M&A activity has increased to a fever pitch. In 2005, there were 10,511 mergers and acquisitions involving U.S. companies alone, with an aggregate value of more than $1 trillion—a 28% increase over 2004's $781 billion.[3]

However, there is trouble in "M&A land." Simply put, mergers and acquisitions don't work as advertised. Most studies and surveys paint a gloomy picture of the after-deal scenario. Between 70% and 80% of the M&A initiatives end up in failures—most of them within the first 18 months.[4] Companies generally do well at realizing the hard synergies; for example, consolidating the borrowing, restructuring the taxation, pooling the working capital, purchasing at higher volumes, and so on. The soft synergies—operational consolidation, process improvement, channel merging, technology sharing, staff layoffs, extension of customer base, and so on—are what rarely materialize. Although most M&A failures are blamed on "people" and "cultural" issues, the end result is that such initiatives fail to enhance (and, often contribute to decline in) shareholder value. After the failure, the CEO often exits and a new CEO arrives who starts divesting those previously acquired divisions—and then promptly start acquiring new ones! Like a gerbil in a treadmill, the cycle of acquisitions and divestitures goes on, with the only sure winners being the consultants, lawyers, and investment bankers.

Given the high visibility of many recent M&A failures (remember Time Warner and AOL or Chrysler and Daimler-Benz), many CEOs have changed their tune and now proclaim innovation as the preferred pathway to growth. In a recent CEO survey, 86% of respondents indicated that innovation is definitely more important than M&As and cost-cutting strategies for long-term growth. In fact, many CEOs and senior managers have come to view innovation as their only alternative to achieve sustained growth.[5]

As Howard Stringer, Chairman and CEO of Sony, recently noted, "We will fight our battles not on the low road to commoditization, but on the high road of innovation."[6]

However, despite such public statements about the importance of innovation, when it comes to actual decisions and actions, many companies still take the easy way out—focusing either on cost-reduction initiatives that promise short-term profit increases or on mergers and acquisitions that create an illusion of rapid revenue growth, even if the former is often not sustainable and the latter mostly turn out to be failures. In short, a significant gulf seems to exist between the desire to innovate and the ability to innovate.

AN INNOVATION CRISIS?

The ability of firms to innovate is stymied by two factors—the pace of innovation required to maintain and grow profits is increasing, and the productivity of internally driven innovation efforts is decreasing. These two factors are conspiring to create an innovation crisis in large firms.

THE "RED QUEEN" EFFECT IN INNOVATION

> "Well, in our country," said Alice, still panting a little, "you'd generally get to somewhere else—if you run very fast for a long time, as we've been doing." "A slow sort of country!" said the Queen. "Now, here, you see, it takes all the running you can do, to keep in the same place. If you want to get somewhere else, you must run at least twice as fast as that!"[7]

Despite having hundreds of in-house scientists and engineers working tirelessly on innovation projects, managers are discovering that their innovation pipelines are not delivering the results they need to sustain growth. Innovation productivity is declining while the cost of new product development is increasing day by day. Investing more dollars into internal R&D efforts does not seem to produce the desired payoffs. For example, Kraft invests close to $400 million annually and has 2,100 employees in its internal R&D unit. Despite such large investments, the company has been discovering its R&D pipeline to be less and less effective in fueling firm growth.[8] The story is not much different in many other large firms in both the technology and the consumer product sectors.

On the other hand, the industry cycle times continue to shrink rapidly across the board. For example, in the automobile industry, 48-month development cycles and six-year model life cycles were the norm. But today, concept-to-production times are down to less than 24 months, and industry leaders like

Toyota are talking about 12-month development cycles. In consumer electronics markets (for example, cell phone, digital audio player, and so on), product life cycles are often measured in weeks, not months.

Added to this acceleration is the impact of globalization—global markets breed global competitors. Companies such as Samsung from Korea (in mobile phones and televisions), Tata from India (in automotive), and Lenovo from China (in computers) have upped the ante by producing innovative products at significantly lower costs, driving the rapid commoditization in many product categories.

These forces—rapidly decreasing product life cycles, decreasing internal innovation productivity, and global competition—together are creating a Red Queen effect[9] in innovation: Companies have to invest more and more just to maintain their market position.

Consider a simple simulation done by Dave Bayless, an entrepreneur and our friend, to understand the crippling effect of shrinking product life cycles on growth. Assuming a company has base revenues of $500 million per year, the simulation illustrates how a 10% annual increase in industry clock speed would necessitate an immediate and sustained increase in the rate of new product introductions of 50% just to maintain that average level of revenue over ten years.[10] And this simulation did not even consider the potential negative impact of reduced innovation productivity or the increasing market risk of new products and services—both clearly evident in many industries. Thus, just one factor alone, shrinking product life cycle, poses a critical innovation challenge. On top of that, if the company wants to grow even at a modest 4% or 5% annual rate, the innovation challenge becomes almost insurmountable.

THE LIMITS OF INTERNALLY FOCUSED INNOVATION

It is not just the Red Queen effect that defines the limits of internally focused innovation initiatives. There is also the potentially debilitating effect of a myopic "world-view" that companies often come to possess—particularly when their "successful" innovation and growth strategies have been around for a while.

Dell's direct-to-consumer business model is a good example in this context. As market pressures continue to climb in the personal computer market, Dell's inability to come up with new business models is what continues to drag down its growth. Dell, to its credit, has started considering new ways of doing business and entering into new product categories and markets—but these efforts haven't been met with much success. Granted, business model innovation is not easy. But it is Dell's ingrained perspectives derived from operating its current business model for a long time that makes such business model innovation doubly difficult. Over time, organizations become prisoners of what they know, especially when they have met with sustained success. They fail to see beyond their limited view of the world.

This limited world-view is becoming more dangerous in the turbulent and dynamic business environment that we find ourselves in. In many industries such as consumer electronics, automobiles and software, products have become more complex in terms of their features, their underlying technologies, and their design. Therefore, the knowledge and skills required to design and develop new products and services have become much more diverse and more demanding. Innovating such new products and services thus calls for not only a command of diverse sets of knowledge and expertise but also the ability to make non-obvious connections between such diverse knowledge bases. This feat is very difficult to pull off inside the four walls of any firm, no matter how large.

Clearly, throwing more and more money at the internal innovation engine is not the most efficient way to address the innovation crisis. Doing more of the same can only result in incremental improvement in innovative output. What is really needed to overcome this crisis is a significant increase in the company's innovation reach and productivity—only such an increase will translate into a dramatic shift in innovation output of one or more orders of magnitude. And to gain such increases in reach and range of innovative ideas, companies need to broaden their innovation horizons by looking outside for innovative ideas and technologies.

Consider the case of Kraft. Profits fell 24% in the time period from 2003 to 2005. Top-line growth stalled, and net income in 2005 was $2.63 billion, down from $3.48 billion in 2003. The company that came up with blockbuster products such as Oreo cookies, Miracle Whip dressing, and DiGiorno pizza is hungry for ideas. It is not lacking any internal R&D infrastructure. Kraft has an extensive internal R&D setup, with thousands of talented researchers on staff. However, internally focused innovation efforts are not delivering the goods. So Kraft has turned outwards in its quest for ideas: The company is inviting unsolicited ideas from its customers or for that matter from anybody who visits its Web site and submits ideas. Whether putting such an invitation for ideas on the company Web site is the right approach is debatable, but what is less arguable is the need to start looking outside. Indeed, the limits of internally focused innovation are well illustrated by Kraft's radical departure from past practice. As Mary Kay Haben, senior vice president at Kraft, noted, "In the past we would have said, 'Thank you, but we are not accepting ideas.'"[11]

The imperative to look outside is not limited to the consumer product sector. Consider Merck, a giant in the pharmaceutical industry. Merck has traditionally been an internally focused innovation organization. However, after a string of failures and a very lackluster R&D pipeline, it made a strategic shift toward looking outside for innovation—specifically, to partner with smaller firms with innovative ideas. Merck's R&D chief, Peter Kim, made it clear that the company's own labs are insufficient to replenish its pipeline for the future, and three years or so back embarked upon a more collaborative and open innovation agenda. Although the results of this approach will likely take years to become evident, the initiative is well underway. Compared to 10 outside alliances in 1999, Merck has entered into 141 such deals between the years 2002 and 2004—an average of 47 each year. And in 2005, Merck reviewed more than 5,000 such external collaboration opportunities.[12]

OVERCOMING THE CRISIS: "LOOKING OUTSIDE"

The opportunities for companies to "look outside" for innovation are increasing day by day. As we noted previously, the Global Brain is rich and diverse—a large number of innovative firms as well as a large pool of innovative people exist in different parts of the world whose knowledge and creativity can be leveraged by companies. Moreover, new types of innovation intermediaries and new technological infrastructure (for example, the Internet) have made tapping into such global networks of inventors, scientists, and innovative firms easier than ever before. Thus, the imperative for sourcing external innovation is matched by the rapidly expanding horizon of innovation opportunities.

Former Sun Chief Scientist, Bill Joy, noted several years back that "most of the smart people in the world don't work for your company." True enough, but increasingly those smart people in other parts of the world represent a global innovation opportunity waiting to be tapped.

This is mirrored in companies, such as by P&G's recent innovation initiatives. As Tom Cripe, Associate Director of P&G's External Business Development group, recently noted:

> "We want to grow efficiently. And at the size we are, it's just not possible to do it all yourself. And even if it was it'd be lunacy to attempt it. There are just too many smart people out there. If we have to grow at the rate we want to, we have to add incremental business of billions of dollars … It took us 100 years to get here and we now have to

do in a few years what we did in 100 years. Even if we could, it would be expensive. And so we've been able to increase our innovative output while reducing our spending as a percent of sales because we're multiplying it by all the people we're partnering with. So the reason for 'looking outside' is to grow most effectively by drawing on the very best ideas out there, rather than trying to compete with everybody."[13]

This message has come through in several other forums, too. For example, the Council of Competitiveness published the National Innovation Initiative report in 2004. This report focused on the implications of globalization for the national innovation agenda for the United States. Among other trends, the committee identified the effective pursuit of highly collaborative innovation as of utmost importance for the U.S. economy. As the report notes, "Innovation itself—where it comes from and how it creates value—is changing:

- It is diffusing at ever increasing rates.

- It is multidisciplinary and technologically complex and will arise from the intersection of different fields.

- It is collaborative, requiring active cooperation and communication among the scientists and engineering and between creators and users.

- Workers and consumers are embracing new ideas, technologies, and content, and demanding more creativity from their creators.

- It is becoming global in scope—with advances coming from centers of excellence around the world and the demands of billions of new consumers."[14]

The key findings of the committee also reflected how the global connectedness and the scale of collaborative innovation will demand the development of a more diverse workforce that is able to communicate and coordinate innovation activities across organizational and geographic boundaries.

Similarly, IBM has been conducting a global conversation on innovation that it calls the Global Innovation Outlook (GIO). The most important finding from IBM's GIO conducted in 2005 and 2006 was that innovation is more global (anyone and everyone can participate without geographical barriers), more multidisciplinary (innovation requires a diverse mix of expertise), and more collaborative (innovation results from entities working together in new ways).[15]

To enjoy the benefits of such a rapidly expanding horizon of innovation opportunities, companies would need to make a gradual shift from innovation initiatives that are centered on internal resources to those that are centered on external networks and communities—that is, *a shift from firm-centric innovation to network-centric innovation*. However, the question remains: Will such a shift address the innovation crisis outlined earlier? In other words, will a network-centered innovation strategy deliver gains that are orders of magnitude higher in innovation reach, range, and effectiveness?

To understand the promise of network-centric innovation, we need to consider its foundational theme or premise—namely, the concept of network-centricity. The concept of network-centricity has very deep roots and very broad applicability. Before we discuss how networks can enhance innovation, let us examine how network-centric capabilities are transforming several other domains.

THE POWER OF NETWORK-CENTRICITY

The university that one of us works at has a library with close to 500,000 books on its shelves. Considering the number of students—around 7,500—it is not a large acquisition. However, the library is part of a network of 13 other university libraries in the area—a system called ConnectNY. The total number of books in the ConnectNY network is 10 million. Each member of the ConnectNY network can request books from any other member library, and if the book is available, it is delivered by a private courier (who travels between the different member libraries) within three to four business days. Thus, in effect, by becoming a member of the ConnectNY network, the library has increased its acquisition by twentyfold—from 0.5 million to 10 million.

Consider another simple example—the task of replenishing a vending machine. A service truck can visit each and every vending machine and then find out whether it needs any servicing or not. This method creates inefficiency because there is no way for the person making the rounds to know whether he needs to replenish a specific machine and what exactly the machine is short of. Imagine if the vending machine could "talk" to the service person over an information network and inform him in advance if it was running out of a specific food or beverage item. This is what Vendlink LLP, a N.J.-based vending service company, has done in Philadelphia. It created a wireless network that integrates information from all the vending machines in the area and produces a servicing plan that optimizes the logistics involved.

Even toys can be made smarter after they are connected to a network. In 1997, Fisher Price and Microsoft created the ActiMates Interactive Barney. By itself, ActiMates Interactive Barney is a cute, purple stuffed animal. But the real fun begins when the toy is used with either of two add-on devices: a TV Pack, which adds a radio transmitter to the user's TV/VCR; and a PC Pack, which does the same to a computer. The toy enables children to improve their vocabulary or language skills. The company also created a network from which the "lessons" can be downloaded into the toy. As the child gets older, parents can connect the toy to the network, download the appropriate components, and thereby extend its use.

These simple examples reflect the essence of network-centricity: the emphasis on the network as the focal point and the associated opportunity to extend, optimize, and/or enhance the value of a stand-alone entity or activity by making it more intelligent, adaptive, and personalized. It should be no surprise, therefore, that the concept of network-centricity has permeated many aspects of our contemporary world and daily-life—ranging from warfare and military operations to social advocacy movements. Let us start with network-centric computing.

Network-Centric Computing

In the field of computer science, the shift from host-centric computing to distributed or network-centric computing has relatively old roots. The concept of distributed computing, pioneered by David Farber in the 1970s at the University of California,[16] evolved into what is now called network-centric computing or grid computing.

Grid computing relates to the ability to pursue large-scale computational problems by leveraging the power and unused resources of a large number of disparate computers (including desktop computers) belonging to different administrative domains but connected through a network infrastructure.[17] The essential idea behind grid computing is to solve computing-intensive problems by breaking them down into many smaller problems and solving these smaller problems simultaneously on a set of connected computers. The parallel division of labor approach can result in very high computing throughput, often more than a supercomputer. Further, this throughput can be achieved at a cost that is significantly lower by exploiting the relatively inexpensive computing resources available at remote locations. And the network-centric computing architecture also is far more flexible, because remote users can decide moment-to-moment how much computing power they need. The promise of grid computing—high computing power combined with low cost and high operational flexibility—is spurring many applications in commercial as well as non-commercial contexts, including financial modeling, weather modeling, protein folding, and space exploration.[18]

Network-Centric Warfare

Network-centric warfare (NCW) is a relatively new theory or doctrine of war developed primarily by the United States Department of Defense.[19] This emerging theory indicates a radical shift from a platform-centric approach to a network-centric approach to warfare.

The basic premise of NCW is that robust networking of geographically dispersed military forces makes it possible to translate informational advantage into warfare advantage.[20] Higher levels of information sharing among the units enhance the extent of "shared situational awareness." In other words, through information sharing, every unit—from infantry units to aircraft to naval vessels to command centers—"sees" the sum of what all other units "see." This shared awareness facilitates self-synchronizing forces, virtual collaboration, and other forms of flexible operations. The value proposition for the military is a significant reduction of combat risks, higher order combat effectiveness, and low-cost operations.[21] Although there is still significant debate about how soon and to what extent the benefits of NCW can be realized, several countries, including Australia and the UK, have embraced the basic tenets of network-centric warfare.

Network-Centric Operations

The term *network-centric operations* (NCO) was originally applied to the field of logistics and supply chain management in business enterprises. The term "value nets" or "value networks" has also been used in this context. However, more recently, NCO has gained a broader interpretation and is often used interchangeably with NCW in the defense and military areas.

In the supply chain management context, NCO signifies establishing dynamic connections between the enterprise, suppliers, customers, and other partners to deliver maximum value to all the entities concerned.[22] It involves integrating enterprise information systems (for example, ERP and CRM systems) with external partners' systems and processes to enhance the information flow and "sense and respond" capabilities. Whereas traditional supply chains emphasize linear and often inflexible connections, network-centric operations or value nets focus on establishing varied, dynamic connections that deliver both efficiency and agility to the enterprise. Supply chain–focused software companies such as SAP, i2 Technologies, and IBM have adapted these concepts to create applications that support such network-centric supply chain operations.

Network-Centric Enterprise

The concept of network-centric enterprise (NCE) owes its origin to the concept of business ecosystems and virtual organizations. It involves establishing an "infostructure" that connects the different partners in a company's business ecosystem and supports the different value creation processes. As such, the concept of NCE is also closely related to NCO.

Companies such as Wal-Mart, Cisco, and Toyota have considerable experience in deploying and operating such a network-centric enterprise. For example, Cisco has evolved its organization into what it calls the "Networked Virtual Organization" (NVO) in its manufacturing operations.[23] Similarly, Toyota has used the NCE model to improve its just-in-time inventory management. The NCE (or NVO) model has three core tenets.[24] First, it puts the customer at the center of the value chain and emphasizes the need to respond rapidly to customers' needs. Second, it calls for the enterprise to focus on those core operations or processes where it adds most value and to outsource or turn over all other operations to multiple partners. Finally, the model requires significant process, data, and technology standardization to enable real-time communication and synchronization across organizational boundaries. Overall, the network-centric enterprise model implies significant strategic and operational agility for an enterprise, thereby enhancing its ability to thrive in highly dynamic markets.

Network-Centric Advocacy

The concept of network-centricity is also becoming evident in the domain of social advocacy movements. Social advocacy groups have realized that the basic tenets of network-centricity can be adopted to enhance the reach, speed, and overall effectiveness of social movements.[25]

Network-centric advocacy (NCA) signifies a critical shift from the direct engagement and the grassroots engagement models of social advocacy to a more network-centered model wherein the individual participates as part of a coordinated network.[26] In NCA, individuals and groups that are part of the network rapidly share information on emerging topics and identify "ripe campaign opportunities." The ability of the network to scale up in terms of resources, expertise, and overall level of public support brings sharpened focus and enhanced visibility to the campaign. Network-centric advocacy provides several advantages: speed of campaign, ability to pursue multiple campaigns with few resources, and ability to rapidly abandon losing efforts. All this brings an element of unpredictability that lowers the ability to counter such social campaigns effectively.

We summarize the promise of network-centric concepts in **Table 1.1**. These examples suggest that, although the concept of network-centricity has found considerable application in diverse domains, all these applications have a common thread in terms of outcomes—greater power, speed, flexibility, and operational capabilities delivered at a lower cost using diverse resources that are spread out geographically. These benefits are the very ones we seek as we examine the appeal of network-centricity in the domain of innovation.

Table 1.1   Evidence of Network-Centricity in Different Domains

Domain	From	To	Implications
Computing	Host-centric	Distributed or grid computing	More computing throughput at lower cost
Warfare	Platform-centric	Network-centric	More combat power with fewer, lower-cost units
Supply chain mgmt.	Linear chains	Value nets	Higher "sense-and-respond" capabilities
Business enterprise	Stand-alone organization	Virtual or networked organization	More strategic and operational agility
Social advocacy	Direct engagement	Network-coordinated engagement	More effective campaigns with fewer resources

NETWORK-CENTRICITY AND INNOVATION

To apply a network-centric perspective to innovation, we formally define network-centric innovation (NCI) as an externally focused approach to innovation that relies on harnessing the resources and capabilities of external networks and communities to amplify or enhance innovation reach, innovation speed, and the quality of innovation outcomes.

Network-centric innovation features principles that are analogous to the examples we mention from other domains. We define these principles in the next chapter. But first, let us look at the evidence of the power of networks to enhance innovation in a variety of industries and markets.

Perhaps the most celebrated example of networked innovation is the Open Source Software (OSS) movement, and its most famous product is Linux, the fast-growing open source operating system that was developed and is continually enhanced by a networked community of software developers. The first release of Linux Kernel, version 0.01, was in September 1991, and it consisted of 10,239 lines of code. By April 2006, version 2.6.16.11 had been released with a whopping 6,981,110 lines of code. In this 15-year period, thousands of programmers spread across the world contributed to the development and release of more than a hundred versions of the Linux Kernel. In fact, within one year— from early 1993 to early 1994—15 development versions of the Linux Kernel were released. Such a rapid release schedule is unheard of in the commercial software world, and it reflects the innovative power of the global Linux community.

A more formal comparison of the development effort between Red Hat Linux version 7.1 (a distribution version) and a similar proprietary product was done in 2001.[27] Red Hat Linux 7.1 contained more than 30 million source lines of code and reflects approximately 8,000 person-years of development time. If this version were developed in a proprietary manner (that is, inside an organization such as Microsoft or Oracle) in the United States, it would have cost approximately $1.08 billion (in year 2000 U.S. dollars).

To provide further evidence of the awesome power of such innovative communities, consider Red Hat Linux version 6.2, which was released just a year earlier in 2000—it had only 17 million lines of code and represents 4,500 person-years of development effort ($600 million in comparative cost). Thus, version 7.1 was approximately 60% more in terms of size and development effort. In one year, the open source community's innovative contributions increased two orders of magnitude—an impossible feat in a conventional proprietary software development initiative.

The creative power of networks and communities is being felt in other domains, too. Consider the community-based encyclopedia called Wikipedia. This online encyclopedia was launched in January 2001, and through the collaborative efforts of tens of thousands of contributors, it swiftly became the largest reference site on the Internet. As of July 2007, Wikipedia had more than 75,000 active contributors working on more than 7,704,000 articles in more than

250 languages. Debate is ongoing regarding the reliability and accuracy of Wikipedia (for example, a peer-reviewed study published by the prestigious journal Nature found that Wikipedia is comparable to the hallowed Encyclopedia Britannica in terms of accuracy,[28] while other studies have shown just the opposite). What is undeniable, however, is the creative power of the community that feeds Wikipedia's exponential growth.

Another example is the world of open source or citizen journalism. The first open source newspaper is OhmyNews—a South Korean online newspaper established in February 2000. The majority of the articles in the newspaper are written by its readers—a community of approximately 41,000 citizen reporters. As a citizen newspaper, OhmyNews exercised considerable influence during the South Korean presidential elections in 2002.[29] An International edition (in English) of OhmyNews was launched in February 2004 with 1,500 citizen reporters from more than 100 countries.

Global networks are also turbo-charging scientific research in the life sciences and material science industries. A well-known example of an electronic R&D network is InnoCentive, a global community of scientists that helps large companies seek solutions to their R&D problems by sourcing solutions from scientists around the world. InnoCentive maintains a community of scientists, in fields as diverse as petrochemicals and plastics to biotechnology and agribusiness, from approximately 170 countries. To understand the power of this network, consider the case of Eli Lilly, which had an R&D problem in the area of small molecules that its internal R&D organization had spent more than 12 person-months of work and failed to solve. Eli Lilly posed the problem on the InnoCentive Web site in June 2003. In less than five months after posting it on InnoCentive, Eli Lilly had a solution in hand—a retired scientist based in Germany had found a solution that had eluded Eli Lilly's internal team of researchers.[30] Through InnoCentive, Eli Lilly had effectively increased its reach to approximately 30,000 scientists and researchers who were members of the InnoCentive forum. Other examples from InnoCentive and similar "Innomediaries" suggest that the innovative power of communities can translate into orders of magnitude improvements in innovation speed, cost, and quality.

Perhaps no other company illustrates the power of network-centricity as well as P&G. The company's aggressive partnership with external innovation networks has translated into highly commendable results. R&D productivity has increased by nearly 60%, innovation success rate has more than doubled, and the cost of innovation has fallen significantly.[31]

These and other scattered examples of the creative power of the Global Brain have encouraged more and more companies to reorient their innovation initiatives to a more collaborative, network-centered approach. However, as most CEOs and senior managers would readily admit, harnessing this innovative power is something that is "theoretically easy" but "practically hard to do."[32]

Let us briefly examine these broad challenges now.

CHALLENGES IN "LOOKING OUTSIDE"

Organizations embarking on a network-centered innovation strategy are likely to be faced with different types of networks and communities with different types of innovation opportunities. The three broad sets of challenges that companies will likely face are *mindset and cultural* challenges, *contextualization* challenges, and *execution* challenges.

MINDSET AND CULTURAL CHALLENGES

Most large companies have considerable experience in partnering with a relatively small set of carefully identified firms—joint ventures, technological agreements, licensing agreements, and so on. However, when it comes to innovation collaboration on a greater scale—for example, a larger number and geographically more widely dispersed set of partners—most companies have limited experience. The first critical issue that senior managers will need to address relates to the broader implications of adopting such a network-centered approach to innovation. How should the organization view such collaboration opportunities? How can senior managers ensure a coherent set of innovation strategies that capture both external opportunities and internal capabilities? What type of broad framework or mindset should be developed that reflects the organization's intent to collaborate with outsiders and defines the broad parameters for such collaboration? And how should senior managers communicate and encourage other members of the organization to adopt such a mindset?

For companies such as 3M, DuPont, and Kodak with a history of significant internal achievements and with a vast array of resident scientists and technical specialists, the dominant threat is the feeling of "We know everything and everyone." This "Not Invented Here" (NIH) syndrome is a serious barrier to acceptance of new ideas from outside the company. The cultural shift needed to overcome the NIH syndrome and to adopt a collaborative mindset is significant.

IBM has acknowledged the simple fact that to partner with open source communities and other such communities of creation, it needs to let go of some of the control it has traditionally exercised in all of its innovation initiatives. Indeed, a recent book by Linda Sanford, one of IBM's senior executives, succinctly captures this spirit through its title, *Let Go to Grow*.[33] Although such a cultural shift might be easy to identify, achieving it in an organization—especially a large organization with a long history of success—is very challenging.

CONTEXTUALIZATION CHALLENGES

The second set of issues involves understanding the landscape of network-centric innovation and relating it to the firm's own unique innovation context.

It is evident that companies such as IBM and P&G have succeeded to different extents in leveraging innovation networks. For example, IBM has subscribed to the open source model and has invested significant resources to align its innovation initiatives in many of its product and service areas with the open source model. Similarly, P&G has garnered significant visibility through its Connect+Develop initiative to partner with external innovation networks such as those offered by InnoCentive and Nine Sigma.

Although these examples indicate specific approaches to a network-centered innovation, they are not the only approaches. The multiplicity of approaches raises many questions: Is there a systematic way to identify and analyze the different approaches (or models) of network-centric innovation? What are these different approaches? How should an organization evaluate and select the most appropriate approach vis-à-vis its particular context? Further, should an organization assume a lead role or a non-lead role in such a collaborative arrangement? What types of internal projects would be ripe for such a collaborative approach? All these issues relate to contextualizing the opportunity offered by the external innovation network or situating the opportunity in the company's particular market and organizational context.

EXECUTION CHALLENGES

Finally, the third set of issues relates to the actual implementation of collaborative innovation projects. When an appropriate network-centric innovation opportunity has been identified, how should the organization go about executing it? How should the organization prepare itself for network-centric innovation? What are the types of capabilities and competencies that the organization would require? How should the organization integrate its internal and external innovation processes? What types of licensing and other value appropriation systems should it employ? What is the appropriate set of metrics that it should use to evaluate its performance in such collaborative innovation projects?

The preceding three sets of issues—mindset and cultural, contextualization, and execution—represent the type of practical issues that most CEOs and senior managers need to address in order to be successful in championing and executing their external network-centered innovation initiatives. Because these challenges originate from the richness and variation that is present in the network-centric innovation landscape, we continue our discussion by examining the different "flavors" of network-centric innovation.

2

Understanding Network-Centric Innovation

The Human Genome project (HGP) is a classic example of the awesome innovative power of networked communities. The HGP was an international research initiative that aimed to identify and sequence the approximately 20,000 to 25,000 genes that make up the human DNA. The project was unique in that it brought together a large number of research and scientific organizations across the globe in a collaborative initiative. The HGP, begun in 1990, was completed in 2003, at least three years ahead of schedule.[1]

The HGP is remarkable not only from a scientific point of view, in that it produced a map of the human DNA, it is also remarkable in terms of how the innovation effort was organized. HGP showcased two distinct themes that underpin network-centric innovation. First, a network of contributors who pool resources and capabilities can produce extraordinary results. Second, the sociological perspective of knowledge creation—that is, the notion of "building on each other's ideas" through interactions—is fundamental to contemporary innovation contexts, which often involve highly complex and diverse sets of knowledge.[2]

The confluence of these two themes is transforming the nature of innovation. On the one hand, businesses are becoming more networked in their operations. On the other hand, Open Source

Software and other similar initiatives exemplify the benefits of "social" knowledge creation. In this chapter, we take a deeper look at these themes and trace the philosophical and historical roots of network-centric innovation.

Like any other new and emerging phenomenon, the evolution of network-centric innovation is also characterized by rapid speciation. Companies experiment by adopting different types of network-centric innovation models. As a result, we are seeing a wide range of approaches to network-centric innovation. We examine these varying "flavors" of network-centric innovation to highlight the richness and diversity of the emerging landscape. This landscape, while presenting many opportunities, also poses a difficult question for companies— which among these is the best approach? To answer this question, we structure the network-centric innovation landscape into a systematic framework in the chapters that follow.

THE HISTORICAL AND PHILOSOPHICAL ROOTS OF NETWORK-CENTRIC INNOVATION

MODES OF PRODUCTION (OF IDEAS)

At its heart, *network-centric innovation* is an approach to organizing for the production of new ideas. As such, the philosophical roots of network-centric innovation can be traced to the literature on the alternate modes of production of goods.

Economists have long maintained that there are two primary modes of producing new ideas or new products: *markets* and *hierarchies*. Ronald Coase, in his classic work, *The Nature of the Firm*, set out the rationale for the existence of the firm (the "hierarchy" mode of production) using the concept of *transaction costs*. Transaction costs are costs associated with conducting a market transaction. They include the cost of identifying a market partner and the cost of defining and enforcing property and contract rights. Coase (and later, in a more rigorous fashion, Oliver Williamson) argued when the transaction costs increase beyond a certain level, it becomes more profitable to conduct and coordinate the production activities inside a firm instead of using a market-based mode of production. In other words, by considering the overall cost of production, which includes the market exchange cost or the organization cost, one can decide whether a market or a firm would be most appropriate. Until the Open Source Software communities came along, markets and firms were the two dominant modes of production.

However, the successful development of Linux and other Open Source Software products in the 1990s implied the existence of a third mode of production for new ideas or new products—one that was not just a hybrid of markets and firms. Yochai Benkler, a law professor at Yale University, wrote a series of articles suggesting that Open Source Software (and other similar open source communities) present a third model of production that he termed the *commons-based peer production* model. Using the same transaction cost logic, Benkler argued that when the "cost of organizing an activity on a peered basis is lower than the cost of using the market, and the cost of peering is lower than the cost of hierarchical organization" the commons-based peer model of production will emerge, as it did in the case of software.[3]

The commons-based peer production model is particularly relevant in contexts where the object of production is information-based (such as software, music, movies, and so on), and when the physical capital necessary for that production (for example, computers) is widely distributed, and the cost of peering is lowered through inexpensive communication facilities (for example, the Internet).

One such context is book publishing. For example, the publisher of this book, Wharton School Publishing, embarked on an innovative project that employs the principles of the commons-based peer production model to create a new book on business management. The book, *We Are Smarter Than Me,* involves collaboration among thousands of business professionals and scholars, including faculty, students, and alumni of the MIT Sloan School of Management and the Wharton School.[4] The output from this collaborative effort will be published in book form in the fall of 2007 by Wharton School Publishing, with all contributors getting equal credit.

We summarize the key differences among the three modes of production in **Table 2.1.**

Table 2.1 The Three Modes of Production of Ideas

Hierarchy-Based Production	Market-Based Production	Commons-Based Peer Production
Producers organized as employees in firms	Producers organized as individual entities in markets	Producers organized as members of a community
Flow of materials and activities coordinated by controlling and directing it at a higher level in the managerial hierarchy	Markets coordinate the flow through supply and demand forces and price signals	Collaborative activities are coordinated following a diverse cluster of motivation drivers and social signals
Example: Ford's famous Rouge River Plant	Example: Markets in financial instruments and other intangibles	Example: Open Source Software development

It is clear that markets, hierarchies, and commons form three alternate modes of production of innovation, too. The development of Windows by Microsoft is an example of innovation organized inside a firm (that is, using managerial hierarchies). Similarly, innovation can also be organized through open markets—companies routinely buy innovative startup firms to access innovative ideas and technologies. And finally, the development of Linux, Apache, and other Open Source Software products are examples of the commons model of organizing innovation.

The emerging models in the network-centric innovation landscape, however, reflect not just the market or the commons approach to innovation but instead the mix or the intersections of these three modes of production—for example, the mix of the commons-based model with the managerial hierarchy-based model, or the market-based model intersecting with the commons-based model. To understand the origins of such hybrid modes of production, we need to understand the history of network-centric innovation.

THE HISTORY OF NETWORK-CENTRIC INNOVATION

The real-world manifestation of network-centric innovation can be traced back to two distinct movements that took root in the 1990s: the Open Source movement (social knowledge creation) and the concept of business networks or ecosystems.

The Open Source Movement

The Open Source concept, in general, relates to the development and production of ideas, artifacts, and systems in a manner that provides free access to the end product's sources and enables free distribution through appropriate licenses.[5] It is based on the fundamental principle that users can be co-developers and that knowledge is created through "a synergistic interplay between individual contributions and social interactions."[6] While the essential philosophy behind open source existed in some form or the other in the 1980s (for example, the Free Software Foundation), the emergence of the Internet and the way it enables communities to come together and pursue collaborative development and production provided the Open Source movement its momentum in the early 1990s.

The software industry is the most prominent among the different fields and domains that the Open Source movement is evident. Open Source Software (OSS) can be defined simply as computer software whose source code is available to everybody for use, enhancement and modification, and distribution.[7] Several types of OSS copyright licenses exist that vary in the type and extent of rights granted for using, altering, and/or distributing the software product. The Open Source Initiative (a non-profit entity formed in 1998 by OSS visionaries Eric Raymond and Bruce Perens) has assumed the role of promoting the Open Source Software movement by certifying products as open source products based on whether they are distributed under any of the alternate licensing schemes listed with the OSI.[8] The number of such OSI-certified products has increased considerably over the past few years and runs into several hundreds now.[9] The steady increase in the number of OS products indicates the overall health of this movement and its wider acceptance by the software business community.

The open source movement is now visible in several other domains, too. For example, the concept of open source intelligence (OSINT)—which relates to gathering information from open or public sources (such as, blogs, Web sites, and so on) and analyzing it to produce usable intelligence—has gained much prominence in recent years. Open source journalism (also referred to as citizen journalism) is another prime example. Other areas where the principles of the Open Source movement have started to take hold include pharmaceuticals or research and discovery of drugs (for example, the Tropical Disease Initiative), computer hardware (open source hardware), education (open source curriculum), and open source filmmaking.[10]

Business Ecosystems

The concept of business ecosystems derives its roots from the fields of biology and social systems. In an article published in the *Harvard Business Review* in 1993, James Moore described a business ecosystem as "an economic community supported by a foundation of interacting organizations ... the 'organisms' of the business world. The member organizations also include suppliers, lead producers, competitors, and other stakeholders. Over time, they co-evolve their capabilities and roles, and tend to align themselves with the directions set by one or more central companies."[11]

A closely related concept is the *alliance constellation*. It describes a firm's set of alliance partners who come together to form a network or constellation. In such an alliance constellation, member companies jointly pursue a number of strategic goals including linking markets, reducing operational costs, sharing risk, and combining complementary skills.[12] A good example of an alliance constellation is the Star Alliance in the airline industry. Such groups enable member companies to compete and win in their markets by drawing on the resources and capabilities of their network of partners.

The key contribution of the business ecosystem and alliance constellation concepts has been to force companies to broaden their perspectives while devising their corporate and business strategies. More specifically, the application of the ecology perspective helped large companies such as Wal-Mart, Intel, Microsoft, and SAP to realize the importance of building robust business ecosystems to further their own future prospects. The ecosystem perspective also highlighted the changed nature of competition—from competition among individual companies to competition among business ecosystems or alliance constellations.[13]

Although business ecosystems and alliance constellations are now familiar terms to most managers, these concepts have mostly been applied to analyze and devise market and operational strategies. However, these concepts also serve to illustrate how companies can champion and orchestrate innovation activities in their industries by establishing and leading a network of partners. For example, Intel's dominance in the semiconductor industry in the 1980s and 1990s can be explained to a great extent by its ability to establish, nurture, and lead a network of partners who collectively contribute to and enhance the value of Intel's technology platform.[14] More recently, the battle for High-Definition DVD players between the Sony-led Blu-Ray consortium and the Toshiba-led HD-DVD consortium will also be won or lost based on the share of the Global Brain that Sony or Toshiba can attract to their ecosystem, including content providers, hardware manufacturers, and retailers.

The Confluence of Open Source Innovation and Business Ecosystems

In recent years, the boundaries between these two movements—open source communities and business networks (or ecosystems)—have begun to blur. On the one hand, companies are seeking out open source communities and other communities of creation (for example, customer communities and inventor communities) as partners in innovation. On the other hand, innovations that have emerged from the open source communities are transitioning into the commercial world (for example, commercial open source). So the neat distinction between "purely open" and "purely proprietary" forms of organizing for innovation is giving way to a more complex and nuanced landscape. A wide variety of networks, players, and roles are emerging: business ecosystems, alliance constellations, open source communities, inventor communities, customer communities, expert communities, and other such communities of creation.

The concept of network-centric innovation embraces these different types of innovation networks and players. But it does more. It also captures the unique approaches to organizing innovation that arise from the combinations of different types of networks and the interactions of companies with different types of innovation networks.

These new approaches to organizing innovation are also characterized by the hybrid modes of production mentioned earlier. In other words, markets, hierarchies, and commons collide in the network-centric innovation landscape and give rise to hybrid modes of production of innovation that underlie the alternate approaches to network-centric innovation. We describe these hybrid modes of production in more detail in subsequent chapters in terms of archetypes or models of network-centric innovation.

With this understanding of the historical and philosophical roots of network-centric innovation, we now turn to the core principles that underlie the different approaches to network-centric innovation.

PRINCIPLES OF NETWORK-CENTRIC INNOVATION

The concept of network-centric innovation has four defining principles: *shared goals, shared "world-view," social knowledge creation,* and an *architecture of participation.* These principles are consistent with the historical roots of network-centric innovation in the Open Source movement and business ecosystems. We briefly describe these four principles and summarize them in **Table 2.2.** Later in the book, we return to these principles as we describe the different models of network-centric innovation.

Table 2.2   Principles of Network-Centric Innovation

Principles of Network-Centric Innovation	Description	Examples
Shared goals and objectives	One or more goals that help bring the network members together and channel their diverse resources and activities	*Customer community:* Identify product flaws and contribute to product enhancement
Shared "world view"	Common assumptions, and mental models related to the innovation and its external environment	*Open source community:* Shared understanding about the software product's ties with other technologies and products
"Social" knowledge creation	Places the emphasis on inter-actions among the network members as the basis for value creation and on the cumulative nature of knowledge creation	*Inventor networks:* Interactions among individual inventor, innomediary, and large firm for the development of new product concepts
Architecture of participation	Defines a set of systems, mechanisms, and processes to facilitate participation in value creation and value appropriation	*Open source software community:* Modular product architecture and GNU General Public License scheme

SHARED GOALS AND OBJECTIVES

For a set of players to come together to contribute to an innovation initiative, it is essential that they have a common set of goals and objectives. These shared goals and objectives act as the glue that keeps the community together—giving direction, enabling coordination of activities, and facilitating the development of a common set of norms and values. For example, the shared goal of a community of customers might relate to providing innovative ideas and inputs to the product developer (vendor) to improve the quality and value of the product features. These shared goals and objectives might develop in different ways—in some networks, a central entity might devise and promote those goals, whereas in other networks, the shared goals might emerge through interactions among the players.

SHARED AWARENESS AND "WORLD VIEW"

The network members also need to share a common "world-view" or shared awareness of the external environment. These might include business assumptions, evaluation methods, and frameworks. A shared awareness is critical for the network to capitalize on the synergies among the diverse set of expertise and capabilities in the network. For example, in the case of an Open Source Software development community, the shared world-view might include knowledge about competing and complementary products and technologies, and how the products being developed should relate to or integrate with existing products and technologies.

The world-view in an innovation network is dynamic. It continually evolves in response to changes in the environment. The connectedness of the network facilitates rapid information sharing that in turn facilitates the maintenance of a shared awareness of the environment in which the network operates.

"SOCIAL" KNOWLEDGE CREATION

New knowledge is increasingly created through interactions among the different types of players or members in a network. For example, open source communities rely on the theme that all users can be co-developers and that innovative concepts evolve from building on one another's ideas or contributions. Such a concept of "social" knowledge creation is evident in customer communities, too, where dialogues among peer customers become the context for product improvement ideas and new product concepts.

Although we use the term "social" here, it is not necessarily limited to open source communities. Instead, this principle reflects the collaborative and cumulative aspect of knowledge creation that is evident in many other types of innovation networks. Even in a market-based model, innovative ideas evolve through interactions among the network members. For example, even in inventor networks, interactions among the individual inventor, the innovation intermediary, and the larger firm provide the context for new product ideas to bubble up and get transformed into commercially feasible product concepts. The key idea is simple—knowledge is created and enhanced socially as people build on each others' contributions, and a social or network infrastructure needs to be in place to facilitate social knowledge creation.

ARCHITECTURE OF PARTICIPATION

The fourth principle of network-centric innovation relates to the way innovation work is distributed among the network participants and the way "rights" from the innovation are shared by the participants. This principle goes beyond just identifying the core and non-core tasks as in outsourcing innovation. Instead, it relates to the development of an *architecture of participation*—a term coined by Tim O'Reilly[15]—that provides a road map for the different players to come together to innovate. The architecture of participation provides the mechanisms and methods for the contributions of participants to be coordinated, integrated, and synchronized in a coherent manner.

Two key aspects of such architecture of participation are the modularity of the innovation system and the granularity (size or scale) of the innovation tasks. Whereas modularity enables distributing and coordinating the innovation processes, granularity assures that a diverse set of members (that is, members with diverse types of resources, capabilities, and time commitments) can contribute to the innovation. The architecture of participation also has to define the means by which the participants will be "rewarded" for their contributions. This reward could range from establishing different types of incentives that drive participation in certain networks (for example, customer communities) to new value appropriation methods for sharing the innovation proceeds among the participants (for example, patent pools, Creative Commons license, and so on).

THE DIFFERENT "FLAVORS" OF NETWORK-CENTRIC INNOVATION

If we look at the history of automobiles, it becomes clear that the period from the mid-to-late 1800s was the "era of ferment" in the industry—the stage before one or more dominant designs emerge.[16] Such an era of ferment is characterized by prolific experimentation. In the automobile industry, inventors experimented with different types of fuels (wood, alcohol, gasoline, and electricity), different types of engines, different types of body structure, and so on. Some of these inventions worked, others did not. But all of them contributed to the evolution of the design that became the dominant model in the early 1900s.

Similarly, considerable experimentation is going on in the network-centric innovation landscape. The new models and approaches that are emerging are characterized by a wide range of structural arrangements, innovation activities, and outcomes. Let's look at some of these forms of network-centric innovation, with an example of a company that is pursuing each form.

OPEN SOURCE SOFTWARE COMMUNITIES AND IBM

In the early 1990s, at a time when the open source phenomenon was still in its infancy, IBM made key changes to align itself more closely with the emerging Open Source Software movement. An excellent example of that shift was the 1996 Atlanta Olympics where IBM was responsible for building and deploying the first Olympics Web site—the results from all the competitions were available in real-time on the IBM-designed Web site. When it came to choosing the server platform for the Web site, IBM chose Apache, an open source solution, despite the fact that IBM had a competing proprietary product for serving Web sites. In recent years, IBM has made conscious decisions to promote and align its own strategies to leverage the power of the Open Source Software communities—in markets ranging from Web servers and operating systems to scripting languages and development tools.

IBM's approach to open source is not a philanthropic approach; instead, it is a considered business decision. In the words of Irving Wladawsky-Berger, IBM's former Technical Vice-President, it is a decision made "after considerable analysis of the technology and market trends, the overall quality and commitment of the community...and the quality of its offerings."[17]

In working with the open source communities, IBM is pursuing a network-centric innovation strategy that involves itself with a vast global network of software developers who make different types of innovative contributions. IBM does not set out the innovation agenda for the open source community nor does it directly benefit from the products developed by the community. Instead, IBM plays the role of a sponsor or patron, whose interest is to sustain the overall energy and health of the open source movement. Of course, as Dr. Wladawsky-Berger notes, it is a "business decision"—IBM does indirectly benefit from the offerings of the open source communities. For example, IBM's revenues from Linux-related services have increased exponentially from 2001 when it started investing in an open source–based business model. By 2004, IBM realized more than $2 billion in revenues from Open Source–related businesses.[18]

CUSTOMER COMMUNITIES AND DUCATI

Ducati's involvement and relationship with its innovative customer community provides another flavor of network-centric innovation strategy. Ducati Motor is a world-renowned motorcycle company based in Italy. The motorcycle is a lifestyle-intensive product and as such most successful motorcycle companies focus on building extensive relationships with their customers to foster a sense of community that complements the actual product.

However, Ducati views its relationship with its customer community not just as a customer relationship management initiative but as part of its innovation strategy—Ducati considers its customers as partners in innovation. In early 2000, it set up a separate Web division to coordinate its Internet-based customer collaboration initiatives.[19] Ducati employs different types of virtual customer environments (all part of its Web site) to involve customers in both the front-end and the back-end of the innovation process (see **Figure 2.1**). Ducati's customers have deep technical knowledge and some of the customers even come up with complex technical and mechanical design improvement ideas—ideas that can be (and have been) translated into real product features. In addition, at the back-end of product development, customers also participate in product testing through the virtual customer environment.

Applicability to Stage of New Product Development Process

		Front-end (Ideation and Concept)	Back-end (Product Design and Testing)
Nature of Collaboration	Deep/ High Richness	Tech Café Advisory Programs Supported by Product Engineers Ducati Service Technical Forum and Chat	Design Your Dream Ducati Focalized Contest Ducati Garage Challenge Virtual Teams
	Broad/ High Reach	Online Survey to Improve the Web site Polls and Feedback Sessions My Ducati Virtual Scenarios	Mass Customization of the Product Web-Based Product Testing

From Mohanbir Sawhney, Gianmario Verona, Emanuela Prandelli, "COLLABORATING TO CREATE: THE INTERNET AS A PLATFORM FOR CUSTOMER ENGAGEMENT IN PRODUCT INNOVATION"; The Journal of Interactive Marketing, p. 8, Vol. 19, No. 4, Autumn 2005. © 2005 Wiley Periodicals, Inc. and Direct Marketing Educational Foundation, Inc. Reprinted by permission.

Figure 2.1   Ducati's Customer Community Initiative

Ducati thus pursues a network-centric innovation strategy wherein it hosts, facilitates, and promotes an active customer community, and coordinates the innovation activities and resources (customer ideas and expertise) to enhance its innovation agenda.

INVENTOR NETWORKS AND STAPLES

Staples Inc., the leading office supplies company, has marketed private-label, low-price generic products with Staple's name on the package from the 1990s onwards. This strategy has served them well in the past—revenue contributions from Staples-branded products accounted for 18% of its total sales of $16 billion in 2005.[20] However, with more competition in the office supplies market, Staples has started changing its strategy in the last few years. But Staples does not want to limit itself to low-cost, me-too products. Instead, it wants to pursue the development of more innovative products—products that will position the firm as an innovator with national brand recognition.

How can a company without a vast internal product development group pursue such an ambitious innovation agenda? Staples believes that innovative ideas are out there in the marketplace. As Jevin Eagle, the Senior Vice President of Staples brands, notes, "Our job is to scour the world for ideas."[21] To hunt for those ideas, Staples holds an "idea" contest called InventionQuest—individual inventors are invited to submit their ideas to Staples, and winning ideas are commercialized by Staples under Staples brand name with the inventor receiving 8% of revenues of royalty (see **Figure 2.2**). Staples also employs third parties such as PDG LLC., to reach out into the inventor community and bring back promising ideas to Staples for potential commercialization.

In pursuing this form of network-centric innovation, Staples sources ideas from the large inventor community, significantly increasing its potential to generate valuable ideas. In a recent contest, about 10,000 individual inventors submitted ideas. Ron Sargent, Staples' CEO, believes that this innovation strategy—centered on external inventor networks—will form its main weapon to fuel Staples' revenue growth in the future. It has already enabled Staples to surpass its main competitor, Office Depot, in revenues and become the top retailer in the office superstore market.

In Stores Now

Staples has received 22,000 ideas from amateur inventors in the past few years. An assortment of products that made it to shelves:

Staples Rubber Bandits
Extra long rubber bands with a write-on label
Invented by: Adrian Chernoff
Introduced: May 2005
Price: $2.99

Staples WordLock
A combination lock that uses letters
Invented by: Todd Basche
Introduced: June 2005 Price: $5.98

Staples Handy Strap Stapler
Has removable base and a Velcro strap on the back
Invented by: Nancy Garner
Introduced: July 2005 Price: $9.99

Staples TackDots
Small rubber disc with adhesive on the back
Invented by: Neil Grimwood
Introduced: May 2005
Price: $3.99

© Staples, Inc. Reprinted by permission.

Figure 2.2   Staples and the inventor network (from *The Wall Street Journal* Online, July 13, 2006)

DEVELOPER NETWORKS AND SALESFORCE.COM

Yet another flavor of network-centric innovation is the creation of an ecosystem of developers who can innovate on a common platform. Consider how Salesforce.com, a leading vendor of customer relationship management (CRM) solutions, has leveraged the power of independent software developers. Founded in 1999 by former Oracle executive, Marc Benoiff, Salesforce.com offers CRM software that enables businesses to track and analyze all of their interactions with customers in real-time. The unique aspect of Salesforce.com is that it provides this solution exclusively "on demand"—in other words, client firms access the application software as a service through a Web browser over the Internet.

More recently, Salesforce.com has created a unique approach to tap into the creativity of independent software developers to enhance its software offerings. In 2005, it launched AppExchange, a forum for external developers to create add-on applications that can link into or integrate with the main Salesforce.com system. More than 600 such add-on applications are available, ranging from e-mail marketing tools to sales analysis tools to finance tools.

Unlike other large software firms such as Microsoft and Oracle, Salesforce.com does not just provide a forum for external developers to develop applications on the platform. Instead, it actively participates in it by marketing the tools offered on the AppExchange to its clients and even conducts the sales transactions and appropriates the proceeds back to the external developers. In many instances, it also provides guidance and direction for innovation efforts of its software partners by channeling potential application ideas from clients to the external developers. The company also plays the role of a community sponsor and promoter by facilitating interactions among the developers as well as by providing the infrastructure for writing and sharing customized solutions.

Thus, in establishing AppExchange, Salesforce.com pursued a network-centric innovation strategy wherein its primary role was to provide the broad vision and the basis (that is, the technology platform) for the innovation and to orchestrate the activities and interactions among its global partners. What does Salesforce.com gain from doing this? Two things—first, the tools and solutions offered through the AppExchange clearly add value to the basic software application that Salesforce.com offers to its clients. Second and more importantly, the community of developers in AppExchange enhances the overall innovation reach and range of Salesforce.com. The company does not offer the full and integrated range of enterprise solutions that firms such as Oracle and SAP offer. But through AppExchange, Salesforce.com can now extend its services to other and more profitable applications areas, such as human resources and finance, as well as to markets such as the healthcare industry. By following a network-centric innovation strategy, Salesforce.com is able to derive innovation gains that are orders of magnitude higher than would be possible with its limited resources.

ELECTRONIC R&D MARKETPLACES AND 3M

In recent years, a number of electronic R&D networks like InnoCentive (www.innocentive.com) and NineSigma (www.ninesigma.com) have sprung up as another interesting flavor of a network-centric innovation mechanism. These networks play a matchmaking role between "seekers" of solutions to scientific problems (typically large R&D-intensive corporations) and "solvers" of these problems (typically individual scientists or small research laboratories spread across the world). Large companies often have very specific technical issues and R&D problems that they are unable to solve internally at an acceptable cost or time frame. When potential solutions from inside the company dry up, they use electronic R&D networks as a vehicle to look outside for those answers by tapping into the global talent pool of scientists and engineers.

Consider the R&D problem that the large industrial manufacturer 3M recently faced—it wanted an adhesive system that would be capable of durably adhering a polyester film to an oil-laden natural stone or fired clay surface.[22] The adhesive needed to be resistant to oils, cleaning chemicals, high pH detergents, and standing water. The adhesive system also needed to remain bonded to the oil-soaked surface for at least 18 months. Unable to find an appropriate internal solution to this problem, 3M turned to NineSigma, an electronic R&D marketplace. NineSigma hosts a global community of scientists and technologists with deep expertise in different fields. NineSigma prepared a Request for Proposal (RFP) based on 3M's requirements. Thousands of relevant scientists viewed the RFP and five potential solutions were offered through the NineSigma Web site. 3M evaluated the solutions and selected one as the most appropriate.

In this network-centric innovation scenario, the relevant part of the Global Brain consists of a global pool of scientists and technologists with 3M playing the role of a solution seeker and NineSigma playing the role of a marketplace operator.

DIFFERENT NETWORKS, DIFFERENT APPROACHES, DIFFERENT OUTCOMES

The earlier examples portray the different forms that network-centric innovation can assume—different types of networks or different types of the Global Brain involved, different types of roles for companies to play, different types of relationships among network members, and different types of innovation outcomes or returns (see **Table 2.3**).

Table 2.3   The Different Flavors of Network-Centric Innovation

Example of Network-Centric Innovation	Nature of Network	Firm's Role in the Network	Nature of Innovation Returns for the Firm
Open source software community and IBM	Global network of software developers	Sponsor and promote the open source movement	Synergies from the open source offerings
Customer community and Ducati	Community of customer co-innovators	Facilitate and coordinate customer participation in product innovation	Innovative ideas for product enhancement
Inventor network and Staples	Network of individual inventors	Seek out and commercialize promising new product concepts	New product or service ideas
AppExchange community and Salesforce.com	Global network of external software developers	Orchestrate and market external developers' add-on offerings	Extend the reach and range of the innovation (software) platform
NineSigma and 3M	Global network of scientists	Buyer of solutions to R&D problems	Solutions to clearly defined technical problems

These differences hold important implications for companies pursing the network-centric innovation strategy. Let us consider some of these implications.

IMPLICATIONS FOR REACH AND RANGE OF INNOVATION

The different flavors of network-centric innovation offer very different levels of the firm's *reach* into the Global Brain and the *range* of innovative ideas it can source from it. For example, Ducati has direct ties with its network of customer co-innovators whereas both 3M and Staples interact with much larger networks (comprised of scientists and individual inventors, respectively) through intermediary organizations.

Similarly, the range of innovative ideas also differs in the preceding examples. In the case of 3M, the focus was on a niche technical problem that needed to be solved. The nature of the problem space was clearly defined by 3M—in other words, there were few uncertainties regarding what the solution should achieve.

In the case of Staples, it was a much more ambiguous innovation space. All that Staples had in view was innovative product concepts that would align well with its existing brand and channel. On the other hand, Salesforce.com had defined the basic innovation platform and the broad design parameters (that is, its main CRM software application) and the network partners were responsible for coming up with innovative product designs or add-ons that adhered to these broad parameters and extended the value of the platform.

Thus, several important questions can be posed: Where are the innovative ideas situated? What type of network should the firm "connect to"? What is the company's reach into that network? And, what is the range of innovation that can be sourced and pursued collaboratively?

IMPLICATIONS FOR ORGANIZATIONAL CAPABILITIES

It is also evident that companies play different roles or participate in different types of innovation activities in network-centric innovation. They also have different types of relationships with the members of the network. These different roles and relationships imply the need for different types of organizational capabilities.

For example, whereas Salesforce.com has to provide leadership for its network of global partners, 3M plays the role of an innovation seeker and leverages the expertise available in the network of scientists. In contrast, IBM seeks to promote and champion the open source software movement and not overtly coordinate the software development activities. Similarly, consider the relational capabilities. The capabilities needed by Salesforce.com to interact with a set of global partners are different from those needed by Staples or Ducati to interact with a larger network of inventors (or customers, as the case may be).

In sum, different types of players in network-centric innovation require different types of capabilities. Understanding the nature of the role your company plans to play in network-centric innovation is important to figure out the nature of organizational capabilities and competencies that need to be developed.

IMPLICATIONS FOR INNOVATION RISKS AND RETURNS

The different examples also imply different types of risks and returns from the resulting innovation. For example, certain approaches seem to be designed to reduce the business, market, or technological risk assumed by a company. Consider Salesforce.com's initiative. By getting external software developers to invest capital into developing complementary products and committing to the basic software platform, the company is able to share some of the innovation risk with its partners. On the other hand, some other approaches are designed to seek out really creative and new concepts—for example, Staples takes relatively "raw" ideas from the inventor network to commercialize and in doing so it trades-off the higher market risk for a more innovative product portfolio.

Thus, clearly, different forms of network-centric innovation imply different types of innovation risks and returns and pose some interesting questions for a company. What types of returns is it expecting from collaborative innovation? What is its risk threshold? Or, what types of risks is the company willing to assume?

BRINGING A METHOD TO THE MADNESS

As evident from our discussion in this chapter, the varied approaches to network-centric innovation imply different opportunities with different implications. Naturally, the question then is, how should a company go about deciding what is the most appropriate network-centric innovation opportunity?

To answer this question, firms need to go beyond simply trying out different approaches and seeing what works, or copying what works for other companies. Instead, we recommend a more systematic approach that starts with a good understanding of the broad structure of network-centric innovation opportunities. With this knowledge in hand, managers can then narrow their focus to select a place in the landscape that is most relevant for the firm's innovation context.

What do we mean by a company's "innovation context"? The context includes the industry, technology, market, and internal organizational characteristics that together define the frame within which firms define and pursue their innovation agenda.

For example, consider technology and market-related attributes. How dynamic are the company's core product technologies? How diverse are the product and technology knowledgebase? What is the nature of the customer base? Are complex and expensive infrastructure required for ideation in the industry? How capital-intensive is (product) commercialization? Similarly, consider organizational attributes. What is the nature of innovation that the organization is hoping to pursue collaboratively? What is the existing innovation infrastructure of the company? What is the collaboration experience of the company? What type of relational skills has it developed? What type of innovative contributions is the company expecting from outside? What type of value appropriation mechanisms and "property rights" systems is it comfortable with?

The answers to these and other similar contextual questions will indicate what type of innovation network would be most appropriate for the company to participate in, what types of roles the company can play in it, what types of capabilities it should develop for those roles, and more importantly, how the returns from those collaborative innovation activities will contribute toward the company's goals and objectives.

However, before we start looking at the company's innovation context, we need to develop a deeper understanding of the broad structure of the network-centric innovation landscape. In the next chapter, we do just that by defining the four fundamental models or archetypes of network-centric innovation.

II

The Landscape of Network-Centric Innovation

Chapter 3 The Four Models of Network-Centric Innovation   51

Chapter 4 Innovation Networks: The Players and the Plays   67

3

The Four Models of
Network-Centric Innovation

When you last saw a movie or a documentary on your TV, did you wonder how it was made? Probably not—because we assume that all movies are produced in more or less the same way. Here is the typical production process: A film production studio like Miramax Films acquires the rights to a movie script and decides to produce the movie. Then the studio looks for a director for the movie as well as the lead cast members. After these key people are lined up, other cast members are selected. In parallel, the studio signs up other specialists, including people who do the lighting, catering, select locations, and so on. When the production starts, these specialist service providers are called upon as needed. The studio's role is to coordinate the activities of all the participants. Although the studio uses the movie script to broadly define the theme and the budget of the film, it tends to leave sufficient leeway for creative input from the movie team, including the director, the actors, the cinematographer, the make-up artists, the special effects team, and the film editor. After the movie is completed, the studio contracts with the distributor (for example, Sony Pictures) who in turn works with exhibitors (for example, AMC Theaters) to distribute and market the film. The studio also ensures that revenues that the movie produces from the theatrical, video, international, cable, and other channels are shared among the participants in the production and distribution, based on contractual terms.

That's the conventional model for movie production—where a central player (the studio) defines the context for the movie and orchestrates the production activities. However, this isn't the only model for movie production. In recent years, several interesting new movie production approaches have popped up.

One approach is the antithesis of the traditional studio production—a model of film making in which there is no single, dominant player like a movie studio. Instead, all the participants in the production come together to provide the direction and the coordination for producing the movie. The script for this model could be "Open Source Meets Hollywood!" Consider the case of a British film project called *A Swarm of Angels,* which has the objective of attracting 50,000 people to collaboratively create a £1 million film.[1] A preliminary movie script or a story sketch is posted on an online forum. All the members of the online forum are then invited to contribute to the further script development, production, and distribution. The project director is a Brighton-based digital film pioneer, Matt Hanson, who conceived the idea. The project has three stages: Fund (collect initial funding from members); Film (develop the script and execute pre-production/production/post-production); and Flow (market and distribute the film; create spin-off materials, and so on). Through a dedicated online forum (called Nine Orders), members are invited to contribute £25 each and officially become collaborators on the project. Why should anybody contribute money to such an "open" project? A collaborator can become involved in the creative process of making the feature film—right from writing the script to making the movie to marketing and distribution. The movie is made using digital techniques and the finished film is shared or distributed worldwide on a Creative Commons license that allows free downloading and viewing, free sharing, and free remixing. Currently, two sci-fi-based scripts, titled *Unfold* and *Glitch,* are under production.

Yet another model for movie production features a central player like a movie studio, but the creative contributions come from a community of contributors. In this model, the central entity markets and distributes the content, but the content itself emerges organically from the community. Unlike the traditional movie studio production model, there is no predefined theme, script, or director. In fact, production occurs in reverse—the *audience* produces the movie content, rather than the studio producing the movie and marketing it to the audience.

An excellent example of this "reverse" production model is a media startup firm called Current TV (www.current.tv) that is the brainchild of former U.S. Vice President Al Gore. Gore and his business partner Joel Hyatt founded a media company called INdTV with the objective of offering an independent voice for a target audience of people between 18 and 34—a highly prized target audience in the entertainment industry. The original intent was to provide this audience with a forum to "learn about the world in a voice they recognize and a view they recognize as their own."[2] INdTV acquired a channel from the Canadian network NewsWorld International (a part of Vivendi Universal) for a reported $70 million.[3] In April 2005, Gore and Hyatt changed the name of the network from INdTV to Current TV. Programming on Current TV was launched on August 1, 2005 in the U.S. (as of July 2007, it was available in approximately 30 million homes nationwide) and on March 12, 2007 in UK and Ireland.

Most of Current TV's programming features short-duration videos or "pods" that are anywhere from three to seven minutes. The videos are submitted by the viewers themselves—Current TV calls this programming Viewer Created Content or VC^2. Viewers are invited to submit their videos for potential broadcast and the company decides which videos it will broadcast on its cable channel. After a video is selected for broadcast, Current TV buys exclusive rights for the video using a tiered pricing structure (payments range from $500–$1,000). Current TV engages viewers in the selection process by asking them to vote on the videos. These viewer ratings decide whether a video is shown again or not. More recently, Current TV extended its strategy to get its viewers involved in creating advertisements for the Current TV program sponsor companies. These viewer-created ads also carry compensation up to $1,000. If the ads are good enough for use elsewhere, creators can get up to $50,000 from the sponsor company.

In the Current TV model of production, the creative output (pods) of independent contributors is acquired and commercialized (broadcast) using a proprietary infrastructure (the Current TV network channel), and the company owns the rights to the content. The incentives for contributors, according to the company, are three-fold—cash, fame, and creative freedom.[4]

Yet another model of filmmaking takes a different approach to both the production process as well as to the ownership of the output. In this model, the participants are given the building blocks to make a movie, and are then allowed to create, distribute, and view the resulting movies as they see fit.

To see how this innovative model works in practice, consider the example of MOD Films, a new-generation film company. MOD Films was founded by

Michela Ledwidge, a British-based media producer, in 2004. The business model of the company involves producing a regular movie and then offering it to the global audience over the Internet in a form malleable enough to allow them to edit, modify, or remix it to suit their taste. As *Wired* magazine noted, MOD Films offers "a massively multiplayer online movie."[5] The first such film is *Sanctuary*—a ten-minute virtual reality sci-fi film shot in Australia in 2005. The film is about a girl, her computer, and a mysterious murder. The original film, released under the Creative Commons license, provides a story framework that the audience can play with—they can disassemble and reassemble materials themselves to create their own interpretation of the story.[6] And, the resulting output will also be available under the Creative Commons license. Sanctuary is distributed as DVD-Video as well as in the HD Video format along with a vast library material. Specifically, more than nine hours of production footage and 90 minutes of sound effects and dialog along with storyboards, still photos, and so on are available for viewers who have subscribed to the online forum maintained by MOD Films.[7] Viewers can play around with these cinematic elements using a downloadable software tool called Switch that the company provides. More films are on the anvil including *The Watch* (a drama) and *Extra Fox* (a comedy).

These four models for movie production are very different in terms of how they are organized, how the process works, and who owns the output. But they have something in common—collaboration among a network of contributors to create an innovative product. More importantly, these models from the entertainment industry are examples of emerging innovation models that lie at the confluence of social or commons-based production methods and hierarchical/market-based production methods. As such, they are harbingers of the network-centric innovation approaches that we are likely to see in the mainstream business world.

Indeed, the entertainment industry has always been a trendsetter in managing and organizing creativity. In a classic article published in 1977 in the *Harvard Business Review*, Eileen Morley and Andrew Silver described a film director's approach to managing creativity and distilled a set of wonderful insights for business managers.[8] Over the next three decades or so, several of those concepts and practices based on successful film projects from Hollywood have found their way into the business world.[9] And, as the preceding examples indicate, the film and the TV industry continue to pave the path in managing innovation and creativity.

FRAMING THE LANDSCAPE OF NETWORK-CENTRIC INNOVATION

Taking inspiration from the entertainment industry, let us consider some of the common themes that emerge from the different models of movie production, and how these themes help us to frame the landscape of network-centric innovation in the movie industry and beyond.

When we compare the traditional model of film making with the one followed by Current TV, we note that there is no predefined theme or script for the movie. Even though the studio still calls the shots in terms of what gets aired, the content of the movie is not controlled by the studio. Instead, it emerges as a result of the collaboration among the contributors. Although script-driven movies and documentaries still form the majority of the output from the industry, examples like Current TV suggest the rise of audience-defined content, where consumers take on the role of producers.

Initiatives like the *Swarm of Angels* go even further, in that the studio plays an even lesser role—that of an enabler and the facilitator of collaboration among individual contributors. In this model, individual contributors exercise greater influence on all or some aspects of filmmaking. Another example of this type of initiative is the Echo Chamber Project, an experiment in documentary production. The Echo Chamber Project is an investigative documentary about "how the television news media became an uncritical echo chamber to the executive branch leading up to the war in Iraq."[10] The project, led by Kent Bye, a documentary filmmaker based in Winterport, Maine, involves a collaborative editing process wherein the lead creator provides a preliminary set of video segments and other collaborators help in categorizing the video segments into different thematic clusters and creating the sequence (storyline). The edited sequences are then exported for final production.

The emerging models and trends in the movie industry illustrate two key dimensions of creative endeavor along which we see change happening. The first dimension relates to the nature of the movie itself—that is, how the overall storyline and content of the movie is defined and how it evolves. The second dimension relates to the structure of the network of contributors to the project; that is, how the talent comes together and shares in activities related to producing, marketing, and distributing the movie.

Generalizing these dimensions to the broader innovation context, we can think of two key dimensions in organizing innovative efforts—the *nature of the innovation* and the *nature of the network leadership*. These two dimensions help us to structure the landscape of network-centric innovation. We now explore these two dimensions in more detail.

THE DIMENSIONS OF NETWORK-CENTRIC INNOVATION

Structure of the Innovation Space

Different types of projects can be pursued collaboratively in innovation networks. As you saw in Chapter 2, "Understanding Network-Centric Innovation," some of the projects involve making well-defined modifications or enhancements to existing products, services, or technology platforms. In other projects, the innovation space tends to be less defined and the outcomes of the innovative effort are not well understood at the outset.

Based on this, we can think about the innovation space as a continuum ranging from "defined" on one end to "emergent" at the other end (see **Figure 3.1**). On the defined end of the continuum, the definition might occur around a technology platform or a technology standard. Such is the case of AppExchange, the development platform created by Salesforce.com to harness the creative efforts of independent software developers. The innovation space can also be defined by dependencies created by existing products or processes. For example, Ducati engages its customers in innovation primarily to generate product improvement ideas for its existing products. Similarly, 3M's engagement with NineSigma.com was defined in terms of the properties of the adhesive material that the company was seeking. In all these examples, the innovative efforts are defined and limited by existing products, processes, or technology platforms.

At the other end of the continuum, the structure of the innovation space can be less defined and more uncertain. Although the broad contours of the innovative space might be specified or known—for example, the target market for a new product or service or the existing commercialization infrastructure—there might be fewer restrictions on the nature or process of the innovation. For example, when Staples looks around for innovative ideas, it is seeking new product concepts for the office supplies market. Similarly, in the Open Source Software arena, many of the projects relate to developing totally new software applications—whether it be developing a new development tool or developing a new operating system.

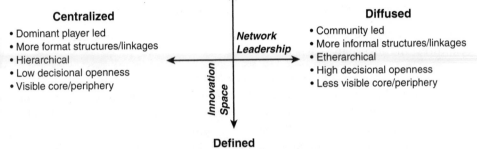

Emergent
- Less defined/unstructured problem space
- Exploration, novelty
- Focus on creating new knowledge/assets
- Emphasis on 'unknown connections' in knowledge-base

Centralized
- Dominant player led
- More format structures/linkages
- Hierarchical
- Low decisional openness
- Visible core/periphery

Network Leadership

Innovation Space

Diffused
- Community led
- More informal structures/linkages
- Etherarchical
- High decisional openness
- Less visible core/periphery

Defined
- Clearly defined/structured problem space
- Exploitation, efficiency
- Focus on utilizing existing knowledge/assets
- Emphasis on 'known connections' in knowledge-base

Figure 3.1   Dimensions of network-centric innovation

Another way to understand this continuum is to think about its implications for capabilities and knowledge. The more well-defined the innovation space is, the more the focus on *exploiting* an existing knowledge-base or leveraging existing technologies. On the other hand, the more emergent the innovation space, the more the emphasis on *exploration* of opportunities in the innovation space and on making creative connections among disparate knowledge domains.

Now, consider the second dimension—the structure of the network leadership.

Structure of the Network Leadership

An innovation network—whether it is an open source community, an electronic R&D marketplace like NineSigma.com, or an ecosystem of technology firms as in the case of Salesforce.com—consists of a set of independent actors with varying goals and aspirations, diverse resources and capabilities, and different business models.

For all these entities to play together in the innovation initiative, there has to be a mechanism to ensure some coherence among their activities, capabilities, and aspirations. This mechanism can go by different names—network leadership, governance, or management. Whatever the precise term, the essence is the need for a mechanism that can provide the vision and direction for the innovation and establish the rhythm for the innovation activities.

Thus, the name we give to the second dimension—the *Network Leadership*—captures this governance aspect.

Network leadership can be thought of as a continuum of centralization, with the two ends being *centralized* versus *diffused*. At the centralized end of the continuum, the network is led by a dominant firm that leads the network. Leadership may be exercised in different ways—envisioning and establishing the innovation architecture, making the critical decisions that affect or shape the nature and the process of innovation, and defining the nature and membership of the network itself. For example, in its technology ecosystem, Salesforce.com provides the leadership by establishing and promoting the technology platform and by facilitating the activities of its external developers.

At the "diffused" end of the continuum, the leadership tends to be loosely distributed among the members of the network. All members of the network share responsibility for leading the network. For example, many Open Source Software projects have a democratic leadership structure wherein the different members of the community share the decision-making powers.

To further understand the distinctions between these two ends, think about the concept of the *core* and the *periphery* in networks. The core of a network can be thought of as one or more members of the network who are connected to one another more closely and form the central part of the network. The periphery consists of those members of the network who have limited ties with other members of the network and are more distant from the center of the network.[11] For example, consider your own social network. A small set of people forms the core of your social network. These people might include your immediate family, your close friends, and your colleagues. Then there are more casual acquaintances, your relatives and distant family members, the people at your workplace who interact with you, and so on who form the periphery of your social network.

As we move from the left to the right on the continuum of network leadership, we think about innovation networks that have a clearly defined core with a single dominant firm to networks where the core and periphery are less well defined or where the core consists of all or most of the members. For example, at the extreme left, we might consider networks such as Microsoft .NET or Intel's microprocessor platform network—contexts where a single firm forms the core of the network, provides the leadership, and makes all the key innovation decisions. As we move toward the center, we think of networks such as IBM's Power chip innovation alliance (www.power.org) wherein IBM forms the core of the network but shares more decision-making rights with other members of the network. As we go further to the right, the core might consist of more than one member, and at the extreme, the core might include most or even all of the members of the network. For example, Open Source Software projects have leadership structures that lie at different points on the right part of this continuum.

INTRODUCING THE FOUR MODELS OF NETWORK-CENTRIC INNOVATION

The two dimensions—innovation space and network leadership—when crossed together, define four archetypical models that help structure the landscape of network-centric innovation. With a bow to the entertainment industry, we call these four models the *Orchestra* model, the *Creative Bazaar* model, the *Jam Central* model, and the *Mod Station* model (see **Figure 3.2**).

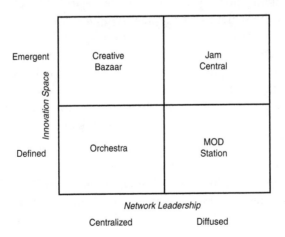

Figure 3.2 The four models of network-centric innovation

We now paint a picture of the defining characteristics of each of these models, drawing parallels from the music and entertainment world. We will explore each model in greater detail in Chapters 5 through 8 of the book.

THE ORCHESTRA MODEL

When we think about an orchestra, we visualize a conductor holding sway with his wand, directing a group of musicians—each a specialist in a specific musical instrument. The musicians come together to play scripted (often, classical) music. The scripted music—whether it is Beethoven's Eroica Symphony or Mozart's Symphony No. 40 in G Minor—provides a well-defined structure for the performances of individual musicians. Although individual musicians might have some leeway in interpreting the music creatively, they are generally supposed to follow the script. And to a large extent, the responsibility of coordinating the musicians falls with the conductor. The conductor communicates with individual musicians (usually through gestures), and this communication determines whether the music that the audience hears is just a mechanical rendition of the script or a moving and elegant interpretation of the script. As the critic Eduard Hanslick noted in the 1880s, the best conductors are able to control and shape "every note and inflection emanating from the musicians under their command."[12]

The Orchestra model for network-centric innovation closely resembles the organization and the structure of a typical symphony orchestra (see **Table 3.1**). In this context, the structure of the innovation space is fairly well-defined and the network leadership is centralized with a single dominant firm. The innovation context provides a clear basis for structuring the activities of the individual actors in the innovation network. And just as the musical instruments in an orchestra need to resonate with each other, the innovative contributions of network members in the Orchestra model also complement one another.

Just as an orchestra is led by a conductor who orchestrates the musical performances of individual musicians to create a coherent symphony, in the network-centric innovation context, the leadership provided by the dominant firm is crucial to ensuring that the innovative contributions of individual contributors add up to a valuable whole.

Table 3.1   The Orchestra Model of Network-Centric Innovation

Symphony Orchestra	Orchestra Model of Network-Centric Innovation
Consists of different types of instrumentalists, each playing a specific role	Consists of a diverse set of partners, each responsible for different types of innovation activities (or components)
The composition or the script provides the structure for the musical performances	Innovation architecture provides the structure for the innovative contributions of network members
Conductor or maestro orchestrates the musical performance of individual musicians	Dominant or lead firm orchestrates the innovation activities of network members
Hierarchical relationships exist between and across the instrument subgroups	Formal relationships or ties exist between network members

Further, in an orchestra, often there is a hierarchy of leadership or a set of generally accepted (formal) relationships or ties between the instrumentalists. For example, each instrumental group or section has an assigned leader (principal or soloist) who is responsible for leading that group. Often, there is also a hierarchy between the instrument groups. For example, the violins are divided into two groups, first violins and second violins. The leader of the first violin group is considered the leader of the entire string section. Moreover, this leader is also the second-in-command of the orchestra, and is responsible for conducting the orchestra if the maestro is not present. Similarly, the principal trombone is considered the leader of the low-brass (trombone, tuba, and so on) section, whereas the principal trumpet is generally considered the leader of the entire brass section.[13] Even though such a set of hierarchical relationships might not translate directly into the network-centric innovation context, the analogy lies in the formal relationships or ties among the members of the innovation network.

The Orchestra model of network-centric innovation describes a situation wherein a group of firms come together to exploit a market opportunity based on an explicit innovation architecture that is defined and shaped by a dominant firm. The innovation architecture typically emphasizes efficiency over novelty, so there is a heavy emphasis on modularity of the innovation architecture.

Innovation processes tend to be highly organized and coordinated with significant investments made in infrastructure to support the roles and activities of the members of the network.

Examples of the Orchestra Model range from Microsoft .NET initiative and Salesforce.com's AppExchange network to Boeing's development of the Dreamliner 787. These examples represent several variations of the Orchestra model. In Chapter 5, "The Orchestra Model," we will examine the Orchestra model and these variations in more detail through specific examples.

THE CREATIVE BAZAAR MODEL

When you listen to your favorite new music artist, have you wondered how he or she got noticed from among the crowd of struggling artists, and ended up launching an album with a major record label? Record labels look for "diamonds in the rough" in lots of ways. They might look for promising but unknown artists through talent scouts and talent contests like the *American Idol*. Or they might opt for tried and trusted performers who have a new album or single and who have a ready-made audience. In both situations, the record company typically only specifies the broad category of interest—the genre of music and the target customer segments—and not the lyrics or choreography of the music. However, the label does have the final say in selecting, developing, and marketing the albums. In other words, while the record label still plays the role of a dominant player, it takes a flexible and open approach to finding talent and letting them come up with innovative music. In effect, the record label shops around in the talent bazaar.

This model of music production is what we think of as an analogy in proposing the second model of network-centric innovation—the *Creative Bazaar* model (see **Table 3.2**). This model describes a context wherein a dominant firm shops for innovation in a global bazaar of new ideas, products, and technologies and uses its proprietary commercialization infrastructure to build on the ideas and make them "market-ready." The commercialization infrastructure might include design capabilities, brands, capital, and access to distribution channels.

Table 3.2 The Creative Bazaar Model of Network-Centric Innovation

Music Recording Studio or Label	Creative Bazaar Model of Network-Centric Innovation
The studio is the dominant player and makes the critical technical and market decisions	The company is the dominant member of the innovation network and makes the critical decisions regarding commercialization of the innovation
Music offerings acquired from a wide range of sources and in varied forms—from talent to market-ready songs	Innovative ideas (products, services, technologies) sourced from a diverse network of inventors and in varied stages of maturity—from raw ideas to market-validated concepts
A range of mechanisms to source music—from talent scouts to talent contests to music agents	A range of innomediaries used to source innovation
The specific nature of the music is more emergent—the only constraint is that it should fit the studio's broad market strategy	The nature of the innovation is emergent—the only constraint is that it should fit the company's overall target market and brand portfolio

In much the same way as a music studio sources new musical compositions from a wide variety of artists, companies that use the Creative Bazaar model to source new product/service use lots of mechanisms to source new ideas and technologies from inventors. For example, product scouts and licensing agents identify promising new product and technology ideas and bring them to large companies for further development and commercialization. Companies can also shop for more market-ready products (that is, product or technology concepts that have been prototyped and market validated) and acquire them from incubators and venture capital firms. Regardless of the sourcing approach, the company plays the dominant role in the innovation network by offering its infrastructure for developing and commercializing the innovation. However, the nature of the innovation space is not that well-defined, because the target markets or technology arenas are defined relatively broadly, and it isn't clear where the idea will come from, or what it will look like.

In summary, the Creative Bazaar model aims to seek out and bring to fruition innovation opportunities that meet the broad market and innovation agenda of the dominant firm. The term *bazaar* implies a dizzying array of wares on offer, ranging from raw ideas and patents to relatively mature or "market-ready" new product concepts, as well as the presence of different hawkers that companies can deal with, from idea scouts, patent brokers, and electronic innovation marketplaces to incubation agencies, venture capitalists, and so on.

THE JAM CENTRAL MODEL

Consider a musical jam session. It typically involves a group of musicians getting together to play or "jam" without extensive preparation and without the intention to follow any specific musical pattern or arrangement. Improvisation is the key to a good jam session. Musicians often follow a "call and response" pattern—that is, a succession of two distinct notes or phrases played by different musicians, where "the second phrase is heard as a direct commentary on or response to the first."[14]

The term *jam* can be traced back to 1929 when it was used to refer to "short, free improvised passage performed by the whole band."[15] The term signifies two key themes: It is a group activity and it is improvisational. The degree of improvisation might vary from being loosely based on an agreed chord progression to being completely improvisational. Further, unlike an orchestra or other musical contexts, typically, there is no single leader in a jam session. All the musicians share in the responsibility to keep the time or the rhythm.

The jam session is our inspiration for the third model of network-centric innovation—the *Jam Central* model (see **Table 3.3**). This model involves individual contributors coming together to collaborate in envisioning and developing an innovation. The innovation space is typically not well structured and the objectives and direction of the innovation tends to emerge organically from the collaboration. There are no dominant members, and the responsibility for leading and coordinating the activity is diffused among the network members. Even if the leadership is not equally shared by all members, key decisions that shape the innovation processes and outcomes tend to evolve from the interactions of the network members.

Table 3.3 The Jam Central Model of Network-Centric Innovation

Musical Jam Session	Jam Central Model of Network-Centric Innovation
Group of musicians get together to perform music in an improvisational manner	Members of an innovation network get together to innovate in an improvisational manner
The nature and form of the music evolves or emerges from the "call and response" among the group members	The structure of the innovation (goals, architecture, processes, and so on) are emergent; that is, it evolves from the continued interactions of the members
All the participants of the jam session share in the responsibility for coordinating the music	The leadership of the innovation network is diffused among all or a group of the network members

In sum, the Jam Central model is characterized by a shared exploration of an innovation arena by a peer group of contributors who share in the responsibility of directing and coordinating the innovation effort.

THE MOD STATION MODEL

The term *mod* originally stood for modernism and was used to refer to a youth lifestyle based around fashion and music that developed in London, England, in the late 1950s.[16] But the term had a rebirth in the computer gaming industry in the early 2000s. Computer-based games that were modifications of existing games were referred to as "mods." In other words, mod stood for modification. And, this is the perspective that we adopt here when using the term *mod*.

By offering the source of a video game to a community of gamers, a company can enable the creation of variations of the game. These modifications can involve adding new characters, new textures, new story lines, and so on. Depending on the extent of modifications, they can be "partial conversions" or "total conversions." Total conversions typically turn out to be completely new games that happen to use some of the basic content or structure of the original game. Mods are made by the general gaming public or *modders*. Increasingly, the gaming companies have started assisting modders by providing extensive tools and documentation. The mods are then distributed and used over the Internet. The most popular mod is *Counter-Strike*, a game that originated as a modification of another game called *Half-Life* produced by Valve Corporation, a software firm based in Bellevue, Washington.

Based on the mod idea, we define the fourth and final model for network-centric innovation—the *Mod Station* model (see **Table 3.4**). This model has two key characteristics. First, it largely involves modifying or leveraging an existing (product, process, or service) innovation—that is, activities that occur within the boundaries of a predefined innovation space, and aim to add, enhance, or adapt existing products or services. Second, it occurs in a community where the norms and values that govern the innovation are established by the community and not by any one dominant firm.

Table 3.4   The Mod Station Model of Network-Centric Innovation

Mod Forums in Computing Gaming Industry	Mod Station of Network-Centric Innovation
Involves modification of existing computer-based games based on the source provided by the original creator	Innovation that is based on an existing, well-defined architecture—the nature of the innovation is incremental
The mods are created by the general gaming public	The innovation is carried out by a community of users and experts
The coordination for the innovation is diffused within the community	The leadership is diffused among the members of the innovation network

In sum, the Mod Station model is focused on exploiting existing innovation or knowledge to address market/technological issues by a community of innovators (innovation users, customers, scientists, experts, and so on). Examples of such network-centric innovation range from commercial open source communities such as SugarCRM to open source projects such as OpenSPARC wherein networks of scientists and experts innovate within the boundaries defined by an existing product or process architecture.

FROM THE PLAYS TO THE PLAYERS

These four models help us to structure the landscape of network-centric innovation. But our framework is not yet complete. In each of the models of network-centric innovation, firms can play different types of roles. What is an innovation role? And, what are the broad categories of such innovation roles? Further, all innovation networks require some basic operational infrastructure for creating as well as capturing value. This includes the mechanisms for managing intellectual property rights and the systems for sharing knowledge. What are the general elements of the network operational infrastructure? In the next chapter, we address these questions.

4

Innovation Networks: The Players and the Plays

Think about the last big home remodeling project you undertook. The project probably involved a number of actors—the general contractor, the subcontractors, the architect, the mortgage company or bank, the workers, and the material suppliers. Each of these actors, including you, played a clearly defined role in the project. And to manage the project, you needed to figure out how to coordinate and communicate with everyone. This might have included defining the contract terms, setting out the rules of engagement, and making sure the project stayed on track. A remodeling project, like any collaborative activity, brings together a set of independent players with clearly defined roles, who operate within a supporting system to manage the project.

Similarly, network-centric innovation requires participants in the network to play specific roles. These innovation roles are characterized by the types of activities involved or the type of innovative contributions that are required. Understanding the nature of these different innovation roles is important because they define the capabilities that players need to bring to the innovation project.

A collaborative project also requires a system to facilitate and coordinate the activities in the network. Someone needs to decide how the project will be managed or governed. And someone needs to manage the knowledge that is created and decide who owns what intellectual property.

In this chapter, we consider the different types of players in an innovation network, and the different types of activities that need to be performed to manage the network. We identify three distinct roles that network members can play—*architects, agents, and adapters*. And we highlight the three key elements of network management—*network governance, knowledge management,* and *intellectual property management*. We reflect upon the differences in these roles and activities based on the type of network-centric innovation model.

PLAYERS IN NETWORK-CENTRIC INNOVATION

Even though an innovation network can be complex, there are only three key categories of roles that members (firms, individuals, and so on) can play in the network: *architects, adapters,* and *agents* (see **Table 4.1**).

Table 4.1   Types of Innovation Players

Type of Innovation Player	Nature of Activities	Example	Characteristics
Architect	Trigger and catalyze innovation Envision and direct innovation Tend to the innovation network	Platform leader, innovation portal, innovation steward	Typically situated at or near the core or central part of the network; assumes higher risk and enjoys greater returns from innovation
Adapter	Provide specialized knowledge/services and infrastructure services	Complementor, innovator, expert	Typically situated away from the central part of the network; exercises limited direct influence on the innovation
Agent	Mediate interactions, knowledge transfer, and innovation	Idea scout, patent broker, innovation capitalist	Tied to diverse types of members in the network; typically assumes lower risks and enjoys smaller returns from innovation

ARCHITECTS

To construct a house, the first person you need to hire is an architect. He envisions the blueprint for the house and defines the key elements of how the rooms fit together into a logical design. And so it is with innovation networks. The *architect* is the central member (or set of members) who designs and influences the evolution of an innovation network. The architect has a ring-side seat at the innovation game because it carries out or influences activities that are central to the innovation agenda of the network. These include defining the innovation architecture and standards, and deciding how to commercialize the creative outputs of the innovation network. In other words, the architect envisions and implements the "architecture of participation" in the network.

The members playing the role of an architect typically tend to be positioned in or near the central part of the network with direct linkages to the other key players in the network. Due to the nature of their activities and contributions, typically, the architects assume greater innovation risks than other members in the network and also derive greater returns from their participation than other members.

Architects perform three sets of activities: trigger and catalyze innovation, envision and direct innovation activity, and "tend" the innovation network.

The first set of activities, "trigger and catalyze innovation," relates to providing the initial impetus to create the innovation network and to define the innovation agenda. It also includes supporting and playing a catalytic role to build momentum and ensure success of the innovation project. For example, when the Human Genome Project (HGP) was launched, apart from the involvement of the U.S. government and scientific agencies such as the DoE and the NIH, a key entity was the U.K.-based Wellcome Trust. During the early 1990s, Welcome Trust played a central role in triggering the genomic research activities in the U.K. In October 1993, the Welcome Trust funded and co-sponsored the Sanger Institute (at Hinxton, south of Cambridge, U.K.)—the center later became one of the major sequencing labs in the international consortium. As the project progressed, Welcome Trust continued to play a catalytic role in the project by funding, bringing together, and facilitating the interactions of other key partners in the project, particularly in the U.K.

The second set of activities, "envision and direct innovation," relates to providing structure and bringing coherence to the activities of participants in the innovation network. This might range from establishing and maintaining the innovation architecture to making the crucial decisions related to the evolution or the commercialization of the innovation. For example, IBM and Microsoft play this role in many of the innovation networks that they lead—whether it is IBM's Power chip architecture or Microsoft's .NET architecture. In the consumer product sector, companies such as P&G and J&J play a similar role through their commercialization capabilities—in effect, offering their commercialization infrastructure as a portal for bringing to market external innovative ideas and technologies.

The third set of activities, "tending the innovation network," involves maintaining and supporting the innovation network as a whole. Consider the activities performed by a gardener. He or she decides which plants to seed in the garden and what position or place they should occupy in the garden. The gardener also nurtures and fosters the growth of the plants and makes sure that the weeds and other plants that might inhibit the overall health of the garden are identified and promptly removed. Further, a good gardener will also know the merits of *companion planting*—plants that complement one another should be planted close to each other. For example, in a vegetable garden, basil and tomatoes should be planted together. Basil acts as a fungicide and can slow the growth of or repel milkweed bugs, aphids, mites, and so on—thereby improving the growth and flavor of the tomatoes.

Similarly, the "gardening" role played by an architect in an innovation network involves managing the membership of the network and providing a nurturing environment for the network to flourish. Duties include promoting a shared set of norms and value in the network, communicating a common "world view" to network members, weeding out members who are detrimental to the health of the network, and bringing together members whose capabilities and resources complement one another. These gardening activities shape the overall success of the innovation project.

Some of the activities that underlie the preceding themes might overlap and some of the activities might appear in different forms in different networks. Furthermore, some of the players might carry out activities that relate to more than one of the preceding themes. Thus, we can identify *different types of architects* based on the nature of activities they assume in a given model of network-centric innovation. While we provide a few examples of these players in **Table 4.1**, we will identify and describe specific types of architects later on in the book (Chapters 5 to 8) when we discuss each of the four models of network-centric innovation in detail.

ADAPTERS

Every queen bee needs a number of worker bees who take direction from her and perform a specific task in making a bee colony work. Similarly, every architect needs a set of firms who take direction and contribute to the network. We call these players *adapters* because they adapt to the direction of the architect and play a supporting role that is less central, but nonetheless important, in the network. Adapters are typically located away from the core of the network and maintain a limited number of ties or relationships with other members of the network.

The activities of adapters can be grouped into two broad themes: provide specialized knowledge or services and provide infrastructure services.

Some adapters bring highly specialized knowledge and expertise to innovation programs to solve unique R&D problems or to create novel components and services that complement, extend, or enhance the innovation. For example, Intacct Corp. plays such a role in Salesforce.com's CRM platform network; it has developed and published a financial management add-on component that works on the CRM platform. Similarly, a scientist who taps into his/her specialized knowledge to provide a solution to a critical R&D problem posed by a company in an electronic R&D marketplace also plays such a role. Or, in an Open Source Software community, an individual might play the role of adapter by writing code that addresses a specific feature or requirement of the software product.

Adapters can also offer other support services in the network. Consider innovation networks in the semiconductor industry. In such networks, often, a member firm might assemble and offer design and testing libraries as infrastructure services to support the design and development activities of other member firms. For example, TSMC (Taiwan Semiconductor Manufacturing Company), the world's largest foundry for semiconductor components, offers such a Web-based library of third-party circuit designs to the other firms—the fabless chip design firms—in its network.[1] Similarly, in a network of individual inventors, companies such as Eureka Ranch play such a supportive role by offering market validation services for new product concepts.

Table 4.1 provides a few examples of the adapter role. We will describe these and other types of adapter roles in more detail in Chapters 5 to 8.

AGENTS

Innovation networks require very different sets of actors to come together. Instead of relying on serendipity and chance to bring these actors together, hiring a broker or an intermediary makes sense. We call these entities *agents*.

An agent is an innovation intermediary that mediates the interactions and innovation activities in an innovation network.[2] Agents serve as brokers, bridges, or go-betweens in innovation networks. However, they can also play more subtle roles that go beyond simple brokering.

Agents perform three sets of activities in network-centric innovation: linking members or *mediating interactions*, technology brokering or *mediating knowledge transfer, and* innovation transformation or *mediating the innovation*.

The first set of activities relates to the traditional role of an intermediary—linking two network members who are not otherwise connected to one another. As in the case of brokering a real estate transaction or executive recruiting, agents also help to "search and filter" in the innovation landscape. For example, idea scouts are agents who troll inventor communities to seek out and filter new product concepts that might be of interest to a large client firm. When they find a promising idea, they bring together or connect the inventor and the client firm.

Agents can also facilitate or mediate the transfer of innovation-related knowledge from one member to another; that is, they can play the role of a knowledge or technology broker. This activity involves not just making connections between two members but also making connections between the different types of knowledge (or technologies) held by those two members, and thereby promoting an innovation that capitalizes on that connection.

A well-known knowledge broker is IDEO, a leading design-consulting firm. Consider IDEO's work as an agent in transferring a "smart fabric" technology developed by a company called ElekSen to a new application area.[3] ElekSen is the world leader in touch-sensitive interactive textiles, which are built around the combination of conductive fabric and microchip technologies. The company's core technology is ElekTex, a unique electro-conductive, flexible, durable, and rugged "smart-fabric." While the technology has diverse applications, its entry into the computer market was brokered by IDEO. IDEO brought together ElekSen and Logitech (the developer of computer mice, keyboard, and other accessories) and facilitated the transfer of the ElekTex technology to Logitech for application in the computer accessory market. Using ElekTex technology, Logitech developed KeyCase, a fabric case for PDAs that unfolds into a keyboard. Thus, in this case, IDEO's role as an agent was not just to bridge two members, but also to serve as a conduit for the technology transfer.

The third set of activities, "mediating the innovation," relates to the innomediary not just mediating the interactions or mediating the knowledge transfer, but mediating the innovation itself. For example, consider an agent that acquires an innovative idea from one member, builds on the idea, and then passes the transformed idea to another member for further development. Compared to the earlier activities, in carrying out this activity, the agent takes a position that is much closer to the innovation—and, in part becomes the innovator, too, rather than just an intermediary. We will identify such an agent role called the *innovation capitalist* in Chapter 6, "The Creative Bazaar Model."

IMPLICATIONS OF INNOVATION ROLES

"What's in a role?" you might ask. Or, "Why is it important to understand the nature of the different innovation roles in network-centric innovation?" An innovation role is an *opportunity* to participate in network-centric innovation. So, understanding different innovation roles allows firms to assess two questions: First, do we have what it takes to play this role? Second, what role should we play to maximize our gains from the innovation network?

To answer the first question, firms need to understand the important resources and capabilities needed to perform the role. As we will discuss in Chapter 10, "Preparing the Organization," preparing the company for network-centric innovation involves identifying and developing these role-related organizational capabilities and competencies.

To address the second question, firms need to assess the risks and returns associated with the role. Understanding the nature of risks and returns is critical for a company to evaluate whether a network-centric innovation opportunity is worth pursuing even if it has the requisite capabilities to be a player.

In addition to these questions, there is a third reason why firms need to understand the innovation roles. Sometimes, firms might play different roles in different networks. Take the example of IBM. In the Power chip alliance network (power.org)—a network that is based on promoting and enhancing Power architecture—IBM plays a leading role. On the other hand, in the Linux open source community, IBM plays a more secondary and supportive role. Such multiple roles lead to the questions, "Do we need the same set of organizational capabilities for the different roles?" "Are there synergies between the roles that we can exploit?"

In Chapters 5 through 8, when we discuss each of the four models or archetypes of network-centric innovation, we will identify the set of roles that apply to each of the models and discuss their implications. This discussion allows us to analyze later in Chapter 9, "Deciding Where and How to Play," an individual firm's network-centric innovation strategy vis-à-vis the types of roles possible in that space.

ELEMENTS OF NETWORK MANAGEMENT

To run a network, the players need a set of systems and mechanisms to support and facilitate collaborative innovation. The three elements of network management are network governance, knowledge management, and IP rights management (see **Table 4.2**).

Table 4.2　Elements of Innovation Network Management

Elements of Innovation Network Management	Objective	Types of Systems	Criteria for Selecting Appropriate Systems
Network governance	Ensure common patterns of behavior among members and coordinate intermember exchange of knowledge and resources	Formal mechanisms (contracts and agreements, rules and procedures, standards) Informal or social mechanisms (restricted access to network; macroculture; collective sanctions and reputational systems)	Nature of interdependencies between network members; nature of the innovation space
Knowledge management	Facilitate the generation, codification, and utilization of knowledge in the network	Mechanisms that facilitate member dialogue; provide common vocabulary; facilitate knowledge transfer, interpretation, and integration	Degree of overlap of domain knowledge; nature of innovation; technological/domain "distance" between network members

Elements of Innovation Network Management	Objective	Types of Systems	Criteria for Selecting Appropriate Systems
IP rights management	Enable innovators (or creators) to control the use of their innovation and its derivatives	Traditional legal instruments such as patent, trademark, copyright, and so on, and more flexible licensing schemes such as Creative Commons, General Public License, and so on	Nature of innovation; nature of relationships among network members; structure of the network

NETWORK GOVERNANCE

The word *governance* is often associated with policing or control. Network governance does involve monitoring and controlling potentially deceptive or opportunistic behavior of individual members that might be detrimental to the other members and the overall network agenda. But governance is more than just policing. It also involves creating an environment that is conducive to interacting and exchanging information and resources. The systems and mechanisms for governance shape the pattern of interactions between members, as well as the flow of resources between the members.[4]

Consider your personal network at the workplace—the network of colleagues and business partners. Your relationships, interactions, and exchanges in such a network are governed both by formal and informal mechanisms. For example, the organizational structure might specify or shape the nature of your relationships with other members in your organization. Your employment contract, any confidentiality agreements that you have signed, and the rules and procedures in your department might also govern your interactions with employees in the company and beyond.

On the other hand, the widely accepted but implicit "do's and don'ts" might also shape your relationships and exchanges in the network. Remember the scene from the TV series *Seinfeld* when the character George Costanza is caught having sex with the office cleaning lady? When asked about his questionable tête-à-tête, George's reply was, "Was that wrong? Should I not have done that? I tell you, I gotta plead ignorance on this thing, because if anyone had said anything to me at all when I first started here that that sort of thing is frowned upon. . . ." Well, as George soon found out when he got fired, some things are not written down or made explicit, but still guide the nature of the relationships and exchanges among members of an organization or a network. So would the potential threat of sanctions or losing credibility for pursuing activities that are beneficial to you but not necessarily beneficial for the overall organization. These constitute the more informal or social mechanisms of governance.

In innovation networks, both formal and informal mechanisms are relevant, though their relative importance depends on the specific model of network-centric innovation. Formal mechanisms for governance include legal contracts, partnership agreements, agreements on exchange rules and procedures, shared set of standards, and so on. For example, innovation networks led by companies such as Intel and Cisco often have a charter of member rights and responsibilities that a potential partner has to sign before being accepted into the network. Similarly, in the software industry, the standards and metrics specified by the Capability Maturity Model—developed and promoted by the Software Engineering Institute—has been used as a mechanism to coordinate and govern large-scale co-development projects. Formal mechanisms not only define what is acceptable but also provide a framework to coordinate interactions and exchanges.

When it comes to informal or social mechanisms for network governance, there are several choices. These include restricting access to the network, developing and establishing a macro-culture, imposing collective sanctions, and using other reputational mechanisms. One option is to restrict membership to players who have demonstrated their competence through past associations with existing members or their broader status in the industry or sector. For example, many country clubs use such a "gated network" approach. They restrict club membership to those people who are well-known to the existing members of the club (or who are influential members of the broader society). If network membership is based on such criteria, typically the members will have more commonalities in their expectations and attributes. Thus, monitoring and/or coordinating each and every exchange in the network will be much easier and less frequently required. In other words, the nature of membership itself serves as a governance mechanism.

Another alternative is to establish and promote a culture that reflects the overall innovation agenda of the network. This might range from shared business/innovation assumptions to norms and values that can bring about a level of coherence in the actions and decisions of individual members in the network. For example, how should members critique one another's contributions in an open source community? The culture of a network gets defined over time through repeated interactions among the network, leading to a definition of "acceptable" behaviors and norms in the innovation network.

Collective sanctions and reputational systems form another set of governance mechanisms. Consider eBay. The ability of eBay merchants (that is, members) to rate one another based on the nature and the quality of the exchanges they have had with one another serve as the mechanism to govern future interactions in the network. Ratings that lower the credibility and reputation of the member can prove to be very costly in the longer run. Further, sanctions might also be imposed on eBay members who operate contradictory to the commonly accepted norms and values. Such collective sanctions can range from temporary exclusion from the eBay boards to outright ejection and loss of privileges to buy and sell on the network.

The threat of collective sanctions encourages members to adhere to acceptable behaviors. The more efficient the information flow about member behavior, the more costly it becomes for individual members to destroy their reputation in the network through deceptive behavior.

Which of the preceding possible governance mechanisms are appropriate for a specific innovation network? This depends on the type of interdependencies between members in the network—in other words, on the nature of the network-centric innovation model. Further, most networks require a portfolio of formal and informal mechanisms. In Chapters 5 to 8, we identify the appropriate portfolio of governance mechanisms for each of the four models of network-centric innovation.

KNOWLEDGE MANAGEMENT

Consider the case of Ducati Motor and its innovative customer community, which we described in Chapter 2. When Ducati engages its customer community to innovate in the design and development of new motorcycles, it does so by ensuring three basic aspects related to innovation and knowledge creation:

- First, Ducati realizes that interactions and dialogue in the customer community form the basis for new knowledge creation. Therefore, it facilitates such dialogue among the customers by establishing different types of online and offline forums that bring together the customers and by hosting their interactions.

■ Second, Ducati also realizes that for such customer dialogue to be effective—for such dialogue to lead to a coherent set of innovative ideas—customers have to "understand" one another's ideas. This requires a common vocabulary. To achieve this coherence, Ducati provides a set of design templates and standards for the customer community.

■ Ducati also understands that, in order to convert customer ideas into products, customer knowledge has to be transferred into the organization and interpreted and integrated with other design knowledge. For this, Ducati has established new organizational roles as well as created new programs staffed by product engineers to enable effective and appropriate utilization of customer innovation.

Three knowledge management themes underlie Ducati's customer-based network-centric innovation initiative: dialogue, common vocabulary, and transfer and interpretation.

The preceding three themes are not, however, unique to Ducati's innovation context. They apply equally well to all other network-centric innovation contexts. In fact, the three themes reflect the three broad knowledge management activities that must be supported in any innovation network: knowledge generation, knowledge codification, and knowledge utilization.[5]

The systems and mechanisms established in the innovation network for managing knowledge have to support these three activities. For example, as interactions among network members increasingly form the avenue for knowledge generation, systems and mechanisms that "connect" members and facilitate rapid and frequent interactions assume importance. These need not always be online or information technology–enabled communication. For example, Intel conducts compliance workshops (called *PlugFests*) that bring together vendors of different hardware products and components that are based on Intel's technology platform.[6] These workshops provide the context for the dialogue to occur among these companies (that is, Intel's network members) to ensure that the different products (or prototypes) are compatible with one another and interoperable. The knowledge generated through these interactions is taken back to individual companies and incorporated as design modifications.

Similarly, the need to codify (or make explicit) the knowledge that is generated allows sharing and building on such knowledge. Such codification is enabled by a common vocabulary ranging from technology standards and technology architecture to common market metrics.

Finally, for members to utilize the knowledge generated, systems and mechanisms for transferring such knowledge to appropriate members in the network need to exist—that is, members have to know where the knowledge is located and how to access such knowledge. Further, after the knowledge is transferred by a member, it has to be interpreted and integrated within the member's own context. For example, in the case of Staples we discussed in Chapter 2, the company acquires new product concepts from individual inventors through a range of mechanisms, including product scouts and idea contests. And after the idea is acquired, Staples has to interpret and integrate it within its own context—a context that is defined by its target market, existing brand portfolio, and its commercialization infrastructure.

Facilitating the generation and flow of knowledge is a critical role in managing network-centric innovation. As the number of members in the network and the diversity of their expertise (or knowledge base) increase, so does the complexity and importance of the systems and mechanisms to facilitate knowledge management in the network.[7]

There are different types of knowledge management systems and mechanisms, and their appropriateness depends on several factors, including the "distance" between members, the nature and extent of overlap of the knowledge transacted, and the nature of the innovation. In Chapters 5 to 8, we identify and discuss specific knowledge-management mechanisms that apply to each of the four models of network-centric innovation.

IP RIGHTS MANAGEMENT

The history of intellectual property (IP) can be traced back to ancient Greece in 700 B.C., when the chefs in Sybarites (a Greek colony in what is now Sicily) were granted one-year monopolies on the preparation of a "new or delicious dish."[8] Other elements of modern IP rights such as patents, trademarks, and trade secrets were evident in ancient Rome as well as during the Renaissance period. For example, laws were enacted in Rome in 100 B.C. to protect trademarks on cloth, lamps, glass, and livestock. Similarly, the first patent ever for a technical invention was granted in 1421 to Filippo Brunelleschi, the architect of Florence's cathedral, for a new and efficient way to transport marble by riverboat.[9] These and other examples indicate that the economic and societal motives to protect and manage rights associated with creativity and invention has a long history.

Although these systems and mechanisms for managing IP rights have evolved considerably in form as well as format over the centuries, their fundamental basis has perhaps remained largely unquestioned—that is, until very recently.

With the emergence of "free software" and "Open Source Software" in the 1980s and 1990s have come fresh and radically new perspectives and interpretations regarding IP rights management. And the primary motivation for these new perspectives has been the increasing level of collaboration in innovation.

Indeed, one of the most vexing issues that companies face in collaborative innovation projects is that of partitioning the rights to the innovation. In other words, who will own what? Or who gets what share of the profits from the innovation? As the numerous patent-related and other IP law suits and cases have shown, issues related to IP rights management is tricky even with two collaborators. If we throw in a few more collaborators, the issue becomes much more challenging. Thus, systems and mechanisms to support and facilitate IP rights management are of utmost importance for all participating members in network-centric innovation.

The extent to which a company (or network member) can capture the returns from its innovative contributions is a function of the *appropriability regime*— the term economists use to indicate the ways and means of protecting the innovation and its profitability. The legal IP regime is comprised of four instruments: trade secrets, patents, copyrights, and trademarks. Patents offer the lowest duration of protection for the innovation, followed by copyrights, trade secrets, and trademarks. In addition, IP contracts form another avenue for companies to derive returns. For example, IP licenses specify the terms of IP use between two or more entities.

In certain contexts, such legal instruments might have limited effect; instead, the nature of the technology or the knowledge that underlies the innovation might serve as a more practical appropriability regime. For example, in the surfing equipment industry, a key knowledge in the manufacturing of surfboards relates to the rigid polyurethane foam cores, or the "blanks" as it is known in the industry. The dominant player in this market until very recently was Clark Foams. The company was highly innovative and had perfected the creation of blanks to the extent that most other surfboard makers depended exclusively on Clark Foams. Indeed, Clark Foams had 80% to 90% of the U.S. blanks business for custom-shaped surfboards. Clark Foams was led by Gordon "Grubby" Clark, often referred to as the "Howard Hughes of surfing." The success of Clark Foams was not due to the protection of its intellectual assets by legal instruments such as patents or trade secrets; instead, it was the highly tacit knowledge involved in the very process of making the blanks. As one surfing industry commentator noted, "Blowing foam is a black art."[10] In other words, in the case of Clark

Foams, the nature of the technology (knowledge base) served as the main element of its appropriability regime. In short, the availability, strength, and effectiveness of the appropriability mechanisms—whether legal instruments or otherwise—can vary across industries and sectors.

Another limitation of the traditional IP regime became obvious with the emergence of collaborative innovation structures and the emergence of new digital technologies to acquire, access, modify, and distribute innovative knowledge. Such radical changes in innovation contexts brought about by new technologies tend to weaken the controls that can be exercised through traditional legal instruments.

The Open Source Software community took the lead in addressing the demand for new IP regimes and introduced several innovative licensing schemes that enable software developers to publish the source of their product and allow others to use it or modify it on flexible terms. For example, the GNU General Public License (or GPL) is an early and perhaps the dominant licensing scheme in the Open Source Software arena. A GPL license grants the recipient the rights to use, modify, improve, and redistribute the product. And, importantly, GPL seeks to ensure that the aforementioned rights are preserved in the derivatives, too; that is, it is a "copyleft" license. Unlike this license, the more permissive "free software" licensing schemes such as the BSD license not only grant the rights to use, modify, and/or distribute the software product, it also allows derivative works to be redistributed as proprietary software (that is, it is a "copycenter" license). Apart from these two broad licensing schemes, numerous other "open" licenses have been developed—for example, Mozilla Public license, Common Public license, Open Source license, OpenSSL license, and Eclipse Public license—either pertaining to particular products or to particular parts of the open source community.

These alternative licensing schemes have paved the path for the development of innovative IP regimes in domains outside the software industry. Most notable in this regard are the Creative Commons and the Science Commons initiatives that have extended many of these IP rights management concepts to the domain of arts, entertainment, sciences, and so on. For example, Creative Commons has taken the notion of copyleft and introduced six different licensing schemes that vary on the nature of the attribution and the rights granted to the recipient for derivative works and commercial use.[11]

As the application of the Creative Commons license and other such emerging licensing schemes is rapidly expanding into other domains—from music and arts to journalism, academic curricula, and medicine—the options for managing IP rights in different network-centric innovation contexts are also expanding. Accordingly, in this book, we consider a range of IP rights management systems—from traditional legal instruments to the newer and more flexible licensing schemes—and, identify and describe the appropriate portfolio of mechanisms for the different models of network-centric innovation.

CONCLUSION

In this chapter and the previous chapter, we presented a framework for analyzing the structure and the opportunities in the emerging network-centric innovation landscape. We first defined the two dimensions of network-centric innovation and identified four archetypical models of network-centric innovation. Next, we offered a typology of innovation roles and also identified the three elements of the network management infrastructure—network governance, knowledge management, and IP rights management. In subsequent chapters, we apply this framework to delve deeper into the different models of network-centric innovation.

The Four Models of Network-Centric Innovation

Chapter 5   The Orchestra Model   85

Chapter 6   The Creative Bazaar Model   113

Chapter 7   The Jam Central Model   139

Chapter 8   The MOD ("MODification")
             Station Model   157

5

The Orchestra Model

Think about the last potluck dinner you were invited to. The host probably decided the theme—for example, a barbeque or an Italian dinner—and requested that each person bring a dish, dessert, or supplies that contribute to the overall theme. And the host probably contributed a main dish, and other people's contributions were meant to complement the main dish.

Now consider the story of the "stone soup." Legend has it that a wandering soldier came upon a famine-ridden village, and found that all the people were jealously hoarding their food. At first, the soldier thought of moving on because there was nothing for him to eat, but he decided to try a creative strategy to get a meal. He announced that he had everything he needed to make soup, and proceeded to fill an iron cauldron with water. He placed a stone inside the cauldron, and built a fire under it. A curious villager approached the soldier and asked what he was doing. The soldier answered that he was making stone soup, which would taste wonderful, although it still needed a little bit of cabbage to improve the taste. Soon another villager approached and offered him cabbage. The soldier added it to the soup and mentioned that it might need some potatoes and onions. Another villager soon offered these for the soup. And so it went, from vegetables to seasoning to garnishes. Finally, everyone enjoyed a delicious pot of soup.

These scenarios have some similarities and some differences. Both involved a central entity (the host family or the traveling soldier) who defined the primary theme for the dinner—a theme that would shape the contributions of other members of the community. In both cases, the contributors (the invitees or the villagers) shared the value derived from the final outcome. However, in the case of the potluck dinner, the host contributed the main dish as the foundation for the dinner and the contributions from other members built on the foundation and enhanced it with complementary contributions. On the other hand, in the case of the stone soup, the contributions of the villagers were cooked together (or integrated) to form one final dish (the soup), which everybody consumed.

These similarities and distinctions are a good analogy for the two types of the Orchestra model of network-centric innovation. As you recall, the Orchestra model involves *a group of firms coming together to exploit a market opportunity based on an explicit innovation architecture that is defined and shaped by a dominant firm.* There are three important concepts in this definition: dominant firm, innovation architecture, and network members. However, based on the role played by the dominant firm, the functions served by the innovation architecture and the nature of contributions made by the network members, the Orchestra model takes on two different forms:

- The *Orchestra-Integrator* model. This model resembles the stone soup scenario. A dominant firm (or network leader) defines the architecture for the core innovation and the network members contribute the different components or elements that make up this core innovation. The network leader then integrates the different contributions or components to build the core innovation and then market it.

- The *Orchestra-Platform* model. This model resembles the potluck dinner scenario. A dominant firm defines and offers the basic architecture, which then becomes the platform or the foundation for the other network members to build on through their own complementary innovations. These complementary innovations extend and/or enhance the reach and range of the basic architecture or platform.

In this chapter, through detailed examples we describe the two types of the Orchestra model including the different types of players (or innovation roles) and the network management systems. We start with the Orchestra-Integrator model. An excellent illustration of this model is the development of the Boeing 787 Dreamliner.

THE ORCHESTRA-INTEGRATOR MODEL: THE CASE OF THE BOEING 787 DREAMLINER

The 787 Dreamliner project was officially launched by Boeing on April 26, 2004. The 787 is designed as a family of airplanes in the 200 to 300 seat class and represents Boeing's entry into the mid-sized, long-range commercial jet market.[1] The first delivery is scheduled for May 2008. The 787 is a big bet that Boeing is placing to win back dominance of the $60 billion jetliner market from Airbus SAS.[2]

The new 787 incorporates several radical advances in terms of basic design and technologies as well as facilities for passengers and crew. It uses a new lightweight carbon composite as the material for building much of the plane.[3] The use of the lightweight material is supposed to translate into at least 20% reduction in fuel consumption compared to that of jets of similar size. The 787 will allow the use of two types of engines—the GE Next Generation (GEnx) engine and the Rolls Royce Trent 1000 engine.[4] In other words, the 787 offers a standard engine interface and a new plane can be fitted with either of the two types of engines without making any other changes elsewhere, thereby providing more flexibility for carriers.

The interior design of the 787 incorporates several innovative features for crew and passengers. For example, the 787 will be an "e-enabled" airplane—it will have electronic flight bags (EFB) to deliver electronic charts, manuals, and reference data to flight crews; a satellite-based communications system to provide Internet access to passengers; and wireless networks for maintenance access as well as for in-flight entertainment. Another interesting feature relates to cabin pressure and humidity. The cabin of the 787 will be pressurized to 6,000 feet altitude instead of the conventional pressurization to 8,000 feet altitude. The higher air pressure is supposed to translate into a more comfortable ride, particularly during long flights. Similarly, the cabin humidity will be maintained at a higher level—between 20% and 30% rather than the 10% humidity that is typical of other airplanes. The 787 can maintain such higher humidity because the carbon composite used to fabricate the structure does not corrode when exposed to moisture. The higher cabin humidity will also contribute to a more comfortable ride for passengers.[5]

Boeing's former CEO, Harry Stonecipher, remarked in 2004 that the new 787 will be "a game changer." Alan Mulally, the former CEO of Boeing Commercial

Airplanes, noted that the new 787 "will allow us to continue to set the standard for commercial aviation in the second century of flight."[6] While both Stonecipher and Mulally were referring to the aforementioned new technologies and features of the airplane, their comments also captured the innovative way in which Boeing went about designing and building this new aircraft.

Indeed, the story of the 787 Dreamliner is also very much a story of "innovating innovation" in the commercial aviation industry—how Boeing redefined the very process by which it developed new airplanes and collaborated with a network of global partners.

ELEMENTS OF BOEING'S NETWORK-CENTRIC INNOVATION STRATEGY

In building the 787, Boeing made a radical departure from its traditional design and development strategy. The 787 program started with the expectation that any external partner that had the responsibility to build a part of the airplane would also be responsible for designing it. This was a major point of departure from previous programs, where Boeing did most or all of the design work and other companies then built the airplane.[7] The 787 project was conceived at the very outset as a highly collaborative innovation program conducted with a network of partners.

Boeing assembled a set of global partners whom it could trust with the process of creating entire sections of the plane, from concept to production. The global partners consisted of companies from all over the world, including Japan, Australia, Italy, and Canada. Each global partner was selected based on a strict set of standards as each company would be assuming responsibility for a higher level of systems and structure—and bringing in their own set of sub-contractors and suppliers.

The design and development tasks were not just outsourced to these partners. Instead, partners made financial investments in those tasks. As Thomas Pickering, Boeing's senior vice president for international relations noted, "We said, 'let's spread the risk and spread the benefit' ... they get the advantages but they also carry the burden."[8] Specifically, each partner was supposed to invest in the project by paying the upfront cost related to design and development. With approximately $10 billion required for the development of the new jet, partners were responsible for investing close to $4 billion—a significant commitment. They were expected to absorb this non-recurring cost of development—in other words, they were not permitted to include those costs in their pricing. And, this was built into the agreements with individual partners. Contracts had common provisions that reflected the central theme of Boeing's network: "What's good for one is good for all."

Boeing's network also includes its customers, although their role is largely limited to providing ideas and suggestions in the product definition phase. Boeing conducts a large-scale meeting with a number of its customer partners (airlines from all over the world) called the Progress Summit, which features open discussions on customer requirements and concepts for standardizing and simplifying the 787 design.[9] The summit is also a venue for Boeing to update its customer partners on the progress of the 787 development project. Each partner (or network member) in the 787 project is directly tied to Boeing, although operationally each one is also linked to one another. The innovation network for the 787 project is highly centralized, with Boeing in the center and the global partners around it.

The development of the 787 follows a three-phase process: conceptualization, joint development, and detailed design. The conceptualization phase started in early 2003 with the appointment of the core 787 project management team within Boeing. Michael Blair, a 24-year Boeing veteran, was appointed as the senior vice president and general manager of the 787 program. Other members of the team included Walter Gillette, another Boeing veteran who is considered the technical and intellectual inspiration for every Boeing jet since the mid-1970s.[10] Gillette was to be the creative force behind Dreamliner, too. During the conceptualization phase, the internal Boeing team interacted with a number of external entities including customers (airlines), suppliers, technical experts, and market experts to identify and define the basic new product concept. The business case for the new 787 was clarified. Boeing also entertained innovative ideas for the systems and the structures from the external entities. For example, the potential for using composites as the material for the airplane structure was explored and a number of alternative materials were tested. After the product conceptualization phase was over, it was time to define the basic structure of the 787.

The second phase, the joint development phase, was the most crucial as it would define once and for all the basic configuration of the new plane. As Michael Blair, general manager of the 787 project noted, "Firm configuration means the airplane's structural, propulsion, and systems architectures are firm or defined."[11] For example, specifying the sweep and size of the wings, the exact size of the fuselage, tail, engines, and all other major components of the airframe. In other words, this phase was when the basic (innovation) architecture would get defined.

Although Boeing will have the final say in all aspects related to the final configuration, the involvement of the global partners is critical as they along with
Boeing start assuming risks (related to the product development) right from
this stage onwards. Boeing and its partners spent the next year or so defining
the 787 architecture.

The 787 program reached the final configuration on September 15, 2005.

The joint development phase not only defined the 787 configuration but also
specified the way in which the *design job would be divided among the global
partners as well as the standards or metrics by which the design would be
evaluated*. The design work for the entire structure of the new jet was divided
into six "integrated assemblies" or work packages. Each of these large components was designed from the bottom-up by one or more of the partner firms.

Boeing took the responsibility for the detailed design and development of only
around 35% of the plane's structure. This included the vertical fin, flight deck,
fixed and movable leading edges of the wing, parts of the forward fuselage, and
wing-to-body fairing. The rest of the structure was the responsibility of a set of
global partners that included Mitsubishi Heavy Industries, Fuji Heavy
Industries, Alenia Aeronautica, Vought Aircraft Industries, Goodrich, and
Kawasaki Heavy Industries (see **Figure 5.1**).

Who makes the parts and where the engineering jobs are

"Who makes the parts and where the engineering jobs are," Reporting by Dominic Gates, Graphics by Mark Nowlin. Seattle
Times, September 11, 2005. © 2005 The Seattle Times Company. Reprinted by permission.

Figure 5.1   The distribution of the 787 design and development

For example, Mitsubishi Heavy Industries was responsible for the main wing box whereas Fuji Heavy Industries designed and developed the center wing box and also integrated the wing box with the main landing gear wheel well. Kawasaki Heavy Industries provided the fuselage section between the wing and the cabin, the main landing gear wheel well, and the main wing fixed trailing edge. Alenia in Italy designed and developed the 64-foot-wide horizontal stabilizer and partnered with Vought Industries to build the aft fuselage.

The global partners were asked to "design and build to performance"—instead of giving each external partner detailed designs that they had to implement, they were now given the broad architecture and the performance standards. The innovation tasks needed to get to these performance standards were now the sole responsibility of individual global partners. Thus, the final configuration and the associated performance standards became the set of *shared goals and objectives* of the network of global partners.

After the firm configuration was defined, Boeing and its partners started on the third and final phase of innovation—the detailed design of the major components. Each partner knew the expectations regarding not only their own contributions (that is, the large components) but also the other partners' contributions. Such a shared understanding of the goals served to bring coherence to the detailed design and development activities of the different partners located in different parts of the world.

The global partners were responsible for the detailed design as well as the final production of the components. The different components of the 787 would then be brought together at Everett, Washington for the final assembly.

The target for the final 787 assembly in Everett is three days. However, Boeing plans to bring down the final assembly time to two days by 2011: that is, a new 787 will roll out every two days![12]

The Role of Boeing and Its Partners in the 787 Program

Let us now examine the roles that Boeing and the other partners play in the 787 program. Boeing developed a master design that defined the general contours of the plane, however, the specific design tasks of the different parts were left to individual partners. In fact, network partners were responsible for more than 70% of the overall design work. More importantly, partners were given the responsibility to design and develop some of the most important structures of the airplane. For example, the Japanese partners developed the entire wing section of the 787. As Boeing's Thomas Pickering noted, "This is the first time we have ever put the full wing ... into the hands of a partner."[13] Indeed, no Boeing plane has ever flown on foreign wings and the company has always held onto such critical knowledge (the "crown jewels") related to building airplanes.[14]

Thus, in building the 787, Boeing made a radical shift in its own role—in the words of Scott Strode, Boeing's vice president of airplane development and production, Boeing made a shift from being a "manufacturer" to being an "integrator." As Strode notes, Boeing's role as integrator requires it to shoulder "a broader range of responsibilities that include assembling the partner team and making work assignments, establishing clear expectations, deciding on common tools and processes, and making the critical technological decisions."[15]

Such a shift in roles is a part of a master plan—the Boeing 2016 Vision—to change the company from a manufacturer to a designer and assembler of high-tech airplanes.[16] And it is a change that Boeing's partners understand very well. Vern Broomall, vice president of quality and engineering at Vought Aircraft Industries, one of Boeing's partners in this effort, notes, "There is a real difference in the business approach—with Boeing taking the role of the integrator and the partners taking the responsibility for the major pieces."

Boeing was also the central decision maker in the network. Although each global partner had a lot of autonomy with regard to the design of their individual components, there was still a need for a single decision maker on important design and development issues. Those decisions were made by Boeing management. Boeing's leadership role is succinctly captured by Steve Shaffer, vice president of Global Partners for Boeing Commercial Airplanes: "We share information with our partners, we listen to them, and we influence each other. But at the end of the day, there's no doubt that Boeing is leading."[17]

Boeing also makes sure that other partners' roles are clearly defined and made explicit. As Vought's Broomall noted, "We've never done a project before where the roles and responsibilities are as clear and consistent as they are on this one."[18] They had better be. Vought is designing two large sections of the fuselage, which then has to be integrated with the components that are being made by Alenia Aeronautica, another partner, in Italy. As Broomall continues, "We (Vought) work directly with the Italian (company), and have an excellent relationship with them, while Boeing facilitates the work for all of us." Thus, while the network partners *build on each other's design ideas*, Boeing has to not only facilitate such cumulative knowledge creation, but also orchestrate the distributed innovation activities.

Boeing's role as the integrator and its limited involvement in the detailed design and development also meant placing different emphasis on its other tasks. For example, as Walt Gillette (787 program vice president of engineering, manu-facturing, and partner alignment) notes, assuming the role of the integrator allowed Boeing to concentrate more on attending to "the voice of the customer" through the product development phase.[19] In this role, Boeing could focus its efforts on maintaining the integrity of the overall product vision vis-à-vis the dynamic external environment and market needs.

What was the role of the global partners in the network? Their primary role was that of an *innovator*—to help Boeing define the overall configuration of the air-plane and to innovate in the design and development of the individual compo-nents. They were also responsible for selecting and overseeing the second- and third-tier partners (or suppliers) in the network—a task traditionally carried out with the involvement of Boeing. In fact, the 787 project will be the first time an entity other than Boeing will control the selection of the second- and third-tier suppliers in a Boeing commercial aircraft program.[20]

Managing Collaboration Among Partners

Coordinating the work on three continents of the partner firms raises some critical challenges related to information flow and communications. The glob-ally dispersed partner companies needed to converse in real-time using the same vocabulary, interpret the design information gained from others, and inte-grate that knowledge with the design of the components that they themselves were responsible for. In other words, what was needed was a system for collab-orative design that facilitated the dialogue among the companies, provided a common vocabulary, and allowed rapid transfer and integration of design knowledge. And as the leader of the network, Boeing had the responsibility to provide such a knowledge-management infrastructure.

Boeing addressed this challenge by creating a sophisticated virtual Global Collaboration Environment for its partners to share information and collabo-rate on design on a real-time basis. The Global Collaboration Centers at Boeing and in each of the partner locations were linked to one another for live video-conferencing (with encrypted transmission for additional security).

The end solution brought together a variety of technologies and tools. For example, Boeing partnered with the Dassault Systems, the French software company, to put together a suite of Product Lifecycle Management tools to support the collaborative design and development tasks. This includes CATIA (V5) the computer-aided design tool; DELMIA, the manufacturing solution; and ENOVIA, the engineering interface. The global partners also made use of collaboration tools available through Exostar, an online trading exchange for the aerospace industry. Similarly, database and communication tools from Radiance Technologies were used to transmit high volumes of data among partners. In addition, a visualization application developed by Boeing allowed global partners to conduct real-time design reviews without any lag time for the models to load.

These tools helped create a highly collaborative environment. The facilities for real-time interaction facilitated and promoted continued dialogue among the partner firms. Further, the configuration or the architecture of the airplane and the design interfaces were embedded in common databases that were shared by all partners. And many of the tools employed a standardized engineering design language to facilitate interpretation and integration of design done by the different members.

Steve Shaffer, vice president of Global Partners for Boeing Commercial Airplanes, noted that the 787 project emphasized a "situational awareness" among the partners.[21] Each partner was kept continually aware of the design activities underway in other partner firms as well as the impact of the external environment on the business and technological assumptions. This "situational awareness" or a *shared world view* is one of the cornerstones of network-centric innovation. In the case of the 787 program, the Global Collaboration Environment facilitated building and maintaining such situational awareness throughout the lifetime of the project.

Building a Trust-Based Environment

Formal contracts signed between Boeing and each one of the partners explicitly outlined the nature of collaboration and the expectations regarding the outcomes. In addition, Boeing also invested heavily in developing a trust-based environment in the network. As the global partners soon realized, it is a very complex undertaking to just get everybody to come together as a team and agree on technical matters, let alone to integrate the different cultural mindsets. A key ingredient of success is the trust and the understanding of one another's work processes and culture that evolves over time.

Consider the development of the wing box, which is the responsibility of Japan's Mitsubishi Heavy Industries (MHI). The wing for the 787 will be the largest composite structure ever built for a commercial aircraft. In developing and testing the wing box, MHI had to interact and coordinate closely not only with Boeing but also with other partners in the network. When the wing box testing came up during development, MHI had a different approach for proto-typing and material testing than Boeing. The wing box test article measures roughly 18 feet at its widest point and is half the length, approximately 50 feet, of the entire wing. The use of new materials created two challenges: the challenge of designing a new component and the challenge of understanding the new material that will be used to produce that component.

As Dan Smith, Boeing's 787 wing test and technology LCPT leader noted, "We took some time early in the (design and development) process to build the trust between Boeing and MHI."[22] For example, Smith called upon both the MHI and Boeing teams to complete the initial development of the equipment prototype in six weeks—Boeing had the job of developing the prototype while MHI had the task of building the tooling to support the testing of the prototype—and set up a "beer/sake challenge." If MHI met the schedule and Boeing did not, the Boeing team would buy sake for MHI team members, whereas if the reverse was the case, MHI would buy beer for the Boeing team. Such team-building challenges help to build a level of trust among partner firms. As it happened in this case, both teams met the timeline and so everybody had both beer and sake. And more importantly, in the process both teams gained better appreciation and trust of each other's capabilities and expertise.

Such trust and shared understanding of the unique work and cultural contexts of the partner firms have to be developed across all members of the network, not just between two partners. This requires adopting new perspectives on risk sharing and information sharing. Steve Huggins is a senior vice president of strategy and business development in Goodrich Corp, a key partner of Boeing. Huggins noted that component providers used to keep their strategies and information to themselves, like poker players holding cards close to the vest. But such an approach went against the goals and objectives of the 787 program. As Huggins commented, "The degree to which our companies share forecasts and visions of the future today is more like talking with a colleague than telling the 'boss' what you think they want to hear."[23] Such open sharing of information and ideas contribute to the development of trust and higher level of shared world view that is fundamental to the success of network-centric innovation.

The flip side of the trust developed in the network is the long-term risk that Boeing might be assuming with regard to the critical knowledge and technologies that it will be sharing with its partners in the 787 development. For example, technological knowledge related to wing design is considered the crown jewel of aircraft building. In the 787 project, the Japanese companies that will be involved in the wing design have their own long-term agenda in the aviation industry.

For example, Kawasaki has future plans to enter into the commercial aviation industry independently. Similarly, MHI plans to use the knowledge it gains from the 787 project related to the new composite technology to fuel its own future plans in this area. Junichi Maesawa, executive director of MHI, notes that the 787 "is a cornerstone for Japan to become a stand-alone aircraft manufacturer in producing a 30 to 50 seater aircraft in a few years."[24] So will Boeing's collaboration with these companies lead to knowledge spillover and create new competitors in the future? That remains to be seen.

COMPARISONS WITH AIRBUS A380 AND BOEING 777 PROJECTS

In sum, the 787 Dreamliner exhibits all the key characteristics of the Orchestra-Integrator model of network-centric innovation. Table 5.1 captures the essence of the model vis-à-vis the network-centric innovation framework presented in earlier chapters.

Table 5.1 Boeing's 787 Dreamliner Network

Elements of Network-Centric Innovation	Boeing's 787 Dreamliner Network
Nature of the innovation space	Product market focus and the firm configuration of the new airplane are defined by Boeing with assistance from external partners. These specifications structure the nature of the innovation space and incorporate the modularity needed for the collaborative design and development of the jet.
Structure of the network leadership	Boeing is the leader of the network and all the key decisions, including the firm configuration, are made by Boeing alone. In other words, network leadership is highly centralized in Boeing.
Innovation Roles	
Architect	Boeing plays the role of integrator—the only leadership role in the network.
Adaptor	Global partners such as Kawasaki and Fuji play the role of innovator by innovating large components of the new air jet.
Agent	There are no firms playing the role of intermediary or agent as Boeing maintains formal direct ties with all the key adaptors (innovators).

Elements of Network-Centric Innovation	Boeing's 787 Dreamliner Network
Network Management	
Network governance	Formal agreements between Boeing and each of the global partners; trust-based mechanisms also serve to facilitate network governance and coordination; restricted network access and reputation-based systems are also used.
Knowledge management	Global Collaborations Centers at all locations, including partner locations, facilitate and enhance the quality of partner dialogue, knowledge transfer, and knowledge integration.
IP rights and value appropriation	Patents and other formal instruments of IP rights management are used. Some of the IP related to 787 are owned by Boeing, some by individual global partners, and some are jointly owned by Boeing and the partners.

Before concluding this discussion, it might also be useful to highlight Boeing's unique approach in the 787 project by comparing and contrasting it with the development strategies related to two other projects: the development of Boeing 777 and the development of a competing aircraft by Airbus—the Airbus A380 mega jumbo. **Table 5.2** compares these three projects.

Table 5.2   Comparison of Boeing 777, Boeing 787, and Airbus A380 Development Approaches

Characteristic	Boeing 777	Boeing 787	Airbus A380
The project	Launched in 1990; cost of $6–$7 billion	Launched in 2004; cost of $13–$14 billion	Launched in 2002; cost of $10–$12 billion
Broad approach	"Build to Print" approach	"Design and Build to Performance" approach	Combination of "Build to Print" and "Design and Build to Performance"

continues

Table 5.2   Continued

Characteristic	Boeing 777	Boeing 787	Airbus A380
Relationships	Boeing as the prime contractor is in control of all suppliers, including second- and third-tier suppliers	Boeing decides on its key global partners; global partners will in turn select and monitor second- and third-tier suppliers	Airbus as the prime contractor selects and controls all suppliers
Risk/reward sharing	Suppliers assume limited innovation or financial risk; (suppliers bid on fixed-price contracts basis)	Global partners assume significant technological and financial risk (partners invest in and absorb cost of development)	Suppliers assume considerable financial risk (contributing $3.1 billion to development)
Leadership role	Boeing designs, develops, builds, and assembles from ground up; suppliers provide component-level build services	Boeing as the Orchestra-Integrator envisions and coordinates innovation activity	Airbus corporate headquarters (Toulouse, France, supposed to coordinate activities)
Nature of design distribution	Boeing's share of design and build was 76%; building of the most critical components remain with Boeing	Boeing's share of design and build is 35%; even components such as wing section is given to global partners to design	Airbus bears majority of the design responsibility; building of critical components remain with Airbus

In developing the wide-bodied jet airliner 777, Boeing followed the traditional "build to print" approach wherein suppliers were required to manufacture to fit the detailed design requirements specified by Boeing. The 777 involved significant technological achievements. However, many of these advancements came from Boeing. External suppliers played a very limited role in the development of the 777. For example, the Japanese companies contributed to the building of less than 20% of the 777 components. Further, unlike in the 787 project, much of the most closely guarded technologies and design components (for example, wing design) remained with Boeing. Also, in the 777 project, the suppliers assumed very limited risk—related to the technologies or to the investment needed for new design and manufacturing facilities.

The development of the A380 reflects a more network-centric approach, but it falls significantly short of Boeing's approach in developing the 787. Why do we call it a network-centric approach? Technically, Airbus S.A.S. is a single corporate entity based in Toulouse, France. However, in reality, its four divisions located in Britain, France, Germany, and Spain still operate as four distinct companies that trace their roots to the four European national aviation firms from which Airbus took its birth. Indeed, in early 2006, former Airbus CEO Christian Streiff noted that "(Airbus) is still in part a juxtaposition of four companies." The company is "terribly balkanized" with the four divisions often prone to national political forces and harboring cross-border jealousies.[25]

The major design and development tasks of the A380 project were spread across these four distinct divisions of the company, with Britain in charge of wing design, Germany in charge of cabin outfitting, Spain responsible for the tail, and France responsible for the final assembly. In addition, a number of external suppliers located in Europe and in other parts of the world were also involved in the design and building of smaller airframe subassemblies. Thus, the A380 development followed a network-centric approach although the design responsibilities of external suppliers were limited compared to the 787 project. However, as in the case of 787, the suppliers of Airbus A380 were also required to contribute to the development costs—to the tune of approximately $3.1 billion.[26]

What do these examples show about the implications of following the Orchestra-Integrator model on innovation outcomes? A comparison of the 777 and the 787 indicates the significant reductions in time, development of innovative technologies and materials, and reduction of overall development cost. Vought's Broomall notes, "We have probably taken more than one-third to one-half of the time out and perhaps 50 percent out of development cost versus historical methods (as followed in 777)."[27]

On the other hand, the case of A380 indicates the central importance of the leadership role played by the dominant firm (that is, the Integrator role). For example, in July 2006, Airbus announced significant project delays that were attributed to problems with the internal wiring designs of the A380. Specifically, wiring that was designed and produced in Hamburg failed to fit the final assembly requirements in Toulouse, France. Investigations showed that this was due to the use of incompatible design software. A detailed analysis of the A380 project showed that while the design and development tasks were distributed across the different divisions or entities, there was nobody to play the critical leadership role of the Orchestra-Integrator. Another issue in the case of A380 was related to the lack of a common knowledge-management system. The PLM software tools used for the development of A380 were outdated and had limited capabilities to support virtual collaboration among the different network entities (for example, the tools did not support creating a digital mockup of the A380). Such lack of knowledge-management capabilities along with highly deficient network orchestration (or network leadership) led to limited shared awareness or world view of the project among the different partners and failure to detect design flaws early enough to avoid project delays and cost overruns.

These and other examples indicate the importance of three broad themes that underline the success of the Orchestra-Integrator model:

- The firm playing the Integrator role has to *provide strong leadership to the innovation activities*—leadership that should be evident in envisioning and clarifying the innovation architecture, facilitating and coordinating the innovation activities of the network partners, and integrating and bringing to market the innovation.

- The key network partners involved in the design and development should be *sufficiently invested in the project*—in other words, the dominant firm should ensure that the partners share in the risks as well as in the rewards related to the innovation.

- The lead firm should also *establish an environment* that supports building trust-based relationships and the ability to rapidly share knowledge thereby ensuring high "situational awareness."

Let us now consider the second form of the Orchestra model—the Orchestra-Platform model.

THE ORCHESTRA-PLATFORM MODEL: THE CASE OF SALESFORCE.COM AND APPEXCHANGE

In Chapter 2, "Understanding Network-Centric Innovation," we briefly introduced Salesforce.com (the customer relationship management solution provider) and its AppExchange forum as an example of a network-centric innovation initiative. More specifically, as we will show here, Salesforce.com is a good example of the Orchestra-Platform model of network-centric innovation.

SALESFORCE.COM—JOURNEY FROM A SOLUTION PROVIDER TO A PLATFORM PROVIDER

Founded in 1999 and based in San Francisco, Salesforce.com is one of the leading software providers in the rapidly growing Customer Relationship

Management (CRM) market. The company's core offerings focus primarily on sales force automation, marketing automation, partner relationship management, and customer service and support automation. The sales force automation services help companies to establish systems and processes to manage customer accounts and to track sales leads, share sales forecasts, and coordinate other tasks with the sales force. The marketing automation services enable companies to manage marketing campaigns. The customer service and support automation services allow companies to track, manage, and coordinate their interaction with existing customers in various areas (for example, requests for repairs, advice about products and services, complaints about faulty goods, and so on).

The unique aspect of the company's core offerings is their availability as "on demand" services that client companies can access through a regular Web browser over the Internet. The market for such on demand or Web-delivered software (also known as *software as service*) is expected to grow rapidly in the next decade or so—for example, one report estimates that by 2011, 25% of the enterprise software market will be on-demand.[28] In the eight years since its birth, Salesforce.com has grown rapidly, riding on the increasing popularity of its particular vision of Web-delivered software. As of July 2007, the company had approximately 32,000 customers using its software and approximately 646,000 paying subscribers worldwide.

Despite its success with the core set of CRM products, Salesforce.com plans to be more than just a CRM solution provider. Starting in 2003, it gradually started evolving into a platform leader. Specifically, the company defined a foundational on-demand architecture that will help external developers to build applications that extend the scope of the company's core offerings. This shift to a platform provider is intended to greatly expand the company's reach into applications areas beyond its customer relationship management roots. Instead of creating and offering all such applications by itself, the platform strategy enables Salesforce.com to harness the innovativeness and the capabilities of external developers and transform itself into an all-purpose enterprise computing infrastructure provider.[29]

As the company's founder Marc Benioff notes, "The strategy is to let 1,000 flowers bloom and look for innovation."[30] The company hopes to get external partners to build applications that are integrated with the company's CRM solutions and mimic the embedded experience of the Salesforce.com user interface, thereby making them an application within Salesforce as far as the user is concerned, and allowing Salesforce's product portfolio to grow without the company building all of them by themselves.

SALESFORCE.COM'S TECHNOLOGY PLATFORM

The on-demand technology platform that the company has developed and made available to external developers constitutes several components. First and foremost, it includes the core sales and marketing application and the customer service and support application. In addition, the platform also includes an on-demand operating system, an on-demand programming language, an integration platform, and on-demand application sharing service.

Consider Apex, an important element of Salesforce.com's technology platform. Apex is a new Java-like on-demand programming language that the company has made available to external developers and customers. Applications built using the language can be made available as a Web service and accessed using XML and SOAP standards. Apex code runs natively on the Salesforce.com hosted server infrastructure and as such it is faster and more powerful than other languages. This enhanced functionality opens up new possibilities for external developers. Further, applications developed using Apex can interact with the access and manipulate data through the standard application programming interfaces (APIs) the company has made available to its core CRM applications.

Salesforce.com's network partners can use Apex to build entirely new applications or solutions and integrate them with the flagship CRM application itself. Apex is derived from the same technologies that the company uses in its internal development activities. As such, the company's current customers can also use the Apex language to customize core features and functions of Salesforce's on-demand applications. Apex enables external developers and clients to create or modify applications in a controlled manner with all code running off the Salesforce platform itself.

Salesforce.com's technology platform also includes other elements that enhance the overall capabilities and range of applications that can be developed. For example, it includes a data relationship API for accessing and managing complex data relationships, real-time messaging and integration for notifying other applications or middleware of business events in Salesforce, and an Ajax toolkit for linking Salesforce applications in "application mash-ups" with other systems such as Google Maps.

The company is clear about its motives behind opening up and offering such a technology platform. "We have a vision for millions of applications on demand," notes Adam Gross, vice president of developer marketing, "but as a company we choose to build only one class of applications called CRM applications. Apex and other elements of our platform will give our partners unburdened freedom and the capability to develop an entire universe of on-demand applications ... ranging from HR and inventory management to transactional applications like ecommerce."[31] Indeed, in releasing Apex, the company wants to have a much broader impact on the enterprise software arena—specifically, it wants Apex to have the same effect on the ballooning market for on-demand or Web-delivered business software as Java did on the consumer Web in the 1990s.

Thus, unlike in the case of the Orchestra-Integrator model, here, the dominant firm's objective in defining the technology architecture is not to specify the innovation components that other network members should develop and contribute. Instead, the "on-demand" architecture serves as a foundation for network partners to build complementary applications that extend the reach and range of the company's suite of products.

However, pursuing such an innovation agenda requires more than just defining a technology platform. It requires playing the role of a platform leader in the network to promote and facilitate the complementary innovation activities of its network partners. In the case of Salesforce.com, the vehicle for exercising such a leadership role is the AppExchange developers' network or forum.

APPEXCHANGE NETWORK

AppExchange is a forum that the company has created to serve as a common ground for all the different members of its network to come together. These members include independent software developers, customers, and other technology partners. The AppExchange forum serves multiple objectives ranging from providing a marketplace for complementary solutions developed by external developers to facilitating the sharing of knowledge related to the technology platform.

The primary participants in Salesforce.com's innovation network are the independent software developers who create applications based on the company's technology platform. Their role is that of a "complementor"—building applications that complement the core CRM solution. The nature of the innovation pursued by the complementors is limited only by the specifications of the technology platform and the imagination of the developers and the on-demand community.

To get a sense of the nature and diversity of the applications available on AppExchange, consider the following two examples. Envox Worldwide, a provider of voice solutions, has created a new application called Envox PhoneLink. The application works on top of the CRM solution and enables businesses to add screen pop-ups and click-to-dial capabilities to their customer contact centers.[32] Another external developer, DreamFactory Software, makes add-on application components that extend the basic CRM features by including teamwork automation and management capabilities—specifically, project management, collaborative calendaring, and document sharing capabilities.

AppExchange has two objectives:

- **To enable the company to make available the platform technologies as well as the knowledge required to use those technologies.** As the platform leader, Salesforce.com has the sole responsibility to define and lead the evolution of the platform. AppExchange allows the company to maintain its communication with the developer community—educating them about new developments in the platform, capturing the community's emerging needs and issues, and facilitating the overall use of the technologies.

- **To serve as a forum for network members to share or distribute applications built on the platform, making it a marketplace for complementary applications.** It offers the AppExchange directory wherein external developers can list their offerings. Other network members (for example, existing users of the CRM solution) can browse the directory, select an application that interests them, and test drive or install that application for their own use.

As of July 2007, the AppExchange directory listed about 600 such on-demand complementary applications ranging from financial solutions to human resource management and inventory management solutions. And, 7,400 out of the company's 32,000 customers had installed at least one application from the AppExchange directory.[33] While some of these applications are offered free of cost, others need to be purchased from the external developer. The directory makes it easy for finding, testing, and installing the applications—in very much the same way you would browse the iTunes Web site to sample and download or purchase songs. Thus, AppExchange serves as an online service for sharing business applications built on the company's technology platform.

The company calls its AppExchange an "eBay for on-demand computing"[34]—a community forum that gives an opportunity for external developers to create and offer an "ecosystem of services" that merge well with the company's own core solutions. And, extending the eBay analogy, the company expects viral growth—as AppExchange adds more products, more buyers show up, and in turn, more developers.

Governance of AppExchange

As is the case with eBay, offering such a forum for external developers and partners requires Salesforce to provide the appropriate level of governance and monitoring. Several elements make up the governance on the AppExchange network. The company uses the following formal and informal mechanisms to govern the AppExchange network:

- **Registration:** Only registered external developers or partners are allowed to participate in the AppExchange directory service. Thus, while registration is free, it enables the company to maintain a "gated" network that provides the first level of governance.

- **Certification:** All the applications that external developers want to share or distribute through the AppExchange forum have to undergo an extensive review and certification process from the company. The certification ensures that the application meets predefined standards regarding security, reliability, and quality. The certification process incorporates a rigorous 300-point test plan that includes a security audit, integration and functional design review, functional testing, and an audit of a reference customer. The last part—customer audit—aims to incorporate customer feedback in the certification process. After an application has successfully passed the certification tests, the company awards an "AppExchange Certified Application" logo to the developer for that application.

- **Quality Ratings:** Salesforce.com uses its user community to evaluate the quality of the applications. As in the case of eBay, the community acts as the judge of the quality of its members' performance. AppExchange community members can rate an application on a 5-point scale and the average ratings of all customers are shown on the AppExchange directory. Community members can also provide detailed comments and critique on applications.

- **Platform Monitoring:** Salesforce.com also monitors the way its technology platform is used by external developers so that it can protect the integrity of the platform and the solutions based on it. Solutions from external developers can pose the risks of complexity and broken applications and work against the company's norms and values regarding ease of use and trustworthiness. To head off this risk, the company has created measures to guard against developers using Apex to inadvertently wreak havoc with its Salesforce.com deployments. For example, when Apex code is being executed on its on-demand platform, the application is constantly monitored for what it is doing and what resources it is consuming. The company's monitoring of hosted complementary applications from external developers does not stop with the certification process. Rather, it continues during the execution too.[35]

SALESFORCE'S OTHER INITIATIVES AS PLATFORM LEADER

Salesforce.com has adopted several other initiatives in recent years to enhance the nature and quality of the innovation outcomes in the network. Let us take a brief look at some of these.

IdeaExchange

Salesforce.com's customers are also participants in the innovation network. They play the role of an "ideator" by serving as the source of new product or product improvement ideas. The company has created a separate forum called the IdeaExchange to facilitate the dialogue between active subscribers (customers) and the company on product- and technology-related issues. Customers can visit the IdeaExchange and suggest product improvement ideas as well as new product concepts to the company. Comments and suggestions on the forum are continuously monitored by the company to identify promising ideas for implementation. Customers can also weigh in on other customers' ideas by "promoting" them on the IdeaExchange forum—that is, indicating that the idea is useful, relevant, and important. Ideas that are promoted the most get the company's attention and are actively considered for implementation. The forum also enables customers to interact directly with the company's product managers. Thus, the IdeaExchange is a mechanism for Salesforce's subscribers to actively participate in the product innovation in a way that will benefit them the most.

Most importantly, the forum also serves as an idea "garden" for the external application developers. In other words, many of the ideas suggested in the forum relate to complementary functions or products—functions that customers would like to have but are not included in the core suite of products from the company. And as such, they indicate the potential market for specific complementary applications. The company also uses the IdeaExchange to communicate with its customers and other stakeholders about its technology and product development plans. As Kendall Collins, senior vice president of the company notes, the IdeaExchange provides a transparent roadmap of the company's development pipeline and the customer demand for new applications and components.[36]

Co-Marketing and Value Appropriation

AppExchange is a marketplace for complementary applications. External developers can market and trade their applications to potential customers. As such, it serves as a worldwide market for on-demand applications. However, AppExchange is not the only value appropriation vehicle for external developers. Salesforce.com also takes a more active role in marketing external developers' applications to its customers.

For example, after an application has gained the company's certification, the external developer can partner with the company and map out co-marketing plans—event sponsorship, paid placements on AppExchange, and so on. In addition, Salesforce's own internal sales team will actively promote specific complementary applications based on the needs of its customers—in essence, external developers can utilize the company's internal marketing and sales infrastructure to promote and market their complementary applications. In many of these opportunities, the synergy between Salesforce's CRM solution and the external developer's complementary application is leveraged to enhance the overall "value" appeal to the customers. If a sale goes through, the external developers' share of the sales proceeds is channeled through the company.

Other Partner Alliances

Other technology companies are also key partners of Salesforce's innovation network. They include major device manufacturers and security, integration, and computer telephony integration companies. These companies offer complementary technologies that the company can leverage to develop customized solutions for its customers in specific industry niches.

Salesforce brings together these companies to support and promote specific aspects of its technology platform. For example, the company has formed the Apex Alliance to promote Apex, the on-demand programming language component of its technology platform. The Apex Alliance incorporates several of Salesforce's technology partners including Accenture, Adobe, Business Objects, Cingular Wireless, Dell, Deloitte, ExactTarget, Palm, Research In Motion, Satyam Computers, Siemens, and Tata Consultancy Services.

Such forums and alliances serve as a mechanism for the company to share knowledge about its technology platform and to identify opportunities for its external developers and partners to exploit the platform in specific application areas. The alliances also enable the company to signal the commitment of other industry leaders to its technology platform, thereby enhancing its overall status in the market and inducing more external developers to join the network.

AppExchange Central Business Incubator

We mentioned earlier that Salesforce plays an active role in promoting and marketing the complementary applications developed by its external partners. In late 2006, the company announced a much more ambitious initiative, called the AppExchange Central Business Incubator, to cultivate, nurture, and promote the innovation activities of its complementary application developers.

AppExchange Central is essentially an incubation program for partners building applications for AppExchange. Salesforce will invest in creating a physical infrastructure to house its fledgling partners. The incubator will also house Salesforce technical staffers ready to assist in AppExchange application development. The first such AppExchange Central incubator opened in January 2007 in San Mateo, California, near the company's San Francisco headquarters. Partner companies can rent space in the facility for about $20,000 a year, which also includes the cost of access to Salesforce's technical and business resources to help bring products to market. The company plans to set up more such incubators in other locations, including Tokyo, London, Bangalore, and Singapore.[37]

AppExchange incubators are designed to provide entrepreneurs (or external developers) with a package of business services aimed at compressing the development timeline and the go-to-market costs for the incubator companies. These services include access to the Apex programming language and other components of the technology platform, technology infrastructure, product development, sales and marketing support, fundraising, and business development assistance.

The AppExchange incubator represents the very active role that Salesforce expects to play in growing its innovation network. It will not only identify potential external partners but also invest resources in assisting them to develop and get products to the market. In turn, the company expects its incubator strategy to enhance the overall demand for its technology platform and the core suite of CRM products.

The incubation centers also represent another opportunity for the company— it would likely provide a funnel of acquisition candidates, or applications that the company can cherry-pick for future acquisition.

While platform leaders should be careful about showing an appetite for acquiring its complementary solution providers, in many cases, an acquisition can be a win-win situation. For example, in 2006, Salesforce acquired a tiny company called Kieden that had created an add-on to its hosted services for purchasing and managing Google-driven Web advertising campaigns. The add-on solution that became a part of the company's core product suite allows marketing and advertising managers to analyze ongoing campaigns by viewing which of the people who click on Google AdWords keywords become sales leads. Kieden, which was a San Francisco-based four-person company, was able to develop a public beta version of the application and launch it on the AppExchange where it clearly demonstrated the overall market appeal of the solution.

The example of Kieden thus shows that Salesforce can harness the innovative power of its community of developers in more than one way—it can nurture the growth of such applications thereby indirectly enhancing its technology platform as well as acquire highly promising solutions and make them part of its core product.

CRITICAL ELEMENTS OF THE ORCHESTRA-PLATFORM MODEL

In sum, AppExchange represents Salesforce.com's branching out from a position as a CRM-only company to being a provider of an application platform for all types of on-demand solutions, adding value as a platform company and leveraging the efforts of numerous partners in the AppExchange innovation network. Table 5.3 captures the critical elements of Salesforce.com's Orchestra-Platform model of network-centric innovation.

Table 5.3 Salesforce.com and the AppExchange Initiative

Elements of Network-Centric Innovation	Salesforce.com and the AppExchange Forum
Nature of the innovation space	Salesforce.com's core offering (the CRM system) and its on-demand architecture provides the platform for external developers to build applications on. The platform both modularizes the overall solution space and also enables the different applications to "talk to one another."
Structure of the network leadership	Salesforce.com is the leader of the network; it owns the underlying technology platform and makes all the decisions related to the evolution of the platform.
Innovation Roles	
Architect	Salesforce.com plays the role of the platform leader, the only leadership role in the network.
Adapter	External application developers play the role of complementor by developing software applications that complement and/or augment the functionality of the core CRM offering; customers play the role of ideator by providing ideas for new applications and rating the performance of existing solutions of external developers.
Agent	Salesforce.com also plays the role of an innomediary by mediating the transfer of solutions from external partners (independent software developers) to end customers through the AppExchange Directory (an application listing service).
Network Management	
Network governance	Salesforce.com's Partner Program provides quasi-formal ties for external partners with the company and is based on specific selection criteria; the external developer community is moderated by Salesforce.com; AppExchange acts as a market mechanism for transactions between members.
Knowledge management	ADN (AppExchange Developer Network) provides the forum for member dialog and knowledge sharing; it also allows Salesforce.com to diffuse new developments in the platform. Offline forums such as the adn@dreamforce bring together external developers to critique new platform developments. AppExchange Business Incubator helps technology transfer to partners.

Elements of Network-Centric Innovation	Salesforce.com and the AppExchange Forum
IP rights and value appropriation	AppExchange provides the primary market mechanism for external developers. Salesforce.com also promotes and markets complementary applications through its own sales infrastructure and channels sale proceeds to external partners; all rights related to complementary solutions are managed by partners themselves.

The case of Salesforce.com as well as other platform leaders like IBM, Microsoft, Intel, and Cisco highlight the central role of the platform leader in orchestrating the innovation activities of the different players in the network.[38] By clearly explicating the technology platform, the platform leader provides a structure to the innovation space that directs and brings coherence to the innovation activities of the diverse partners. And, as we saw in our case studies, the role involves three important sets of activities: "seeding" and nurturing complementors and other innovation partners, facilitating and supporting innovation, and providing market delivery and other value appropriation mechanisms. We will come back to these themes later on in Chapter 10, "Preparing the Organization," when we discuss the organizational capabilities needed to carry out the role of the platform leader.

CONCLUSION

The two forms of the Orchestra model that we have described in this chapter represent two sides of the same coin.

In both the Integrator and the Platform model, the innovation architecture defined by the dominant firm becomes the context for the network partners to innovate. However, while in the Integrator model, the objective is to constrain partners' activities and channel their innovative efforts to suit the dominant firm's vision of the final product or service offering, in the Platform model, the objective is to expand the opportunities for network partners to innovate and build on the platform so as to enhance its overall reach and range.

In both cases, the tricky part is to bring together a diverse set of capable partners who are sufficiently committed to the innovation architecture and to orchestrate their activities in a manner that leads to outcomes that are beneficial to all the network members. In sum, the dominant firm has to create the impression in the network that it is giving its partners the opportunity to be part of its success.

6

The Creative Bazaar Model

Sometimes, instead of creating an innovative product from scratch, firms might choose to "shop" for innovative ideas available from the Global Brain. Shopping in the "Creative Bazaar"—the global marketplace of ideas, products, and technologies—is particularly useful when time to market is an important consideration, and when the firm's external environment is rich with creative potential.

Shopping for innovation is not unlike shopping for food to satisfy your hunger. You basically have two very different options before you. You could go to a grocery store, buy the ingredients, and cook a meal yourself. Alternatively, you could order a fully cooked meal at a restaurant. Cooking a meal yourself would likely cost less, but it would take more time and effort. Moreover, the quality of the meal would be a little uncertain if you aren't an expert cook. On the other hand, ordering a fully cooked meal from a restaurant would be quick and easy and in most cases would ensure reliable quality. However, your choices will be limited to what's on the menu, and further, you would have to pay a higher price for the convenience and the reduced risk.

Likewise, when a company shops for innovation, it has similar options. It can source "raw" new product and technology ideas from inventors and then go about "cooking" these ideas into commercial products and services. Alternatively, it can acquire "market-ready" products, technologies, or startup firms. As in the food analogy, these options have very different implications for cost, reach, risk, and time to market.

Regardless of the option the firm chooses to shop for innovation, it needs to partner with a network of inventors and innovation intermediaries. In this chapter, we describe the different options that firms have in shopping for innovation in the Creative Bazaar. As we noted in Chapter 3, "The Four Models of Network-Centric Innovation," the Creative Bazaar model involves a large firm sourcing innovative product ideas and technologies from external sources and using its proprietary commercialization infrastructure (including its brands, design capabilities, and access to distribution channels) to build on the ideas and make them market-ready.

THE "CREATIVE BAZAAR" CONTINUUM

Innovative product or technology ideas can be acquired at different levels of maturity, ranging from "raw" ideas or concepts to "market-ready" products. And companies can use different mechanisms or different types of intermediaries for sourcing such innovation. These mechanisms differ in terms of the *cost* of acquiring the innovative idea and the *risk mitigation* that the mechanism allows. In addition, there are additional considerations such as the *reach* of the mechanism (how many ideas can be sourced) and the *time to market* (how much time it will take to commercialize the idea). **Figure 6.1** depicts the continuum of innovation sourcing mechanisms. These sourcing mechanisms represent the Creative Bazaar continuum.

Looking at the left end of the continuum, companies can source relatively undeveloped or "raw" product or technology ideas. They can do this by reaching out directly to individual inventors, as Procter & Gamble has done through its Connect+Develop initiative.[1] P&G invites individual inventors to submit patented product or technology ideas that can potentially be commercialized by the company.[2] Companies such as Kraft, Kimberly Clark, and so on have also announced such initiatives to invite ideas from external entities through their Web site.

Such "raw" ideas or patented inventions can also be sourced through a set of innovation intermediaries that include patent brokers and electronic R&D marketplaces (for example, NineSigma and Yet2.com). These intermediaries largely focus on connecting large firms with individual inventors (or their patents). They are pure brokers, in that they play a matchmaking role, and have limited involvement in the development of the innovative ideas.[3] Similarly, another type of intermediary, idea scouts—entities who trawl for innovative ideas in the inventor community on behalf of large firms—utilize domain or market knowledge to locate promising new ideas without much input into the innovation process. While such brokers and middlemen broaden the reach and range of idea sourcing and lower the cost of acquiring ideas, they typically deal with rather immature ideas that are a long way from being ready for primetime. As such, there is still a lot of market risk that the firm has to mitigate through further development and market testing.

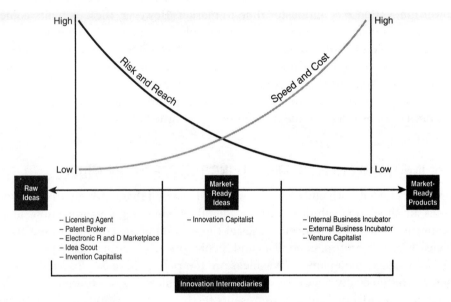

Figure 6.1 The Creative Bazaar Continuum

Now, consider the other end of the continuum. The mechanisms at this end for buying innovation include internal incubators (such as Salesforce.com AppExchange Central Business Incubator), external incubators (for example, university-based incubators), and venture capitalists—entities that invest in and/or incubate new ventures with the purpose of offering these ventures as acquisition candidates for large firms. Typically, the innovative ideas underlying such new ventures are fully developed, market-demonstrated, and married with matching organizational infrastructure.

The classic example here is P&G's acquisition of the SpinBrush product (the novel, low-cost battery-operated toothbrush). The SpinBrush was developed and launched in 1999 by a startup (Dr. Johns Products Ltd.) led by entrepreneur

John Osher and the principals of Nottingham-Spirk (a Cleveland-based industrial design firm) and their in-house patent lawyer. By the time P&G acquired SpinBrush in 2001, the product had been test-marketed and proclaimed a commercial success based on its initial sales performance in Wal-Mart stores.

The sourcing mechanisms at this end of the continuum enable the development of the product concept to a stage where it can be taken to the market directly, that is, a "market-ready" product. Consequently, the large firm can benefit from lower innovation risk and faster time to market. However, these benefits come at a cost. Acquisition costs are high (for example, P&G had to shell out $475 million for the SpinBrush). And the reach of the firm is limited because few ideas make it far enough in the innovation pipeline to be market-ready. Further, the routes to market, the sales organization, and the other commercialization infrastructure that gets added to the product concept might not be needed by the acquiring firms, and often might need to be discarded at a cost.

THE INNOVATION CAPITALIST—FILLING THE GAP IN THE MIDDLE

Having looked at both ends of the continuum, we find that neither extreme provides an appetizing solution to the trade-offs in shopping for innovation. Idea scouts and other such intermediaries at the left end of the continuum sell "raw ideas" whereas venture capitalists and incubators sell "market-ready products" or "fully baked" companies. Raw ideas are too risky, whereas fully baked companies are too costly. As every shrewd politician likes to say—there has to be a *third way*—a mechanism that represents the best of both worlds. Indeed, there is such an entity that fills the gap in the middle of the Creative Bazaar continuum and allows firms to achieve a balance among the reach, the innovation cost, the innovation risk, and the time to market.

We call this entity that represents this "third way" an *innovation capitalist* (IC). An innovation capitalist is an organization that seeks out promising new ideas from individual inventors, transforms those ideas into market-ready concepts, and sells the related intellectual property to large firms. In effect, the IC offers a "market-ready idea" as opposed to a "raw idea" or a "market-ready product." In so doing, an IC adds significant value beyond the brokering function provided by idea scouts and R&D marketplaces. Specifically, an IC invests in the idea, assumes risk, and shares in the rents generated from selling the intellectual property.

ICs act as the extension of the "fuzzy front-end" (that is the initial, unstructured part) of the innovation process of large firms, by allowing them to make effective tradeoffs between innovation reach and business-readiness in innovation sourcing. Revisiting our cooking analogy, ICs sell "step-saver meals"—ingredients that have been assembled into a recipe that looks promising, and only needs a few more steps to make a delicious meal!

Before we discuss the innovation capitalists (and how companies can partner with them) in more detail, let us first consider the two options that companies have to source "raw ideas" at the left-end of the creative bazaar continuum: (a) partnering with the inventor community and (b) partnering with idea scouts (and other such intermediaries). We omit the right-hand extreme of the continuum because the acquisition of a startup firm is traditional M&A, and is outside the scope of network-centric innovation.

PARTNERING WITH THE INVENTOR COMMUNITY: DIAL CORPORATION AND THE "PARTNERS IN INNOVATION" INITIATIVE

Partnering with inventors involves going directly to the source—to individuals who have creative ideas. To understand how this approach works, consider how Dial Corporation, a large consumer product company based in Scottsdale, Arizona, has successfully reached out to inventors through its "Partners in Innovation" initiative. Dial has a presence in three core markets: personal care, laundry care, and home care. Some of its well-known brands include Dial, Purex, Right Guard, Pure & Natural, Borax, and Soft Scrub. Its products have been in the American market for more than 130 years. In 1953, Dial launched one of the best-known marketing slogans ever—"Aren't you glad you use Dial?"—to establish Dial as the nation's best antibacterial soap.

In March 2004, Dial became a subsidiary of Henkel KGaA, a German consumer products conglomerate based in Düsseldorf, Germany. While the parent company afforded it a greater global reach and presence, in the U.S. market, Dial remained a mid-sized company competing against much larger consumer companies such as P&G and J&J. This size disadvantage necessitated that Dial be very aggressive in innovation to stay competitive. In recent years, this drive for innovation has led to a more open approach to sourcing innovation from external sources, and more specifically to the launch of its partnership with the inventor community called the "Partners in Innovation" initiative.

Dial's story of its partnership with the external inventors started with the establishment of a separate organizational unit called the Technology Acquisition group in 2003. Debra Park was appointed as the director of the group with the mandate to seek out new product and technology ideas from external sources and to feed the organization's R&D pipeline with commercially feasible innovative ideas.

The "Partners in Innovation" initiative launched in 2004 was the first step. It originated as a Web site where individual inventors could go and submit patented ideas that Dial would then evaluate for commercialization potential. If ideas were found to be commercially attractive, Dial would pursue those ideas with the individual inventor—in most cases, buying outright the patented idea from the inventor. In 2004, as part of this initiative, Dial launched a contest for individual inventors called the "Quest for the Best." In this contest, individual inventors were invited to submit patented (or patent pending) ideas to Dial. Dial specified the product categories in which it was seeking innovative ideas.

The number of submissions ran into the hundreds. A panel of judges within Dial then screened those ideas and narrowed the list down to 60 inventions. Dial then asked these inventors to create a five-minute video of their idea so that Dial could get a first-hand feel for the idea. Dial asked inventors to answer two key questions—"How does the idea work? And how is it better than what's out there?" Based on these video submissions, Dial further narrowed the list down to the top ten inventors. These inventors were then invited to Dial's corporate campus in Arizona to showcase their inventions to top Dial executives.

Each inventor was assigned a booth to exhibit the prototype of their invention. Judges selected three ideas and the inventors were given awards. Dial agreed to pursue these three top ideas for more formal market evaluation and feasibility analysis. The agreement was that if Dial decided that one of these ideas was commercially attractive, it would buy the patented idea from the inventor.

In 2005, Dial ran another version of the Quest for the Best contest and garnered a fresh set of innovative product ideas for internal evaluation. In the same year, it added another element to the Partners in Innovation program by establishing the "Submit & Win" sweepstakes for online idea submissions. All submissions that met the basic criteria (for example, patented or patent pending idea) were entered into a sweepstake and three winners selected at random were awarded $1,000 each. The objective was to keep inventors coming to the company's Web site and submitting their innovative ideas. So far, the Partners in Innovation program has generated at least five new product concepts that have made it into the official Dial product development pipeline. This feat is quite impressive for a consumer packaged goods company in relatively mature markets.

Dial's initiative embodies several best practices worth noting. The first relates to the nature of the innovation network. The members of Dial's innovation network primarily consist of individual inventors. They are a diverse lot. As Debra

Park notes, "Some of them are retirees who have mulled over these things and now they have time to work on it. But for some of them, it's a side passion. One gave a presentation at the local inventor association here in Arizona. And, these people are from all walks of life."[4]

Dial was able to reach out to such a diverse and widely distributed set of inventors by partnering with local and national associations of inventors. It decided early on that establishing credibility with the inventor community was critical. Partnering with inventor associations signals that Dial is a credible and trustworthy partner. Dial sought and got the support of two inventor associations—the United Inventor Association (UIA), a national body, and the Inventor Association of Arizona, the local association. UIA was instrumental in getting the word out in the inventor community about Dial's "Quest for the Best" contest and other initiatives. According to Debra, "UIA is a much respected organization within the inventor community. So, hearing it from them made inventors feel more comfortable ... in their eyes, Dial is a big corporate entity."

Dial also provided the commercialization platform for getting the innovative ideas to the market. We call this role the *innovation portal*—a role that involves serving as the portal to the market for new ideas and concepts. As the dominant player in the network, Dial made the crucial decisions regarding the commercial feasibility of the innovation and the approach it should take to develop and market the new product. And if the idea or the patent was licensed, Dial assumed the responsibility for appropriating the value from the innovation and sharing it with the inventor.

A key to the success of Dial's initiative was to establish itself as the preferred innovation portal for individual inventors with neat ideas. As Debra Park notes, "To me, one of the mantras of the Partners in Innovation program is—'think of Dial first.' Come to us first with your idea, not to our competitors, and set up Dial as a company that you would want to do business with." To achieve this goal, Dial had to make the process as transparent as possible and also build a long-term, trust-based relationship with the inventor community. For example, it made sure that it communicated the outcomes of the ideas submitted promptly and in a respectful manner to the inventors. Such actions enabled the company to establish and maintain a network of inventors who are likely to bring their ideas to the company in the future.

Although Dial does not use intermediaries, preferring to interact directly with individual inventors, the inventor associations do play a supporting role by facilitating those interactions and promoting Dial's initiatives in the community. For example, they helped to communicate details of Dial's contest and other initiatives to the different chapters of the association across the country. Inventor associations have an incentive to play such a facilitating role as they spend a lot of their resources educating their members on how not to get ripped off by fraudulent patent brokers and agents. By partnering with a reputed and established company like Dial, the association is able to offer a safe and trusted avenue for inventors to shop their ideas. In return, Dial also sponsored some of the associations' educational activities to cement its perception as a "good citizen" of the inventor community.

In partnering with individual inventors, there are no formal linkages among the members in the network, so governance is largely based on trust and reputation. Most individual inventors have limited knowledge about patents or product commercialization. Thus, their trust-based relationship with Dial is crucial in their dealings with the company. On the other hand, Dial has a critical need to maintain its credibility and reputation in the inventor community. Any bad experience that an individual inventor might have with the company would likely travel fast within the inventor community via word of mouth and damage Dial's long-term objective of becoming the preferred portal of innovative ideas.

Dial also made sure that a clear organizational mandate existed to take the promising external ideas into the formal product development channels within the organization. For example, Dial instituted internal systems whereby innovative ideas could be funded for the proof of principle stage even if initial evaluations did not match with Dial's current product portfolio. Without such a mandate and associated systems, externally sourced ideas would likely stagnate within the company and not see the light of the day in the marketplace— thereby discouraging inventors from bringing their ideas to Dial in the future.

Furthermore, with the acquisition of Dial by Henkel, the scope of both idea collection as well as idea utilization has become more global. For example, in early 2007, Henkel launched the *Henkel Innovation Trophy*, a global contest for innovative product ideas. The program was launched in collaboration with U.S. and international inventor associations, including the United Inventor Association in the U.S. and the Deutscher Erfinderverband, the German inventors association. Further, innovative ideas sourced by Dial from the inventor community (in the U.S.) that do not have a direct fit with Dial's current product strategy are shopped around among Henkel's other business units worldwide. In the words of Debra, "We are now not only sourcing ideas for Dial but for Henkel, too." Such a global reach enhances the attractiveness of Dial as the preferred portal for individual inventors.

Dial uses several metrics to evaluate the success of its Partnership in Innovation program. For example, the company tracks the ideas as they progress through the development pipeline—how many ideas were brought in, how many proceeded to concept test, how many were incorporated into a project, and how many actually went into the market. Of course, the ultimate success metric is whether the idea got into the market. As Debra notes, "All of this boils down to that something was put out into the market under the Dial name—that to me is the only meaningful measure of whether I am doing a good job here."

While Dial is definitely one of the pioneers in employing this form of the Creative Bazaar model, other companies such as P&G, Kimberly Clark, and Kraft Foods have also started similar initiatives. The case of Dial, however, suggests that success in this approach requires patiently building trust-based, long-term relationships with the inventor community and seeking the help of inventor associations and other such entities.

PARTNERING WITH IDEA SCOUTS: THE BIG IDEA GROUP AND "IDEA HUNTS"

Another form of the Creative Bazaar model eschews direct interactions with inventors, relying instead on the services of an intermediary, such as an idea scout to seek out innovative ideas or technologies.

The Big Idea Group (BIG), located in Manchester, New Hampshire, is a firm that focuses on identifying innovative product concepts for large companies, particularly in the areas of consumer packaged goods, food and beverages, and personal media and technology. The company was founded by Mike Collins, a former venture capitalist and toy industry entrepreneur, in 2000. Over the years, the company has built a large network of independent inventors, which it mines for new ideas and concepts.

Reminiscent of the popular public television show, "Antiques Roadshow," where antique experts offer appraisals for antiques that people bring in from their homes, BIG conducts "roadshows"—events at different locations of the country where inventors can walk in and present their ideas to a panel of experts who provide a quick and free evaluation of the idea. There are no obligations on the part of the company or the inventor for this preliminary idea evaluation. If the initial evaluation shows that the idea might have potential, the company invites the inventor to submit the idea in a more formal manner and sign a representation agreement with BIG, wherein it takes the responsibility for shopping the idea to large client companies who might be interested in commercializing it. If a company is interested in licensing the idea, BIG splits royalties with the inventor (in most cases, the split is 50-50).

BIG achieves several objectives through the roadshows:

- It provides a free service to individual inventors and establishes its reputation in the inventor community as a trustworthy partner.

- Each inventor who participates in a roadshow—whether or not the ideas get pursued further—becomes part of the "inventor network" that BIG maintains. The roadshows help build BIG's most important resource—its inventor network. As of July 2007, BIG's inventor network was 12,000 strong—an impressive pool of creative talent for any client company.

- Within its vast inventor network, BIG has identified a more focused set of around 500 "strong" inventors—individuals that BIG has evaluated as "highly creative" and whose talent is particularly relevant for the more focused discovery of innovative ideas that the company pursues for client firms.

Such focused discoveries are called *idea hunts*. BIG conducts the idea hunts on behalf of large clients firms such as Gillette, Staples, Sunbeam, and Bell Sports, as well as toolmakers such as Skil-Bosch and Dremel. These "idea hunts" are essentially an exercise in mining BIG's inventor network for promising ideas related to a specific theme or market need that the client firm has expressed. For example, a client firm might specify a broad market need or the need for a particular type of product; BIG then communicates this need to its inventor network, seeking potential product ideas. After the ideas are submitted (usually online), BIG does an initial screening and then forwards them to the sponsoring firm. Such idea hunts might cost the sponsoring firm anywhere from $40,000 and up.[5] So far, these initiatives have led to the creation of more than 60 new products for companies like Staples, General Mills, eToys, Sunbeam, and QVC.[6]

BIG is not the only firm playing the role of such an intermediary. Another idea scout is the Product Development Group (PDG) LLC.[7] PDG plays the role of an idea screener—it receives, compiles, and reviews new product ideas on behalf of companies such as Staples. Its objective is to determine the likelihood of a potential match between the product idea and Staples' needs. PDG does not do any market research on the viability of the ideas. It only screens and aggregates the ideas that it receives before forwarding them to client firms.

A similar role is also played by electronic R&D marketplaces, such as InnoCentive and Yet2.com. Independent inventors list their patented technologies on such sites, which companies can browse through and then evaluate for potential commercialization. A number of other new types of entities have entered this space (see the following sidebar, "Intellectual Ventures: An Invention Capitalist").

INTELLECTUAL VENTURES: AN INVENTION CAPITALIST

Intellectual Ventures LLC (IV) is an *invention capitalist* firm co-founded in 2000 by former Microsoft CTO, Nathan Myhrvold, and scientist, Edward Jung. The company's goal is to invest in a wide range of patents with the objective of selling or licensing those patents to client firms that are interested in commercializing them. Myhrvold and Jung built the company based on the belief that invention or patents is the "most interesting part of the commercial food chain."[8]

However, rather than focusing on marketing individual patents, the company adds value by bringing together patents related to a common market problem.[9] Thus, while the company's focus is not on traditional product development and it does not invest in transforming the patents (invention) to products (innovation), it does help client firms by offering a more complete set of patents that are required in a given commercialization context.

Intermediaries such as IV offer two potential benefits for client firms:

- As in the case of idea scouts, they go trawling for innovative patented ideas and technologies; that is, they do the most difficult job of finding the "diamonds among the rough."

- They make critical connections among the different patents vis-à-vis a commercialization opportunity and then market that portfolio of patents to client firms, thereby accelerating the innovation process and enhancing its success.

However, remember that companies that buy these patents from an invention capitalist still have to do the heavy-lifting of developing and commercializing them into new products (or services).

The role of innovation intermediaries such as BIG and PDG is to mediate between the inventor network and the large company seeking the innovation. As BIG founder Collins says, "Corporations don't want to deal with inventors one-on-one. We saw the need to bridge between all these inventors and clients who wanted innovation,"[10] These intermediaries do not invest any money in developing or validating the innovative ideas. Instead, they add value to the process by seeking out and filtering the promising ideas.

To do this, however, they have to first get access to the inventor community. Thus, the key capability for an intermediary such as BIG is the ability to establish and maintain a network of independent inventors from which the company can source innovative ideas. The larger the network, the more successful the innovation sourcing is likely to be. However, because no formal ties exist between any of the entities in this network, social mechanisms of governance—trust and reputation-based systems—form the glue that holds the network together. Information technology—for example, Web-based forums—can be used to communicate, interact, and share knowledge with individual inventors. Finally, formal agreements based on the sale or licensing of patents form the primary mechanism for the appropriation and sharing of value from the innovative idea.

PARTNERING WITH INNOVATION CAPITALISTS

An innovation capitalist (IC) is an organization that seeks out and evaluates innovative technology and product concepts from the inventor community and other external sources, develops and refines these ideas to a stage where their market potential is validated, and then markets these technology and product concepts to large client firms. In other words, an IC firm transforms the ideas to a stage where a large firm can make a much better judgment of their market potential (see the following sidebar, "Profiles of Innovation Capitalist Firms").

PROFILES OF INNOVATION CAPITALIST FIRMS

Evergreen IP is a firm based in Evergreen, Colorado, that focuses on the innovation outsourcing market in the consumer product sector. Specifically, it seeks out promising ideas and inventions from individual inventors and makes selective investments to upgrade those inventions via market research, product design, and patent work. It then sells or licenses the resulting innovation and related IP to large consumer product companies such as P&G and Dial. The company targets a number of product categories, including health and beauty, household products, pet care and pet accessories, and low-tech gadgets. The founders of the company include an entrepreneur, a financial specialist, and a consumer product marketer. The company has so far reviewed more than 1,600 product ideas, has more than 15 ongoing product development projects, and is in discussions with prospective licensees on 6 of those projects.

IgniteIP (IIP) is a U.S.-based investment firm with offices in New York and California that focuses on IP placement in the technology sector. It seeks out promising IP and invests in them (in the range of $500,000 to $2 million) to upgrade the IP and secure licensing opportunities in existing market channels. For this task, the company brings together a diverse set of knowledge and expertise including technical, industry, marketing, and legal expertise. The company has established an extensive network among senior managers in technology companies and utilizes the network to market and place its candidate IP. Given the risks—largely technological and development risks—it assumes on the IP, the company shares the IP royalties with the inventor. While IIP does not explicitly specify a particular technology sector, the dominant areas include chemicals, energy, environment, and software.

ICs help companies outsource the early stage ideation and development processes, often the most risky and time-consuming stage of the development cycle. Their value proposition centers on four themes—*greater reach, lower risk, greater speed,* and *lower cost.* ICs enable large firms to broaden their innovation reach—the range of ideas they can consider—without requiring direct interaction with the inventor community and the associated investment in relationship management or risks related to IP rights and knowledge spillover. Further, they provide client firms with access to innovative product or technology ideas that are much farther along on the maturity scale (that is, more "market-ready" ideas), thereby mitigating early-stage innovation risks as well as lowering the time to market without significantly increasing the innovation acquisition cost. By selectively investing in and building on promising ideas, ICs allow large firms to lower the overall business risks related to the innovation. Also, ICs lower the cost of acquiring the innovation by not adding any management or other commercialization infrastructure to the innovation, relying instead on the existing brand and operational infrastructure of the client firm for market exploitation. Moreover, ICs source innovation at a fairly early stage, allowing for cheaper acquisitions than buying a fully baked startup firm. In return for this unique value proposition, ICs expect a share of the proceeds from the innovation from the client firm.

How different is an IC from other innovation sourcing mechanisms we have discussed in this chapter? In **Table 6.1**, we summarize the key differences between an innovation capitalist and other innovation sourcing mechanisms. As we discussed earlier, an IC differs from an idea scout or patent broker in that it invests in and adds value to the innovation. And although an IC shares some traits with venture capitalist firms, it is different from them in that its capital investment tends to be very limited and the investment focused only on refining the product idea and not on building an organization (or management infrastructure) around that idea. Further, most of the projects (product concepts or technology ideas) that ICs pursue typically do not fit the "business model" of VCs. They don't have the "size" to justify additional management overheads or the creation of new market channels. Also, the expected payoff tends to fall below the threshold of most VCs—that is, the projects don't exploit or warrant the core competencies of VCs nor do they provide sufficient returns. As Stephan Mallenbaum, a partner at New York–based Jones Day, notes, an "innovation capitalist can serve as an extension of a large client company's innovation engine. Such a service provided by (an innovation capitalist) is really unique and VCs are just not equipped to serve large firms in that manner."[11]

Table 6.1 Comparison of Innovation Capitalist with Other Innovation Sourcing Mechanisms

Characteristics	Idea Scout, Invention Capitalist, and so on	Innovation Capitalist	Venture Capitalist, Business Incubator, and so on
Core objective	To connect companies with independent inventors and patents	To connect companies with "market-ready" innovative concepts	To connect companies with new ventures that have "market-ready" products

Characteristics	Idea Scout, Invention Capitalist, and so on	Innovation Capitalist	Venture Capitalist, Business Incubator, and so on
Key function	Creates a brokering infrastructure in the "raw idea" market	Brings industry and market expertise to idea development	Brings market and financial expertise to new ventures
Value addition	Seeks out and filters new ideas that fit companies' innovation goals	Builds on and transforms "raw" ideas to "market-ready" concepts	Builds an organization around a new idea
Core competencies	Cost-effective "sniff-testing" of new ideas Networking in inventor community	Front-end innovation management Industry and market expertise Relationship management IP rights management	Venture creation Market expertise Financial risk management Networking in inventor community
Capital investment	No investment in concept/patent development (patent-related investment for invention capitalist)	Limited investments in concept development	Substantial investment in building new venture
Risks assumed	None or little (patent-related risk for invention capitalist)	Considerable early-stage idea development risk	Considerable financial risk associated with new venture
IP rights ownership	None or few (invention capitalist owns patent-related rights)	Owns a share of the IP rights	Owns a share of the new venture (including associated IP)
Relationship with client company	Transactional	Long-term partnership	Transactional

Adapted from table "The Differing Roles of Innovative Intermediaries," on pg. 114 of "A Buyer's Guide to the Innovation Bazaar," by Satish Nambisan and Mohanbir Sawhney. Harvard Business Review, June 2007. © 2007 Harvard Business School Publishing Corporation. All rights reserved.

VALUE CHAIN AND COMPETENCIES FOR INNOVATION CAPITALISTS

To deliver such a value proposition, an innovation capitalist has to implement a value chain with three components: Seek and Evaluate, Develop and Refine, and Market the new product/technology concept. **Figure 6.2** shows the value chain of an innovation capitalist and **Table 6.2** lists the key competencies needed. Let us examine these value chain activities and associated competencies in more detail.

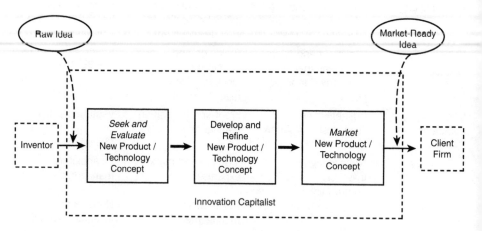

Figure 6.2 The value chain of an innovation capitalist

Seek and Evaluate

The Seek and Evaluate activity relates to sourcing innovative ideas (or patents) from the inventor community and selecting those that have the best potential to develop into a marketable product or technology.

This activity requires two competencies. One is that the IC has to establish and maintain deep roots in different types of inventor communities to allow it to source ideas from a wide range of places. Some of the IC firms are active in attending regional and local inventor club meetings and sponsoring and participating in inventor education events. This direct outreach to inventor clubs builds awareness of the IC firm and establishes a long-term, trust-based relationship with the inventor community. Trust is crucial because historically, intermediaries like patent brokers have earned an unsavory reputation by ripping off inventors who have limited knowledge of the patenting and commercialization processes. Building trust and offering a fair and just idea review process are essential to attract good ideas from inventors. As Brandon Williams, the managing director and co-founder of IgniteIP notes, "The overall approach should be—we win when you win."

Table 6.2 Competencies for Innovation Capitalist

	Nature of Competency		
Innovation Capitalist Value Chain Activity	Industry/Market-Related Competencies	Innovation Project Management Competencies	Network/ Relational Competencies
Seek and Evaluate	Evaluate market risk	Establish transparent review processes	Build and maintain inventor networks
	Identify critical market needs/gaps	Assess and manage IC portfolio risk	Establish trust in inventor community
			Communicate client and market needs
Develop and Refine	Integrate diverse industry knowledge	Manage idea development risks	Build and manage partner network
	Identify critical market success factors	Coordinate idea development activities	
Market	Understand client firm's brand and innovation portfolio priorities	Understand client firm's innovation processes and metrics	Build and maintain long-term relationships with client firms
	Manage IP rights		Structure value appropriation deals
			Communicate market potential of new idea or concept

The second competency relates to the ability to screen or identify ideas that are worth further consideration and investment. Typically, the first screening is a qualitative analysis of the key value proposition of the idea and the potential for building sufficient IP—a five-minute "sniff test." Given the volume of ideas to be screened, it is critical that the IC firm be able to do this as cost effectively as possible. As you saw earlier in the example of the BIG, pre-scheduled events (such as "roadshows") held in different parts of the country where individual inventors can come and present their ideas to a panel of experts for preliminary screening is one such cost-effective mechanism. Evergreen IP, on the other hand, pursues a more community-centric approach—it sends out its "scouts" to places that inventors frequent and provides idea assessments then and there itself. This technique allows EIP to find out through word of mouth "where the ideas are located" and provide rapid assessments, which might help the inventor to further refine the idea and induce him/her to come back to the company later on. The overall objective is to offer a transparent and fair process by which the business potential of new ideas can be quickly evaluated.

The initial evaluation is often followed by a more rigorous quantitative benchmarking test of the market/business viability of the product or technology concept. EIP, for example, uses an idea handicapping tool such as *Merwin*, a benchmarking database from Eureka Ranch, the market research firm, for this screening. It evaluates and provides a score for an idea that reflects its potential market success. John Funk, a co-founder of EIP, describes this initial screening:

> The average market success score is 100 on that scale. The CPG companies that use Merwin, which there's a fair number that do, they get excited when they're at about 120. So we've handicapped ourselves to say it's got to be really north of that. We're looking for 170. And that's our first screen for identifying. And then we use a "spiral risk reduction" model. What's the big show stopper? Is there a protectable asset here? Because if we don't have a protectable asset, we don't have anything to transact around, a license agreement. So sometimes we'll go there first, do the patent search to see if we've got enough green space.

> Is it a big enough idea? Is the size of prize going to be meaningful enough that our royalty stream is going to be worth a hill of beans? And this is where the research tool comes into play. So we can both clarify the product, enhance the product with design in figuring out how to do it, and iterate that through a research loop that'll make sure that we've got the right purchase intent to make it meaningful and to get somebody's attention.

> When we go into a large client company, we can have a wonderful relationship with them. Everybody knows us and likes us and we can get a meeting. But if we don't have something that is worth jumping the queue, nothing will happen .... The inertia factor is huge in these large companies. So we've got to have something that they say this is worth screwing up, or creating chaos internally for me.[12]

Develop and Refine

After the ideas are sourced, they need to be developed or transformed to a stage where there is greater clarity about the commercialization potential, and the ideas can be marketed to a large firm. Typically, this activity starts with the IC firm negotiating a deal with the inventor to own part of the idea as a prerequisite for making further investments in it. Thus, at this stage, the idea becomes a project in the IC firm's portfolio and the firm's ability to manage this project from here on determines its success rate.

While many of the capabilities to develop and refine the product/technology concept can be acquired from outside, an IC firm needs two in-house competencies: relevant domain knowledge and an exceptional market focus. The transformation process often progresses iteratively by identifying and resolving the key risk areas in the innovative idea. Such risks might relate to market risks (which in turn would require market validation), manufacturing risks (which might require prototyping and addressing manufacturability issues), asset protection risks (which might require evaluating the quality of the patent), and so on. The degree or the extent of idea transformation depends on the nature of the product concept or idea, the nature of the industry or market, and the nature of the client firm for which the idea is targeted.

Consider a project that Evergreen IP pursued recently. An inventor brought an idea for a collapsible plastic trash collector—as a solution for temporary trash situations such as parties, picnics, and in community events. The initial evaluation showed that while the idea was promising, the particular solution that the inventor came up with was not economically feasible. EIP checked with a few potential client firms and realized that the inventor had indeed identified a very unique problem—a $250 million product opportunity—although the proposed solution was not the best way to tap into the opportunity. So EIP invested capital in transforming the solution to make it commercially more feasible. The resulting work produced a product design and prototype that attracted serious attention from several large manufacturers in that product market. In this case, the transformation was comprehensive—it involved the development of a new solution.

More interestingly, the preceding example also shows that individual inventors might not always have great product inventions from the outset. However, they can often be excellent "sensing mechanisms" for product opportunities. As such, the IC needs to remain flexible and adapt its strategy to build on and transform the inventor's innovative contribution, whatever be the starting point—a great working product prototype or an important market need.

Market

This part of the value chain relates to placing the product or technology concept (or related IP) within a client firm—in other words, appropriating the value from the innovation through licensing agreements or sale of the patent or other such mechanisms. It calls for seeking out the firm that is most likely to be interested in the innovative idea and marketing and negotiating the IP sale or placement.

This activity requires two competencies. For one, the IC has to have excellent relational skills—they have to establish and maintain long-term relationships with large client firms. An IC firm's understanding of a client firm's competitive context enables it to conduct better analysis of the potential fit of an innovative idea vis-à-vis the firm's commercialization infrastructure. As Dave Bayless of Evergreen IP notes, "It is all about the client's brand window—gaps in the brand portfolio—and their internal hurdle rate. And, we spend considerable effort in getting to know our potential clients ... what are their priorities now, what are they looking out for, and what kind of market size will they accept?" Such an understanding can also enable IC firms to customize their back-end processes to integrate well with the client firm's open innovation processes. The IC firm also needs to develop a trust-based relationship that can help the negotiation process.

Another competency relates to the management of intellectual property rights related to the product concept. ICs have to possess knowledge and capabilities to navigate the IP placement process and to ensure that equitable share of the IP are appropriated. For example, IgniteIP recently assessed a new technology for removing heavy metals from water, which could reduce hazardous waste in the mining industry. The inventors had tried unsuccessfully to create a new business around the technology. When IgniteIP took over the project, it evaluated the market and decided that the greatest challenge lay in overcoming the mining industry's inertia around adopting a new technology like this. So, in addition to modifying the technology to clarify its potential, Ignite constructed an innovative licensing scheme that provided sufficient incentives for a client company to acquire the new technology and also ensured that Ignite and the inventors would receive sufficient return on their investment.

IC firms need to have appropriate skills to negotiate effectively in asymmetrical power situations (that is, with large client firms) to appropriate a fair share of the returns from the innovation. Given that only around 2% of the ideas that an IC firm reviews makes it to the commercialization stage, it is critical that the firm has excellent capabilities to appropriate value from those ideas that do finally get placed within a large firm.

Unlike early-stage innomediaries, IC firms do not operate on service-based fees. Instead, they share the returns from the innovation with the inventor. While this might be structured in different ways, the typical method is to pre-specify the proportion of the licensing royalties (or proceeds from the sale of the IP) that the IC firm will retain. IC firms retain anywhere from 40% to 70% of the revenue stream.

The scale of capital investments that IC firms make in their projects vary widely based on the size of the potential market for the product or the technology, but they range anywhere from $50,000 to $500,000. According to Brandon Williams of IgniteIP, "(our) objective is not to add value through capital investments as venture capitalists tend to do. Instead, we add value through a unique combination of our domain/market, networking, and innovation management skills." It is also important for IC firms to shape this value addition so as to *complement* the innovation strategies and initiatives of large firms. Thus, the IC firm's ability to meld together its varied competencies in a way that complements the internal innovation infrastructure of the large firm is the most important factor in determining its long-term success as an innovation partner of the client firms.

Having examined the IC's value proposition and competencies in some detail, we now look at the IC from the perspective of the large client firm by considering the approaches that large firms such as P&G, J&J, and Unilever can adopt to partner with IC firms.

BUILDING WINNING PARTNERSHIPS WITH INNOVATION CAPITALISTS

An IC can serve as a very effective partner to strengthen the innovation pipeline of a large firm. However, for these partnerships to succeed, the client firm has to play an effective role on its part as a partner.

The first important task the large firm has to undertake is to build and nurture a special relationship with a few selected IC firms (and their associated inventor communities). Another task is to direct or drive the innovation in the network—either by seeking out ideas for specific product markets or by driving the innovative idea using the firm's internal commercialization engine. Let us look at some strategies related to these two tasks.

Client firms need to acknowledge that there are no standing formal ties between any of the members in the innovation network—either between the IC firm and individual inventors or between the IC firm and the client firm. The importance of trust and understanding in the relationship between a large client firm and an IC thus cannot be overstated. One way to achieve this goal is to establish long-term relationships with a selected set of IC firms. This step ensures a smoother negotiation process for product or technology commercialization deals as both partners are aware of each other's decision criteria and processes. Further, a large firm can also build into its relationship an informal agreement that it will give all the proposals brought forward by an IC firm serious consideration, in return for giving the company the first chance to evaluate new ideas—in other words, become the "preferred innovation portal" for the IC firm and its associated inventor community.

Another way to enhance trust in the relationship is for a large firm to share information more openly with ICs. For example, the firm can provide ICs with a window into its product gaps, innovation priorities, and business goals. A shared understanding of the innovation priorities enables the IC firm to match promising ideas and concepts from their inventor networks with the requirements of the large company. It also allows ICs to make better judgments on whether or not a potential idea would meet the internal threshold of the large firm (in terms of market size, profit margins, and so on). The eventual goal of information sharing is to develop a *shared world view* of the large firm's innovation environment.

It is also important for the large firm to educate its internal units (particularly the R&D unit) on the unique role and value proposition of the IC firm. Such internal evangelism (or building the organization's faith in the value of the innovation capitalist) helps to overcome the "Not Invented Here" syndrome that tends to bias internal R&D units against externally sourced ideas. And it promotes better alignment of the firm's internal innovation decision processes with the role played by the innovation capitalist. By integrating the front-end work done by the IC with the back-end development done by the large firm internally, time to market can be further reduced and success rates can be enhanced. For example, one of the ICs we studied used product concept evaluation systems and tools (for example, the Product Lifecycle Management tool) that were already being used by their "preferred" client firm. This allowed faster project transitions from the IC firm to the client firm.

Large firms can also strengthen their partnership with IC firms by adopting a "reverse flow" model—that is, becoming the *source* of innovative ideas for the IC firm. Often, large companies have product or technology concepts that they have developed to different stages (including working prototypes), but for varied strategic or market reasons are not considered high priority and hence sit on the shelf.

John Funk of EIP notes, "Often, when we have gone to our client companies, they tell us that they have something which they would like us to take a look at. These are ideas that they (client firm) have let their people incubate that might not fit with their brands at the time or they have sold off the brand that they originally incubated it under. Sometimes as (these ideas) get farther along they don't fit—strategic reasons, brand fit, resource, size of prize, hurdle rates, whatever it might be. They put them on the shelf. And there's nowhere for those to go today. We come on it and we say we'll take those on. We will develop them further and market to other firms." In other words, the large client firm now becomes the "inventor."

For example, P&G's External Business Development (EBD) group recently initiated such a project with one of the IC firms. P&G had developed a product concept but found that the target market was only around $35 to $50 million worth (well below P&G's internal threshold and also the concept didn't have a natural fit with any of its existing brand portfolio). Because the concept required further work, it negotiated a deal with an IC firm to develop the concept further and market it to other large firms in that product market.

As Tom Cripe, associate director of the EBD group of P&G notes, "We are definitely interested in such deals as they allow us to potentially derive revenue from ideas that are sitting on our shelves but require more concept work before they are business-ready. Such deals also allow us to strengthen our relationship with specific IC firms. ... And, in turn, we want those IC firms to consider P&G as the preferred destination when they come across interesting ideas in the (inventor) community." So this approach for monetizing stranded assets (whether those are patents or just product concepts) has two payoffs—potential new product revenues, and a stronger relationship with the IC firm to become the "preferred innovation portal."

Are there any downsides to partnering with an innovation capitalist? Well, there are definitely some risks that client firms need to keep in mind. Precisely because they are new on the scene, innovation capitalists are still refining their business models and thus must work out some wrinkles. For example, they get much more modest returns than do, say, venture capitalists. That means they need enough ongoing projects in their portfolios to sustain the business. But an overlarge portfolio will reduce the value an IC firm can add in developing any given idea and also threaten its relationships with both client companies and the inventor community. Another risk for the client firm is relational risk. On the one hand, to benefit from the IC firm's capabilities, a client firm has to open up and share its innovation priorities; on the other hand, building the trust needed for such sharing of information will take some time. Thus, this poses some risk for the client firm especially if the IC firm is still very young and not well established.

Table 6.3 shows some of the key elements of this form of the Creative Bazaar model that involves partnering with ICs. The key observation that bears repetition—success in partnering with ICs—depends on the closeness of the partnership the client firm can build with ICs.

In the words of David Duncan, the head of R&D for Unilever's home and personal care division, at best such relationships offer more than a pipeline of new projects and become "a collaborative effort at building the innovation capability" of a client company.[13]

Table 6.3   The Creative Bazaar Model & The Innovation Capitalist

Elements of Network-Centric Innovation	Partnering with Innovation Capitalist
Nature of the innovation space	The ideas that emerge from the inventor community are evaluated for commercialization feasibility and alignment with client firm's corporate innovation goals and priorities.
Structure of the network leadership	The client firm (for example, P&G, Dial, Staples, and so on) makes all the key decisions related to the commercialization of the innovative idea (patent).
Innovation Roles	
Architect	Client firm plays the role of an innovation portal.
Adapter	Independent inventors play the role of innovator and contribute new product and technology ideas.
Agent	Innovation capitalist.
Network Management	
Network governance	There are no formal ties among network members; trust-based and reputational mechanisms serve to facilitate network governance and coordination in the network.
Knowledge management	The innovation capitalist provides the infrastructure to communicate and share knowledge with individual inventors; the client firm shares with the innovation capitalist its innovation goals and priorities.
IP rights and value appropriation	Patents and licensing agreements are used to assign the rights and for value appropriation.

CONCLUSION

The Creative Bazaar model involves a large firm "shopping" for innovative ideas by establishing a network of partners that might range from individual inventors and inventor communities to different types of innovation intermediaries. You explored three partnering models on the Creative Bazaar continuum that represent different points on the continuum of risk and cost and considered the important role played by an emerging class of entities called innovation capitalists.

Although the innovation capitalist is a powerful approach to sourcing innovative ideas, it is just one weapon in the arsenal of a large firm. Most large firms need to pursue not just one but a combination of the different options we have discussed so far. In other words, they need to implement a *portfolio* of innovation sourcing mechanisms. The question then is, how should a large firm go about selecting the appropriate set of sourcing mechanisms and making sure that its overall portfolio of innovation sourcing is balanced? What does the optimal portfolio look like? These are important questions, and while we can state the obvious by saying that the answers would be dictated by industry and market factors, we will address these issues in more detail in Chapter 9, "Deciding Where and How to Play," when we discuss how a firm can identify opportunities in network-centric innovation.

The Jam Central Model

In the Orchestra model, the firm has a very clear sense for the nature of the innovation it seeks to co-create with partners. In the Creative Bazaar model, while the initial innovative idea might emerge from the inventor community, the firm still plays the dominant role in deciding how the innovation will evolve into a market-ready product or service. Sometimes, however, innovations are emergent in nature and involve the community to a much greater extent—taking shape through the collaborative efforts of contributors, and evolving in ways that are not well-understood at the outset. Recalling our analogy from the music business, we look at a different approach to creating network-centric innovation that is akin to musicians jamming together to create new music. In introducing the Jam Central model in Chapter 3, "The Four Models of Network-Centric Innovation," we compared musical jamming sessions to collaborative innovation, and we identified three themes that define the essence of the Jam Central model:

- An emergent innovation vision and goals that evolve from intense interactions among the community members
- A diffused leadership structure that relies on each member of the community
- An infrastructure to support improvisation and sharing of innovation benefits

An innovation initiative that embodies all of these themes is the development of Apache, an Open Source Web server software that runs on most operating systems, including UNIX and Windows. First created in 1996, Apache has established itself as the most popular Web server on the Internet; more than 70% of all Web sites on the Internet currently use Apache, making it more widely used than all other Web servers combined.[1]

The history of Apache can be traced back to the early 1990s when a group of individuals started working on improving the HTTPD server originally developed by Rob McCool at the National Center for Supercomputing Applications, University of Illinois, Urbana-Champaign. When the resulting product—Apache server v 0.6.2—was released in April 1995, it took off immediately in the Web server market as an open source alternative to other proprietary products. In 1999, as the project got wider recognition and attracted more volunteers, the Apache Software Foundation (ASF) was established to better organize and channel the creative contributions of the volunteer community.

An interesting twist in the Apache story is that while the original effort was focused solely on creating and supporting the Apache Web server product, by the early 2000s, a broader vision had emerged in the community—a vision that encompassed projects related to a number of other aspects of the World Wide Web. In this broader vision, the ASF was no longer just a Web server initiative; instead, it had evolved into an innovation community tied together by a common set of values (including meritocracy and openness) and pursuing a more emergent set of software development goals.

As the number of community members (or innovation participants) and the diversity of the innovation projects grew, the Apache community adopted a very open governance structure. Each project has its own separate project management committee, comprised of members committed to that project, which exercises full autonomy on project-related decisions and activities. A central board (again comprised of the most committed set of community members) keeps the community together through appropriate support activities. New project ideas from individual members are evaluated not for the nature of the project (all project ideas are equally welcome) but for the potential for the group associated with that project to adhere to the overall community goals, norms, and values.

The Web-based infrastructure at Apache.org supports the collaborative process and enables the community members to come together and contribute to the various individual projects. Further, all the output from the community's innovation efforts is made available in the public domain under the open Apache license, benefiting the broader community.

The Apache initiative underscores the key tenets of the Jam Central model outlined earlier—an emergent innovation vision being pursued in a community-led environment in a manner that benefits all the community members. Such a collaborative innovation model is clearly evident in many other parts of the software industry, too—from operating systems and Web servers to enterprise applications and end-user tools.

But the Jam Central model has applicability well beyond software. It is being applied with success in a wide range of domains and industries that are quite different from software. In this chapter, we describe examples from two very different industry contexts—the biomedical research field and the consumer interactive-services industry—to illustrate the key aspects of the Jam Central model. By considering such divergent contexts, we hope to demonstrate how broadly this model can be applied.

We start with the case of the Tropical Disease Initiative (TDI)—a community-based innovation initiative in the area of biomedical research.

FINDING CURES BY "JAMMIN" TOGETHER: THE TROPICAL DISEASE INITIATIVE AND THE SYNAPTIC LEAP

Tropical diseases are a largely neglected frontier in the commercial drug discovery arena. Only about 1% of all newly developed drugs are for tropical diseases.[2] Most of the tropical diseases occur in developing countries in Africa and Asia where patients can seldom afford to pay the high prices that are typical of patented drugs. As such, there is limited interest from commercial pharmaceutical firms to pursue drug discovery in this area. As the World Health Organization report notes, tropical diseases represent both the greatest need and the opportunity for open collaborative research, one that is not dependent on commercial proprietary solutions.[3]

The TDI is a Web-based, collaborative innovation effort aimed at identifying cures for tropical diseases such as malaria and tuberculosis. The project was launched by a group of scientists and researchers including Stephen Maurer of the University of California at Berkeley, Arti Rai of Duke University, and Andrej Sali of the University of California at San Francisco. The TDI project aims to bring together computational biologists and other volunteer researchers to work collaboratively on specific tropical diseases and then makes the results of such collaborative innovation available in the public domain, where other researchers could use them to guide their clinical research work.

Drug discovery is particularly well-suited to a collaborative innovation approach because of the dichotomy of tasks involved in drug R&D. The R&D process consists of two broad types of tasks: *knowledge-based tasks* and *rule-based tasks*. Knowledge-based tasks call for deep domain knowledge along with intelligence and judgment capabilities but very limited laboratory or other technical infrastructure. Examples of knowledge-based tasks include identifying promising targets, designing computerized disease models, and so on. As Bernard Munos wrote in *Nature*, such knowledge-based tasks are "about scientists leveraging each other's ideas and using tools to gain deeper insights that might lead to breakthroughs"[4]—in other words, building on and improvising through continued interactions. On the other hand, rule-based tasks involve clinical experimentation and require significant laboratory facilities, equipment, study subjects (patients), and funding. Examples of such tasks include clinical trials, toxicology studies, and other lab-intensive work. Rule-based tasks are also subject to rigid regulatory requirements, so they tend to require highly structured and controlled research environments. Thus, while a Web-based collaborative innovation model might not be appropriate for rule-based tasks, it is an excellent approach to carry out knowledge-based tasks.[5]

Collaborative work in knowledge-based tasks has become even more promising due to the increasing importance of computation in the drug discovery process.[6] Indeed, computing and biology are converging rapidly, opening up new possibilities for organizing collaborative innovation efforts. Computing resources have become cheaper and more widely available. New distributed computing techniques allow spare computing resources distributed across organizational and national boundaries to be integrated into a powerful common infrastructure. And, newer and more powerful software tools are becoming available for drug discovery. These new tools can help scientists identify promising protein targets and lead chemical compounds, mine genomic databases, visualize bind sites, map metabolic networks, and design complex molecules. These tools can work on diverse medical databases and enable volunteers to participate in the innovation project from their homes. Further, many of these tools are now available as Open Source tools. For example, the OpenScience project is dedicated to developing and releasing free scientific software for drug discovery and other research purposes.[7]

These two factors—more computing resources and better tools—have radically changed the face of computational drug discovery. The founders of TDI, Steve Maurer, Arti Rai, and Andrej Sali, draw parallels between computational drug discovery and software development:

Very similar to the way software developers find bugs and write patches in open source projects, biologists look for proteins ("targets") and select chemicals ("drug candidates") that bind to them and affect their behavior in desirable ways. In both cases, innovative contributions consist of finding opportunities and fixing tiny problems hidden in an ocean of code.[8]

THE TDI-TSL NETWORK

The TDI brings together a community of researchers and scientists who have common interests related to drug discovery and are willing to volunteer their time and effort in collaboratively pursuing such interests. The TDI offers a Web-based environment that helps to integrate scientific talent, computing resources (for example, software tools), and a wide variety of chemical, biological, and medical databases. In this environment, TDI partners with another entity called The Synaptic Leap (TSL).

TSL is a North Carolina–based non-profit organization founded in 2005 by Ginger Taylor, a software professional. TSL provides a package of Web-based facilities to support open collaborative biomedical research.[9] The Web site provides the vehicle for organizing the different research tools, technologies, and databases and making them available to the community members (scientists). Members can peruse the research tasks on the Web site, choose the one that they are interested in working on, and register themselves as contributors. Contributors can then download any necessary data and tools and start working on that data. Other Web-based facilities (for example, chat rooms, wikis, blogs, and discussion boards) provide the communication infrastructure for the community to discuss and debate the innovative ideas in each project. Thus, by providing the Web-based infrastructure, TSL complements the resources and capabilities of the TDI. As Taylor notes, "After speaking (with the TDI founders), I discovered that their heart is really in the biomedical science. They have little interest in building and running a collaborative Web site. We therefore combined forces; they provide inputs to us, and we build and maintain the site where they and other scientists can collaborate."[10]

There are three types of players in the TDI-TSL network. A core body of founding members (which includes people from TDI and TSL) plays the role of the *innovation steward* by providing the broad direction for the community and facilitating collaboration and communication among members. Scientists from all over the world contribute to individual projects by volunteering their time and scientific expertise. In so doing, they play the role of *innovators*. Their incentives include reputational benefits, acquisition of new skills and knowledge, expanding their professional network, and the prospect of gaining prominence in the employment market. Finally, external organizations (for-profit as well as non-profit) play the role of *innovation sponsors* by providing funding and other types of resources, including computing resources, software tools, and so on.

TDI has defined a broad focus on tropical diseases. However, the specific projects are left to individual contributors or community members. Any contributor can propose a new project, and as long as the project falls within the broad scope of TDI and there is sufficient interest among the community members, it will be incorporated into the fold. The first active project in the TDI portfolio is focused on malaria.

As noted earlier, the goals and activities of the community are emergent. For example, consider the evolution of the Schistosomiasis project. Soon after the malaria project took off in the TDL-TSL forum, Mathew Todd, a chemist from the University of Sydney, had an idea for an open research project for Schistosomiasis. His objective was to develop a cheaper process for producing Praziquantal, the current treatment for Schistosomiasis. He interacted with the TDI founders and expressed his interest in starting this new project and was encouraged to collaborate with Ginger Taylor to come up with a more formal outline of the project and the design of the community site. His blog post on the proposed project on the TSL Web forum elicited many positive reactions from the community members. One such volunteer was Jean-Claude Bradley, a chemist from Drexel University in Philadelphia. Bradley found Todd's post and began to offer ideas for collaboratively pursuing those research goals. With sufficient interest expressed by community members, it was evident that the project had legs and Todd volunteered to play the role of the Schisto community leader. Over the next few months, he worked with TSL's Taylor to develop an information architecture to serve as the portal for the Schisto collaborative research project.

Similarly, new projects are being defined and initiated as part of TDI. For example, the idea for a project on Chagas, a disease that plagues South America, was suggested by a young biology researcher from Venezuela. Similarly, another scientist, Miguel Mitchell, is leading another new project that relates to tuberculosis. Thus, as new contributors join the community, new research ideas emerge, get shared and built upon, and evolve into individual projects.

MOVING FROM THE LAB TO THE MARKET

A critical issue in the TDI network relates to intellectual property rights and production of drugs. Specifically, who "owns" the output from the TDI projects and how should such outputs reach the "market"? The TDI community members have at their disposal several intellectual property ownership options. Researchers always have the right to publish their ideas in traditional peer-reviewed scientific journals. In addition, the Science Commons offers public domain licenses (similar to the Creative Commons licensing scheme) that can be used to make available the leads or targets generated through the TDI project to other scientists for follow-up work.

Similarly, if a promising lead or a new compound is generated through the TDI project, then its further development can be outsourced. Note that the early drug discovery processes, which form the primary focus of TDI, occur at a pre-commercial stage and typically the output might not have reached a patentable stage. However, here given the niche focus of TDI, the objective is to keep the new knowledge created in the public domain so that all the different options to exploit such knowledge can be exercised. This includes outsourcing the clinical trials and production to non-profit pharmaceutical entities or "Virtual Pharma" entities like the Institute for One World Health and the Drugs for Neglected Diseases Initiative.

The TDI innovation network owes its early success to several factors: the emergence of computational biology as a powerful and sophisticated vehicle to research and discover new drug candidates, the ability of Web-based infrastructure to bring together hundreds of scientists and researchers who are willing to donate their time and knowledge in collaborative research, and the alternative systems and mechanisms available to protect and share the intellectual property rights in the public domain. These forces have enabled the creation of a collaborative research forum that adheres to all three central tenets of the Jam Central model—an emergent innovation vision and goals, a community-led diffused leadership structure, and a robust infrastructure to support collaborative knowledge creation and value appropriation.

OTHER INSTANCES OF THE JAM CENTRAL MODEL IN BIOMEDICAL RESEARCH

Another set of examples of the Jam Central model evident in biomedical research relates to the open databases approach. The more famous examples include the Human Genome Project, the SNP consortium, and the International HapMap project.

Consider the International HapMap project. The project is a multi-country effort to identify and catalog genetic similarities and differences in human beings.[11] The HapMap (Haplotype Mapping) is a catalog of common genetic variants that occur in human beings. Using the information in the HapMap, researchers will be able to find genes that affect health, disease, and individual responses to medications and environmental factors. In other words, researchers can link haplotypes (patterns of genetic variation) to disease phenotypes. The project, started in October 2002, involves scientists and funding agencies from six countries: Japan, the United Kingdom, Canada, China, Nigeria, and the United States. The project releases all information generated by researchers into the public domain. However, the information is released under a "click-wrap" license, which requires those who access the HapMap database to agree that they will not file product patent applications if such patents are built upon, even if only in part, HapMap data.[12] In other words, the HapMap project adopts the "copyleft" licensing scheme.[13]

Although the project does not allow just anybody to get involved—only those who are tied to the affiliated organizations can contribute—the overall structure of the initiative follows the Jam Central model. The network of scientists maintains a broad innovation vision for the project—for example, in this case, to develop a haplotype map of the human genome so as to describe the common patterns of human genetic variation—and collaborate by improvising and building upon each others' research work. The leadership for individual projects is diffused to the local level and the central network infrastructure is used to share as well as protect the rights to the data and the other outputs from the project.

To see how the Jam Central model can be applied to a very different context, we shift our focus to the creation of Web-based consumer interactive services and the case of Second Life.

CREATING CONSUMER EXPERIENCES BY "JAMMIN" TOGETHER: THE SECOND LIFE

In 1992, Neal Stephenson authored a now-classic science fiction novel called *Snow Crash* in which he envisioned a successor to today's Internet—a virtual reality–based Internet that he called the *Metaverse*. In Stephenson's Metaverse, denizens create "avatars" or online virtual bodies and their social status derives from the sophistication of their avatars. The Metaverse inspired several attempts to create such virtual reality worlds and implement some of the concepts he described in his book. By the time the 1990s rolled around, 3-D technologies had also advanced significantly, and such virtual world implementations became feasible.

One of the first Metaverse-like 3-D virtual reality worlds was *Active World*, launched in June 1995. It was soon followed by a host of other implementations including *There, Second Life, The Palace, Uru, Dotsoul Cyberpark, Blaxxun*, and *Entropia Universe*. While some of these no longer exist and some are on their way out, perhaps the most representative—and definitely, the most well-known—is *Second Life*.

Second Life (SL) is a partly subscription-based 3-D virtual world that was launched in 2003 by Linden Lab—a privately held, San Francisco-based company founded in 1999 by former RealNetworks CTO Philip Rosedale. The *Second Life* "world" resides in a vast array of computer servers owned and operated by Linden Lab. The company also provides the Web-based tools and technologies for users to create, view, and modify their avatars and the other objects in the SL world and participate in its virtual economy. The resident population in SL has been growing exponentially since its inception—on October 18, 2006, the population hit the 1 million mark, and by July 2007, it had reached 7 million.

The goal of Linden Lab is to create a user-defined Metaverse-like "virtual world" in which users or "residents" can interact, play, and participate in other activities. However, SL is much more than a 3-D virtual world for entertainment. Linden Lab sees itself as being in the business of hosting and facilitating "consumer experience" innovation. SL offers diverse types of experiences to its residents. These experiences are not created by Linden Lab—they are created collaboratively by the residents through individual creativity and interactions. The role of Linden Lab is to provide the context and the tools for residents to create those experiences. In short, *Second Life* is a massive experiment in collaborative experience innovation. As such, it is an excellent example of the Jam Central model—while the innovation space constitutes "user experiences," the nature of these experiences (that is, the innovation goals) are emergent and the residents (that is, the innovators) "jam together," improvise in innovating those experiences and share in the fruits of the innovation.

THE SL NETWORK AND THE PLAYERS

Let us consider the nature of the innovation network and the players in SL. Broadly, the innovation network in SL consists of three players: Linden Lab plays the role of *innovation steward*, individuals and other residents of SL play the role of the *innovators* and corporations seeking to connect to the community play the role of *innovation sponsors*.

Linden Lab's primary role is to facilitate experience innovation in SL by bringing the collaborators together and providing them with the supporting tools and technologies to innovate and the infrastructure to appropriate and share the value from the innovations. Its success in this role can be traced to three key ideas of Linden Lab founder, Rosedale.

Rosedale's first key idea was to create a live forum that could bring together the residents and host their interactions. These live interactions form the experience—nothing is predetermined or pre-designed. Linden Lab's computers do all the intense computational work that is needed to keep the SL dynamic and as live as the real world.

The second key idea was to support residents' creativity by offering easy-to-use tools and technologies that can be used to create objects (including residents' own avatars) in SL. While the technologies are user-friendly, they are powerful enough to support the diverse creative talent that residents bring to SL. For example, one such tool is a 3-D Modeler that allows residents to create complex objects—ranging from avatar attachments to buildings, sculptures, and gardens—out of a set of basic building blocks. Residents can then use SL's scripting language (called Linden Scripting Language) to apply scripts to shape the behavior of the objects they create. SL also provides tools to add texture to the surface of any 3-D object (for example, tattoos on an avatar's skin) to enhance its richness. Multimedia capabilities (for example, sound) can also be added to such objects. This powerful suite of tools enables residents to create very rich objects in SL that exhibit diverse behaviors and lead to diverse experiences through their interactions.

The third decision that Rosedale made was to allow the residents to retain the right to their creation, whether it be their own avatar or any other object that they created in SL. This feature allowed Linden Lab to develop a truly collaborative innovation environment in SL that emphasizes the residents' role as innovators.

As innovators, residents contribute to the community through the objects they create as well as through the interactions they participate in. Thus, the more diverse the residents, the more diverse the overall experiences in the SL world.

Finally, corporate, non-profit, and other types of organizations participate in SL by sponsoring and catalyzing the collaborative experience innovation. As an innovation sponsor, a firm can directly host and facilitate experiences. For example, American Apparel opened an outlet in SL that allows residents to browse through merchandise and shop for virtual clothing for their avatars.[14] The company is now considering test-marketing new styles of jeans in the virtual environment before they are launched in real-life stores. By catalyzing such virtual shopping experiences for residents, the company contributes to the community—in return, garnering additional company exposure and brand recognition. Companies can also sponsor users' experience innovation. For example, on September 14, 2006, PopSci.com (the online home of *Popular Science*) sponsored a special live concert in SL that featured popular SL musicians including Jonathan Coulton, Melvin Took, and Etherian Kamaboko.

MANAGING "AVATAR" BEHAVIOR AND RIGHTS IN SL

Members of the SL community are tied to Linden Lab through a set of Terms of Service they agree to when they join the network. This formal agreement allows Linden Lab to establish a basic set of "accepted" behavior or ground rules and specifies consequences if such rules are not adhered to. For example, residents who harass other residents or engage in destructive behavior can be ejected from the community. Similarly, residents can also register civic complains in regular town-hall meetings and these complaints will then be acted upon by Linden staff. These formal governance mechanisms enable Linden Lab to ensure an innovation environment that members would want to be a part of. However, such formal mechanisms are only part of the story.

More important as a governance mechanism are the behavioral norms that exist among the members themselves. Such social mechanisms include group-driven culture and reputational systems. For example, SL is composed of numerous "interest" groups. Individual residents can create groups and invite other residents to join them. Groups can be based on a particular interest or activity. The names of the groups that a resident belongs to are displayed in that user's profile. Each group can set up its own group leadership team with titles and responsibilities. The groups through their interactions set up their own norms and values—such group-driven culture forms a powerful mechanism to bring coherence to members' interactions and experiences within SL.

As noted previously, residents own the rights to their innovations in SL—for example, the objects that they create. Even though the actual computer code related to the objects resides on Linden's servers, residents retain the full intellectual property rights for all the digital content they create. Linden Lab employs the Creative Commons license scheme to enable residents to assign rights to their innovations. This gives residents considerable leeway in deciding how, when, and in what ways other residents can use or build on their innovation.

It is important to note that, while residents might own the rights to the objects they create, "consumer experiences" are based on the interactions among the objects created by the different community members. As such, there is sufficient incentive for community members to share their innovations with others and to facilitate such interactions.

Linden Lab also provides the infrastructure for measuring and monetizing value created in the community. SL has its own currency, referred to as Linden Dollars (L$). Residents can acquire L$ by selling the objects they create. The economy that is based on L$ has grown considerably over the past few years with the increased level of activity in the SL "economy." In the SL economy, residents can appropriate value from their innovations by transacting in L$. Linden also provides an exchange called the LindeX for residents to convert L$ into US$.

The case of *Second Life* thus illustrates the application of the Jam Central model in yet another context—the consumer interactive services industry. While the particulars and the details might be different from the earlier contexts of software and biomedical research, the three themes of the Jam Central model outlined earlier forms the essence of *Second Life,* too—SL residents (innovators) collaborate and improvise to create new interactive experiences (innovation) in a community-led environment that is supported by an infrastructure for protection and sharing of innovation rights.

"JAMMIN" TOGETHER TO CREATE MUSIC: MYVIRTUALBAND (MVB)

MyVirtualBand.com (MVB) (acquired by NetMusicMakers.com in December 2006) is a Web portal for musicians to come together and form "virtual bands" to collaboratively write and produce original music that can then be freely shared with others.[15]

MVB was started in 2004 by two Madison, Wisconsin-based friends Kelly Senecal (a guitarist) and Scott Mason (a drummer). The two had started and played in a band together from 1996 onwards. However, when one of them had to move to a different city, they felt they lacked the tools to work on musical projects together. This unmet need gave rise to the idea of building a Web portal to facilitate collaborative songwriting and recording.

MVB offers an online forum for members to advertise their individual projects and invite other members to join those projects by uploading audio tracks of their own instruments or vocals and specifying the type of collaboration that is needed. Members can download the files, add their contributions, and reupload them—so the song evolves over time through contributions from multiple community members. When a song is completed, MVB puts it as an MP3 file on the Featured Songs list, which non-members as well as members can listen to.

MVB operates on a Creative Commons Attribution 2.0 license that it calls the "MVB Open Music Agreement." The license applies to all audio files and other supporting materials (for example, lyrics) that are uploaded on the MVB server. It also applies to completed songs. Thus, any member can freely copy, distribute, display, perform, and of course, add to or modify the songs as long as acknowledgments are made to the original authors of the music. MVB also offers a more formal music showcase or distribution infrastructure called the MVB Radio that is a podcast of the completed songs. Members can vote on the songs for inclusion in the podcast. In sum, MVB represents the essence of the Jam Central model—a community of musicians coming together to improvise and create new music that is openly shared and thus benefits the entire community.

ELEMENTS OF THE JAM CENTRAL MODEL

When we compare the different examples of the Jam Central model that we have described in this chapter, we see some common elements that define the essence of this form of network-centric innovation. **Table 7.1** summarizes these common elements.

Table 7.1 Elements of the Jam Central Model

Elements of Network-Centric Innovation	TDI/TSL	Second Life	Apache
Nature of the innovation space	Drug discovery for tropical diseases and other neglected diseases	Creation of rich and diverse digital experiences for consumers	Development of Web-related software products
Structure of the network leadership	TDI board provides broad guidance; individual project teams exercise complete project autonomy	Individual residents and resident groups make key decisions	ASF council provides broad guidance; individual project teams exercise complete project autonomy
Innovation Roles			
Architect	TDI/TSL as innovation steward	Linden Lab as innovation steward	ASF as innovation steward
Adapter	Individual scientist as innovator	Resident as innovator	Individual developer as innovator
Agent	Pharma companies as innovation sponsor	Consumer companies as innovation sponsor	Software companies as innovation sponsor
Network Management			
Network governance	Trust and reputation-based systems	Formal mechanisms (Terms of Service) and social mechanisms (group culture, trust, and so on)	Apache "meritocracy"
Knowledge management	Web-based facilities to share information on "targets" and co-create knowledge	Online forums for consumers to extend support to peers	Online forums to support knowledge sharing
IP rights and value appropriation	Science Commons; Licensing rights to "virtual pharma" and non-profits	Creative Commons license	Apache Public License

The first common thread in all these examples is the *emergent nature of the innovation goals*, and the need for continuous improvisation through iterations and interactions. The innovation space is only broadly defined—whether it be the focus on tropical diseases in TDI, the Web-based software in the Apache community, or the interactive experiences in *Second Life*. The specific innovation goals then emerge from the community through the continued interactions of the members. This two-phase goal setting (broad innovation focus and emergent innovation goals) was evident in all the domains we studied and indicates the nature of the community-based leadership structure that provides the foundation for the innovation activities. Such emergent goals lend to a sense of belonging and ownership among community members as they work together to evolve the shared goals and objectives. They also imbue the community with the improvisational spirit that pervades the innovation process. Indeed, the actual innovation is marked by a "call and response" pattern—members respond to and improvise on each others' contributions to iteratively evolve the innovation.

The second common thread relates to the *decentralized nature of decision making* in the innovation network. In all the contexts, the diffused leadership is achieved through two mechanisms. The first mechanism enables the entire community to come together to make critical decisions regarding the broader innovation agenda or the community's goals. In the case of TDI, this task is achieved by an informal body that consists of the founding members and some of the most active community members. In the case of Apache, the task is achieved through the Board of the Apache Software Foundation. The second mechanism operates at the individual project or group level and enables localized decision making that involves only those members who participate (or have a stake) in that project. The combination of these two mechanisms ensures the continued involvement of the community members in the evolution of the innovation agenda as well as the necessary flexibility for individual projects to chart their own path.

A third common thread relates to the *nature of the collaboration infrastructure*. Given the improvisation nature of the innovation process, the Jam Central model relies on an effective infrastructure to facilitate the constant "give and take" that involves multiple members of the community. Typically, the infrastructure has elements to support both the "social knowledge creation" as well as the development of a "shared world view" that is critical to keep the coherence of the varied innovation activities in the community.

In most cases, the innovation steward had the responsibility to maintain the collaboration infrastructure—whether it is a simple online forum for community members to interact (for example, discussion boards in the Apache community) or more complex facilities to swap knowledge (for example, the wikis and databases in the case of TDI or object repositories in the case of *Second Life*).

Another important observation in the Jam Central model relates to the appropriation of rewards from the innovation. While there is an emphasis on sharing the fruits of the innovation with the wider community, this doesn't necessarily mean that all intellectual property rights are released to the community (or to the public domain). Indeed, as we have seen in the case of *Second Life,* certain rights related to an innovation might stay with an individual member. However, the community might provide the mechanism for individual members to share some of those rights with other community members so that they can build on those innovations. As is evident from the examples, the ability of the community to devise and deploy innovative mechanisms to share intellectual property rights among the community members is essential to ensure the success of the innovation initiatives.

JOINING THE JAM SESSIONS: HOW LARGE COMPANIES CAN PARTICIPATE

Despite the community-based innovation agenda and governance system of the Jam Central model, abundant opportunities exist for large for-profit companies to participate in such initiatives. However, realizing such opportunities requires companies to understand the specific roles they can play and the competencies they need to perform such roles.

Large companies can play the role of an *innovator* by contributing their employees' time and effort to Jam Central projects. For example, IBM "donates" hundreds of its employees to the Linux community. These IBM employees write code and contribute to the Linux development in the same way any other member of the Linux community would. They participate in the Linux online forums and discuss the different module enhancement ideas with other volunteer developers, write code to add new functionalities, and test finished code written by other community members.

Similarly, companies in biomedical research, can participate as innovators by donating their employees' time and expertise. For example, one company that is participating in a TDI project is Inpharmatica, a midsized London-based biotech company. Similarly, several large pharmaceutical companies including Eli Lilly and Merck are actively exploring opportunities to participate in such community-led, drug discovery projects. In a typical scenario, a scientist employed by the pharma or biotech company would participate as a volunteer researcher in a project—for example, by working on protein "targets" identified in prior research and helping the community advance the drug discovery to the experimental stage. Playing such an innovator role might, however, require the company to make a strategic commitment to the initiative as it is likely to involve contributing valuable and expensive resources (domain expertise, scientific talent, and so on) to the project with limited clarity on any direct economic returns.

Corporations can also promote and facilitate community-led projects by playing the role of an innovation sponsor. They can provide computing, laboratory, or other types of infrastructural support for innovation activities. For example, Collaborative Drug Discovery, a San Francisco-based company that writes software for biomedical research, provides free access to its biomedical databases to the members of the TDI community. This access offers the TDI community members a rich resource to mine targets related to the different drug discovery projects that they pursue. Similarly, in April 2006, Microsoft launched a collaborative initiative called the BioIT Alliance, which aims to unite the pharmaceutical, biotech, hardware, and software industries to explore new ways to share complex biomedical data and collaborate among multi-disciplinary teams to speed the pace of discovery in the life sciences.[16] The other members of the network include Amylin Pharmaceuticals, Applied Biosystems, Geospiza, Hewlett-Packard, Interknowlogy, Scripps Research Institute, Sun Microsystems, and VizX Labs. Microsoft plays the role of the innovation sponsor in this network by providing both data management resources as well as specific technical expertise to the network members. One of the first projects, the Collaborative Molecular Environment, involves building an application environment to capture laboratory data electronically and enable scientists to annotate it and search for it effectively. The project utilizes the software tools and other technical resources provided by Microsoft.

Although corporate organizations can contribute "free" resources to the community, such contributions are not entirely altruistic. IBM's contributions to the Linux development project have earned it the goodwill of the community. It has even earned IBM a seat at the decision-making table in the Linux community. For example, participation in the Open Source Development Lab (OSDL) allows IBM to not just participate actively in the advocacy of Linux but also influence the evolution of the overall community innovation agenda.

Similarly, Microsoft's contributions to the BioIT alliance also have commercial benefits for the company. As Don Rule, platform strategy advisor at Microsoft, notes, "We're looking at the areas where disruptive changes are occurring in the (pharmaceutical) industry, focusing on bringing together proof-of-concept applications that will alleviate some of the bottlenecks we see in the industry. The advances will benefit Microsoft as well as the other companies we are collaborating with."[17]

CONCLUSION

The community-centric Jam Central innovation model holds tremendous promise as a way to organize and shape the innovation activities in diverse industries and markets ranging from software to drug discovery to interactive entertainment. However, an important issue that we have not discussed so far relates to the appropriateness of this model to particular contexts. What are the factors that determine the applicability of the Jam Central model in specific innovation contexts? We will return to this question after we describe in the next chapter the fourth and final model of network-centric innovation, the Mod Station model.

8

The MOD ("MODification") Station Model

In the preceding chapter, we saw how a community of innovators can come together to improvise their way in an innovation initiative. However, not all community-based innovation needs to be managed in this emergent manner. Communities can also come together to innovate around a well-defined technology or platform.

In Chapter 3, "The Four Models of Network-Centric Innovation," we talked about an innovative community-based approach to create a movie, *Sanctuary*. The movie, offered into the public domain under an open license, fueled the creative energy of individual contributors who adapt, interpret, and evolve the original movie. This open approach has two requirements. First, the innovation project should be designed so that elements of the project can be partitioned and handed off to different community members. Second, the project sponsor should provide the tools to modify, adapt, and recombine the elements of the innovation. This community-based modification approach is yet another form of network-centric innovation—one that marries the certainty of a well-defined innovation architecture with the diversity and the creativity of a community of contributors.

In this chapter, we examine this model of network-centric innovation, which we call the MOD Station model. As we noted in Chapter 4, "Innovation Networks: The Players and the Plays," the term *MOD* itself is associated most with "modifications" made to a computer game by the general public (or users) and hence, known as "mods" in the computer gaming industry. Generalizing from this definition, we refer to the MOD Station model of network-centric innovation as *an innovation context wherein a community of innovators come together to create new offerings by modifying, extending, and/or enhancing an existing innovation platform in ways that benefit all members of the network including the creator of the innovation platform.*

To understand how the MOD Station model works, we take a look at the computer gaming industry where this model originated. Later, we consider other contexts including the semiconductor industry.

"MODDING" IN THE COMPUTER GAMING INDUSTRY

An arena where the MOD Station model is quite popular is the computer gaming industry. Many gamers are highly conversant with computer programming, and a fair number of them also believe in the "hacker culture"—pursuing innovative ideas to change the game to add an extra dimension of challenge or excitement to the game, or to improve their odds of success in playing the game. So avid gamers often "hack" or modify the games, and sometimes take the additional step of releasing their modifications to other gamers through online gaming community Web sites. Most contemporary PC-based games are designed so that they can be modified by gamers relatively easily. The combination of the hacking culture and the ease with which games can be modified has given rise to the phenomenon of "mods" in the computer gaming industry.

The benefits from mods accrue to gamers as well as to the developers of the original games. And, this has led to many game developers (for example, Epic Games, id Software, Valve Software, Bethesda Softworks, and so on) taking a more proactive approach to promote and support the innovative activities of the gaming community in ways that open up new commercial possibilities for the original game as well as enhance the overall gaming experience.

THE "MODDING" AND THE "MODDERS"

The original game provides the structure for the innovative activity of the gaming community. However, the precise nature and extent of the modifications can vary widely. Broadly, the mods can be of two types—partial conversions and total conversions.

Partial conversions are relatively minor alterations to a game, in that they do not change the underlying elements or flow of the original game. For example, modifications can change the execution of certain functions of the game including the behavior of specific actors, the operation of particular weapons, and so on. Partial conversions can also involve adding new elements to the game—for example, new weapons, new game maps, new "skins"—that bring more complexity without changing the underlying flow of the game. For example, *Team Fortress*, one of the most popular mods, is a partial conversion of the original game called *Quake*.

Total conversions, in contrast, involve modifying the overall game play as well as the core elements of the game. While a total conversion mod might still employ the basic engine of the original game, the end product can be a completely different game with a different look and feel. Typically, such total conversion projects involve complex development work and a significant amount of development time and thus are often pursued as a group project.

While mods exist for most of the popular games, some games in particular have attracted a lot of attention from the gaming community. A notable example is *Half-Life*, a game produced by Valve Software in 1998. *Half-Life* was a single-player "first-person shooter" (FPS) game with a complicated plot involving a protagonist with an advanced degree in theoretical physics saving Earth from a set of attacking aliens. With more than 8 million copies sold since its release, *Half-Life* is one of the best-selling PC FPS games to date. The success of *Half-Life* can be attributed not only to the pioneering elements of the original game but also to the highly innovative mods that followed in the eight years or so since the release of the original version.

Mods for *Half-Life* have ranged from partial conversions that involved new game maps to total conversion that changed the game from single-player to multiple-player format. The best-known total conversion mod of *Half-Life* is *Counter Strike*, which uses the *Half Life* engine but is a multiplayer-only game. *Counter Strike* is a team-based, first-person shooter in which the players join either the terrorists or the counter-terrorists, and combat the opposing team while fulfilling predetermined objectives. Released shortly after the original game, *Counter Strike* is the most popular online first-person shooter game in history—with more than 94,000 gamers playing at any given time and collectively contributing more than 5 billion minutes of playing time each month.[1] Indeed, *Counter Strike* has become so popular that it has generated its own mods and dedicated gaming communities.

Because most total conversion mods use the basic engine of the original game, playing such mods requires owning the original game, too. However, some of the game engines have become free software allowing the total conversions to become truly stand-alone games—playable without having to own the original game. Examples include the *Tremulous* mod for *Quake III Arena* and the *D-Day: Normandy* mod for *Quake II*.

In this innovation network, the game developer plays the role of an *innovation catalyst* by making the game "moddable"; that is, releasing it in a form that allows modding. For example, game developers can facilitate modding by defining game play variables in non-proprietary file formats and adopting graphics of a standard format (for example, bitmap files). Developers can also make available extensive tools and documentation to assist mod makers. For example, in the case of *Homeworld 2*, a game that requires a very sophisticated tool called Maya to build new in-game objects, a free version of the tool was made available to the modding community.

Similarly, in the case of *Half-Life,* Valve Software provided tools and code to the gaming community. For example, it included Worldcraft, the design tool used during the game's development, as part of the game software. The developer also released a comprehensive software development kit (including texture editors, model editors, and rival level editors) that enabled easier modding. Finally, the source code of the game was also released and has become the base for the many multiplayer modes that have been created for the game (including *Counter Strike*).

The individuals who participate in creating the mods play the role of *innovators*. In the gaming community, they are referred to as *modders*. Most modders belong to the fan community associated with a particular game. The online forums associated with such communities also provide the platform for the modders to promote and distribute the mods.

The online forums also provide the context for a group of modders to come together as a team to pursue projects of common interest. Some of these modder teams go on to create more than one mod. One such example is Team Reaction, a prolific mod team, most notably known for the *QPong* and *Jailbreak* mods.

INCENTIVES FOR MODDING

All computer games involve some combination of intellectual property rights—copyrights, trademarks, patented technology, and trade secrets. However, by and large, a copyright is the most widely applied IP (intellectual property) right management mechanism in the computer game industry. A copyright in a computer-based game protects the source code (either embedded on a physical medium such as a DVD-ROM or as a file made available for download). Many other elements of a game (such as game artwork, musical score, and so on) might be subject to the copyright of a different entity (author).

The IP issues related to the mods are complex and yet to be resolved.[2] Most mods are derivative works as they are built on or use parts of other games. As such, game developers require mods to be non-commercial or free. As noted previously, some game developers have opened up the source code of their games for use by the mod community while other developers have partially opened up the code. For example, the *Quake 2* game engine from id Software has been released to the open source community under the GNU Public License (GPL). Similarly, Raven Software (which licensed the *Quake 2* engine privately to create the game *Heretic II*) released part of the source code of *Heretic II* to the mod community while keeping closed some other parts as they were considered trade secrets.

Despite the issues related to intellectual property rights, game developers have largely adopted a positive approach towards the modding community, because they realize that modding offers important indirect benefits for them. Good mods help to build and maintain a fan base for the game. The larger the number of mods associated with a game, the bigger the player community associated with it. Mods also extend the lifecycle of a game. Each time a new mod is released, the original game attracts a new generation of players. For most mods, the original game is still required to run the mod, so a number of high-quality mods can result in a significant increase in the sales of the original game. For example, in the case of *Half Life,* popular mods such as *Counter Strike, Team Fortress Classic, Deathmatch Classic, Firearms, Ricochet,* and *Day of Defeat* have extended the life of a product that was first released in 1998 by several years, and have helped push the total sales to over 15 million units.

Game developers can also acquire the more popular mods and convert them into distinct products. For example, both *Counter Strike* and *Day of Defeat* were so popular in the gaming community that they were bought by Valve Software and turned into full-fledged retail products. Game developers can save development costs as well as development time. In addition, some game developers have also encouraged mod creation by hiring the star mod creators.

Although all the preceding incentives benefit the game developer, the player community also gains much from the mods created by the community members. Most mods are non-commercial products, so they are free of cost. This means that mods multiply the returns from purchasing the original game. Mods also provide a powerful avenue to channel the creativity of individual developers. With a greater proportion of game code as well as development tools available in the public domain, the development of mods has become easier. Further, the reputational incentives associated with creating high-quality mods serve as a powerful mechanism in attracting more and more talent into the modding community.

In sum, the computer game industry offers an excellent illustration of the MOD Station model of network-centric innovation—a community of innovators coming together to innovate in a clearly defined and structured innovation space and sharing the benefits of such innovation with other members of the network. However, this model is not limited to the computer gaming context. Indeed, it finds application in several other contexts. Let us now consider an example of this model from a project in the semiconductor industry—namely, the OpenSPARC Initiative.

"MODDING" THE CHIP ARCHITECTURE: THE OPENSPARC INITIATIVE

In early 2006, Sun Microsystems Inc. launched the OpenSPARC Initiative—a community-based initiative to promote open and collaborative innovation around its hitherto-proprietary SPARC microprocessor architecture. The initiative involved the creation of a community Web site (www.OpenSPARC.net) where Sun released the source code and other specifications into the public domain under an open source license allowing any contributor to modify and build on the SPARC architecture.

SPARC stands for Scalable Processor Architecture and is a technology that is based on the revolutionary Reduced Instruction Set Architecture (RISC) created at the University of California, Berkeley in the 1980s. The SPARC architecture was initially implemented in workstations, which were high-performance standalone machines used for scientific and financial services applications. Later, it was used to build processors for large servers, a very different application. SPARC machines generally use Sun's Solaris operating system, but over the years, other operating systems ranging from FreeBSD, OpenBSD, and Linux have also been used. One of the more popular SPARC implementations—the SPARCstation1—was introduced by Sun in 1989.

In the same year, Sun also established a separate entity called SPARC International to promote the SPARC architecture and to provide conformance testing. SPARC International owns and manages the licensing of the SPARC architecture and the associated trademark. The organization has been instrumental in the late 1980s and early 1990s in licensing the technology to several manufacturers including Texas Instruments, Cypress semiconductors, and Fujitsu.

Over the years, several versions of the SPARC architecture have been released—the most notable have been SPARC Version 8, the standard 32-bit architecture definition released in the late 1980s; SPARC Version 9, the 64-bit architecture released in 1994; and UltraSPARC Architecture 2005, an extended architecture definition, released in late 2005.

In late 2005, Sun also introduced UltraSPARC T1, a new microprocessor implementation that conforms to the UltraSPARC Architecture 2005 specification and executes the full SPARC V9 instruction set. UltraSPARC T1 is designed as a multithreading, multicore CPU and is at the heart of Sun's newest server line, the Sun Fire T2000 and Sun Fire T1000 servers.

On March 21, 2006, Sun made the UltraSPARC T1 processor design available under the GNU General Public License (GPLv2) through the OpenSPARC project.

Sun pursued the open license strategy for two reasons. First, Sun realized that the revenues it could derive from its proprietary internal "builds" and support services could be significantly enhanced by the complementary external innovation that could be created for its architecture. Second, the company also realized that there were diverse new application areas for its SPARC architecture chips, ranging from consumer electronics to health informatics. Entering such new markets would be far easier if the company adopted a more open approach toward its technology architecture and encouraged community-based innovation initiatives targeted at such new application areas where Sun had limited expertise.

Thus, the primary objective of the OpenSPARC initiative was to enable a community of innovators to take the source code and specifications of the 64-bit UltraSPARC T1 processor and modify and build on it to design and develop a new generation of multicore, multithreaded chips and complementary software products. The newer chips and software products would open up newer markets for the UltraSPARC T1 design, benefiting all community members.

While modifying and improving the basic SPARC architecture is one of the primary objectives of the OpenSPARC initiative, another equally important objective is to facilitate the "System On a Chip" (SOC) design. The SOC design movement is dictated by the need to lower product costs as well as to speed up product design cycles in the semiconductor industry. It involves integrating on to a single chip a number of functional modules that in the past have been spread across several chips. A key challenge in this design approach involves getting access to the IP related to the separate pieces (needed for integration on a given chip) in a format that facilitates easy customization and ready integration. The OpenSPARC initiative is aimed at building momentum for such an SOC design movement.

Thus, the innovation space in the OpenSPARC project is clearly defined and structured by the SPARC architecture specifications and the instruction code set that Sun released into the public domain. Specifically, Sun released the source code in Verilog language of the 64-bit, 32-threaded UltraSPARC T1 processor. This new open source version is called the OpenSPARC T1. Along with this version, Sun also released the full UltraSPARC Architecture 2005 specification (that is, the instruction set) as well as the full OpenSPARC simulation environment and verification suites. In addition, several other support tools and technologies that facilitate innovation on the architecture including Sun Studio software and SPARC-optimized compiler were also released. All of these technologies were released under the GPLv2 license, which gives the right to use, modify, and/or redistribute the technologies, thereby enabling a wide range of innovation activities. To understand what these activities are, let us take a closer look at the operation of the OpenSPARC community.

THE OPENSPARC COMMUNITY AND THE INNOVATION ACTIVITIES

Membership to the OpenSPARC community is open and free to any interested entity—firms as well as individuals. By registering at the community Web site, contributors can get access to all the code and the tools. They can also participate in any of the open projects. In mid 2007, more than 200 registered members were in the OpenSPARC community, a majority of them being firms.

Who are the key players in this community? The first key player is Sun itself. The company plays the role of an *innovation catalyst* by contributing the base architecture upon which all the innovation activities will be based, and by creating the Web-based infrastructure to support the community activities. Sun also actively participates in the community governance and provides a broad roadmap for the evolution of the SPARC architecture.

The second key role is that of the *innovator*. All community members who contribute to the enhancement of the SPARC architecture play this role. These community members or innovators range from software and hardware firms to individual developers and academic researchers who contribute in different ways. For example, software firms take the source code of the SPARC architecture and create innovative software applications that are highly optimized and tightly integrated with the hardware. Microprocessor chip designers and manufacturers (foundries) take the SPARC architecture and modify it to develop newer chips. Similarly, other hardware vendors use knowledge of SPARC architecture specifications to design highly customized benchmarking tools and verification suites. Finally, individual developers and researchers build on the SPARC architecture and specifications to research and develop next generation chip architectures. Many of these individual developers tend to work for firms or research institutions.

The nature of the OpenSPARC community is such that members do not necessarily have to have any formal relationships with Sun. OpenSPARC.net is an independent entity and as such all the members develop their ties with one another through the community. Further, there are no intermediaries in the community. Ties among community members are developed over time based on the nature of the projects they are working on.

Members in the OpenSPARC community are free to innovate either within or outside the architecture. Within the architecture, members can, for example, add or delete cores, add new instructions to the instruction set, modify the different types of interfaces (memory interface, Input/Output, cache/memory interface, etc.). Members can also innovate outside the architecture by designing additional components that extend the architecture—for example, video or graphics components, networks interface, and so on.

As of July 2007, there have been more than 4,700 OpenSPARC T1 RTL downloads through the community Web site. Typical projects in the OpenSPARC community have ranged from porting operating systems to the current SPARC chip to developing newer chips that build on the SPARC architecture.

For example, in Italy, a small company called Simply RISC designed and published the first derivative product of the OpenSPARC chip design. Simply RISC is a company that develops and supports CPU cores, peripherals, and interfaces released under the GNU-GPL (open source licensing scheme) to build free hardware designs of microprocessors, Systems-on-a-Chip and Networks-on-a-Chip. In 2006, a team of engineers at Simply RISC created a cut-down (single-core) version of the OpenSPARC T1 processor called the *S1* core, which can run on Ubuntu Linux and can be used in embedded devices such as PDAs, set-top boxes, and digital cameras. This version can be freely downloaded and implemented on a Linux host.

Another project relates to operating system software. David Miller, an individual software developer, led the Linux community in creating a Linux port for the OpenSPARC T1 processor that was added to the mainline Linux kernel. The port allows a very diverse set of applications to run on the OpenSPARC architecture and also paves the way for a broader adoption of the technology. And, based on this work, two Linux distributors—Ubuntu Linux and Gentoo Linux—have already brought out OpenSPARC-specific Linux distributions.

Finally, a more ambitious project based on the OpenSPARC open source is being pursued by a set of researchers at the University of California, Berkeley. The project, called Research Accelerator for Multiple Processors, or RAMP, is aimed at developing a new multicore, microprocessor architecture that is focused on parallel computing. The researchers are working on building a massively powerful and complex architecture that involves chips that hold one to two dozen cores. The RAMP team has adopted the OpenSPARC T1 processor as a target processor for its project because it is available in the public domain.

COMMUNITY GOVERNANCE AND INFRASTRUCTURE

Although Sun is the initiator of the OpenSPARC project, it is a community-led initiative. The community has established a formal mechanism, an elected community advisory board, to exercise such community leadership. Reflecting the community-based governance structure, the advisory board is expected to solicit input from the community on a regular basis and use this input to shape the evolution of the initiative. The OpenSPARC charter explicitly states that "The board shall be selected and shall conduct its affairs in accordance with democratic principles and shall represent the interests of the OpenSPARC community."[3] As such, the role of the advisory board is similar to that of advisory councils that are common in Open Source Software communities.

The advisory board helps to set a coherent innovation agenda for the community—an agenda that embodies the will and the interests of the overall community. As David Weaver, Sun's representative on the OpenSPARC board noted, "The board is there to help foster the development of the community and as a final arbiter in case of any disputes that might arise."[4] The board also helps in promoting a set of community-wide principles to guide the collaborative innovation activities and practices. These guiding principles include equal rights and opportunities for all members, fair processes in all community projects, and the obligation to make available, whenever possible, the IP (intellectual property) rights to all community members to build upon and share.[5]

So how can a member initiate and participate in a collaborative project in OpenSPARC.net? Any registered community member can start a new project. When a member makes a request to start a new project, the request is evaluated by a community manager to ensure that the proposed project meets the guiding principles of the community. After the project is approved, the members who participate in that project have all the rights and responsibilities to manage the activities and make all the project-related decisions. Members can play different contributing roles in a project—from project owner to developer to content developer.

OpenSPARC.net constitutes the central forum for members to interact, download and use the tools and technologies. It lists the ongoing projects and their details to allow members to join the projects. It also provides different types of interaction facilities to members ranging from community discussion boards to blogs and wikis. And it offers tools to support collaborative development, including mailing lists, source code version control, issue tracking, and file sharing.

The community is also in the process of developing an "open book" on OpenSPARC T1 that is licensed under the Creative Commons Attribution License. The objective is to describe the architecture in detail (a sort of user manual) to assist the developer community.

IP RIGHTS MANAGEMENT AND VALUE APPROPRIATION

Sun made the OpenSPARC architecture and the specifications available to the community under the GPLv2 license. The GPLv2 is an open source license that has been approved by the Open Source Initiative and provides wide latitude to the user to run, copy, distribute, or modify the technology. The GPL is built on the "copyleft" principle, which gives every person the permission to reproduce, adapt, modify, or distribute a work (a software program, an art, a piece of text, and so on) as long as such rights are preserved for any resulting modifications or adaptations as well.

Community members are allowed to make private modified versions of the technology, without any obligation to divulge the modifications, as long as the modified technology is not distributed to anyone else. However, if a member chooses to modify and redistribute the technology, then the modified technology must also be licensed to the OpenSPARC community under the same GPLv2 license. This practice ensures that the whole community benefits from the innovative effort. Note that members are allowed to distribute a modified technology and charge a fee for it as long as the modified technology is also released under GPLv2 to the community.

All contributors to the OpenSPARC community are also required to sign a *Contributor Agreement* (CA) before contributing code to the community.[6] The CA ensures that the community has a patent license for all contributions made to the project. The CA establishes a joint copyright assignment in which the contributor retains copyright ownership while also granting those rights to Sun as the project sponsor. However, the CA does not change any of the rights and responsibilities that are due from the GPLv2 or any other open source license used in the community Web site.

The SPARC trademark remains the property of SPARC International. As such, while modified or new designs based on the OpenSPARC architecture can be marketed by community members, they will need to license the trademark if they want to associate such new or modified designs with the SPARC name.

An interesting question here is how does Sun benefit from the OpenSPARC initiative? Or, in what ways does Sun appropriate value from this project?

One benefit is that because Sun still develops and markets systems that are based on the UltraSPARC T1 architecture, by opening up the architecture and establishing a vibrant community around it, the initiative will lead to the creation of new markets that the company can target. For example, with the porting (implementation) of Linux on the OpenSPARC platform, the market for Sun's UltraSPARC-based systems broadened considerably. As David Weaver of Sun's Architecture Technologies Group noted, "Our hope is that the creativity that gets unleashed on the open platform would lead to new and innovative applications—applications that Sun has never thought about (and may never will)—that expand and enhance our broader ecosystem. An overall bigger pie and an increased slice of the pie for everyone." Another benefit is that the OpenSPARC initiative enables more external "eyes" to be focused on researching the challenges and opportunities around multithreading and 64-bit processes (for example, the RAMP project) thereby enabling these technologies to evolve more rapidly and creating newer opportunities for Sun's own internal technology development projects. Further, by increasing the number of people who can obtain the SPARC architecture code, the OpenSPARC initiative also increases the number of deployments and the base of customers likely willing to pay for systems, software, and services from Sun.

For contributing members, the community provides other types of incentives. The OpenSPARC Web site offers a marketplace to exchange or trade products and technologies developed by community members on the OpenSPARC architecture. Members can market free as well as "paid for" products. For individual developers as well as other community members, returns can also come through exposure to other firms. By participating in and contributing to the community, firms can enhance their reputation among their peers as well as track the technology evolution and market dynamics that in turn might inform their own internal technology development strategies.

COMBINING OPENSPARC WITH OTHER SUN INITIATIVES

Sun has extended the OpenSPARC model to its other technologies—most notably, its operating system Solaris—through the OpenSolaris community project and its Java technology through the OpenJava initiative.

The Solaris OS is Sun's operating system distribution and is branded, tested, maintained, and supported as a Sun product. The OpenSolaris project provides the open source code base of Solaris, the "build" tools necessary for developing the code, and an infrastructure for communicating and sharing related information.[7] Over time, Sun expects most (if not all) development of the source to take place in the OpenSolaris community. Since launching the OpenSolaris initiative, Sun claims a significant increase in the installed base of Solaris (up to nearly 6 million registered licenses).[8]

In May 2007, Sun released its implementation of the Java technology as free Open Source Software under the GNU GPLv2 license—effectively replicating the same community-based collaborative innovation model that it used for the OpenSPARC and the OpenSolaris technologies. The source code to all three implementations—the Java Platform Standard Edition (Java SE), the Micro Edition (Java ME), and the Enterprise Edition (Java EE)—were released to the community for modification and enhancement.

The success of these community-based initiatives will depend on Sun's ability to be an effective innovation catalyst—offering an appropriate innovation infrastructure, being creative in devising IP rights management systems, and being a responsible community partner. In addition, Sun's ability to find potential synergy among the three initiatives would also shape the growth and success of these initiatives.

MODDING IN THE WEB SERVICES ARENA: THE "MASHUP" MOVEMENT

A more recent example of the MOD Station model of network-centric innovation is the *Mashup movement* that has emerged in the Web services market since 2005 or so. The Mashup movement represents the creativity of independent developers and entities in mixing and matching data and presentation elements from multiple Web information sources to offer new and innovative Web services.

The innovation architecture in this context is defined by the data and presentation elements of popular Web information sites such as Yahoo!, Google Maps, Flickr, Virtual Earth, Technorati, YouTube, Zillow, and Amazon. The innovation activities involve combining different elements of these architectures to create *mashups* or new services.

There are two types of players in the Mashup community: The large Web information companies that play the role of innovation catalysts and the individuals and small firms that play the role of innovators by creating the mashups. The application programming interfaces (APIs) published by the large companies provide the primary mechanism for the innovators to combine elements from multiple sources. Furthermore, these large companies also provide free access to their data (as well as the presentation formats) thereby promoting the Mashup movement. In many cases, they also provide visibility to such innovative effort by linking such mashups to their Web sites.

Consider Mappr, one such mashup.[9] Mappr was developed by a team of San Francisco–based designers and programmers. The Mappr service uses the Flickr APIs and sifts through the tags of all the photos posted on Flickr.com (by more than 300,000 Flickr.com customers) and then transposes them against the U.S. map—in effect, creating a photo guide of the different places and people in different parts of the country.

As of July 2007, there were more than 2,000 mashups ranging from map mashups to news mashups.[10] More are being innovated every day, at an average rate of around three per day—indicating the richness of the innovation space.

What is the incentive for the large Web companies such as Flickr to offer such free access and play such a sponsoring role? Mashups allow them to tap the creativity of external developers in a way that enhances the visibility and usage of their own products. For example, through the Mappr service, Flickr.com can get more Web surfers (or customers), some of whom might be willing to pay more for premium services. In other words, the Mashup movement enables large Web companies to expand the reach of their Web services platforms to newer markets and customers. As Paul Levine, general manager of Yahoo! Local notes, "We want to encourage community participation (through mashups). It's essentially research and development and marketing for us."[11]

As a true community-based initiative, the Mashup movement also maintains an expectation to give back to the community. For example, in the case of Mappr, the service publishes its own APIs that other developers can use. In short, one mashup can build on top of another mashup by using the appropriate APIs, thereby forming a truly collaborative innovation process.

TYING TOGETHER THE COMMON ELEMENTS OF THE MOD STATION MODEL

The three examples of the MOD Station model of network-centric innovation are different in many respects, but they have some common themes (see **Table 8.1**). We briefly discuss these three key themes.

Table 8.1 Comparison of the Three MOD Station Examples

Elements of Network-Centric Innovation	OpenSPARC Initiative	Computer Games	Mashup Movement
Nature of the innovation space	Defined by the SPARC architecture	Defined by individual computer games	Defined by the data and presentation architecture of key Web information service providers
Structure of the network leadership	OpenSPARC community led	Community of modders	Community of developers
Innovation Roles			
Architect (innovation catalyst)	Sun Microsystems	Game developers	Web information service providers
Adapter (innovator)	Individual and firm innovators	Individuals and mod teams	Individual and firm innovators

continues

Table 8.1   Comparison of the Three MOD Station Examples

Elements of Network-Centric Innovation	OpenSPARC Initiative	Computer Games	Mashup Movement
Network Management			
Network governance	Advisory board provides broad community guidance; individual projects managed autonomously	Modding community forums associated with individual games devise norms and values and validate/regulate mod quality	Mashup aggregator forums serve as the platform for the broader community to devise "do's and don'ts" and to evaluate mashup quality
Knowledge management	OpenSPARC.net provides all the infrastructure	Online forums serve to share tools, documents, and so on related to the game	APIs provide the primary mechanism to share data and integrate knowledge
IP rights and value appropriation	Open licensing scheme: GPLv2	Mix of open (for example, GNU-GPL) and proprietary licensing	Individual developers decide the IP rights of their mashups

One theme is that, in each of the examples, the platform for the innovation activities was clearly defined or well specified—for example, the OpenSPARC architecture or the *Half Life* computer game. The availability of such a structured innovation space serves as a catalyst to bring together a community of innovators and also provided coherence to their creative contributions. While a single entity is generally responsible for releasing the innovation platform to the public domain, the nature of the innovation activities on such a platform is largely left to the community. For example, in the case of computer games, individual mod teams decide the specific nature of modifications they would make to the game.

Another common theme is the presence of some form of community governance. In the case of the OpenSPARC community, a formal mechanism—a governing board—channels and facilitates community leadership. In the case of computer games, the mod communities are more loosely organized around the different online mod forums. The interactions of the community members in these forums provide the context for devising and applying the common norms and values of the community. Community interactions also serve to regulate or validate the quality of the mods and indirectly allow the community members to formulate a shared vision of the desired nature of innovations. In all three examples that we considered, the success of an innovation is largely based on the use of that innovation by the community members. As such, community members exercise considerable influence on the overall innovation agenda and the outputs.

The third common element relates to the intellectual property rights and the incentives associated with the innovative contributions of the community. Our examples suggest that the MOD Station model demands a mix of IP rights mechanisms and incentives applied to promote and sustain community-based innovation activities. It is also evident that open (left) and closed (right) IP rights mechanisms can coexist in many of these contexts and help channel the innovative contributions of the community to specific areas of the innovation platform. For example, by opening up certain parts of the code, game developers can encourage the development of mods related to specific elements of the game. Similarly, in the information services industry, by carefully opening up certain elements of information delivery architecture, technology firms have been able to encourage and promote the creation of innovative mashups. These examples suggest that application of the appropriate mix of IP rights and incentives can help to catalyze community-based innovation activities in ways that benefit all the members of the network, including the firms that contribute the platform for such innovation.

LARGE COMPANIES AND THE ROLE OF THE INNOVATION CATALYST

Our examples clearly demonstrate that companies that play the role of the innovation catalyst by contributing the innovation platform to the community can realize several benefits—both direct and indirect. For example, we outlined some of the benefits that Sun derives from its OpenSPARC initiative—expansion of the company's existing customer base, greater reach into newer markets, exploration of the application potential of the SPARC architecture, and so on. We also indicated the different types of benefits that game developers might obtain from mods associated with their game products—higher sales, longer product lifecycle, larger and more diverse fan community, brand recognition, and so on. In effect, by opening up certain parts of their product or technology architecture for community-based innovation, companies can create win-win situations for all the members of the network.

How can companies adopt the MOD Station model to promote such community-based innovation initiatives focused on certain parts of their product or technology architecture in ways that benefits all the entities involved? What specific capabilities and resources do they need to bring as an innovation catalyst?

We address these questions in detail in the next two chapters. A key observation is that the successful use of the MOD Station model requires a clear understanding of the incentives for the community members to innovate on the platform and to devise and apply the appropriate mix of IP rights mechanisms that would support such incentives. It also demands that companies serve as a true "partner" of the innovation community, and be comfortable with operating in a context where the innovation goals, objectives, and activities are largely shaped by the collective desires of the community members.

CONCLUSION

The MOD Station model of network-centric innovation is a relatively nascent phenomenon. Most of the applications of this model have thus far been limited to information-based products and services (for example, software, computer games, computer hardware, movies) that are more readily amenable for deploying such a partitioned, community-based innovation initiative. As the trend toward increasing the information intensity of products continues, we are likely to see this model extended to other products and markets.

We have now completed describing the four core models of network-centric innovation. Beginning with the next chapter, we focus on the logical next question—which model is the most appropriate for a specific company? And what does it take to make each model work? We explore these issues by showing how to match the model to the context of the company's market and environment, and by detailing the competencies and best practices associated with specific roles in each of the models.

Executing Network-Centric Innovation

Chapter 9   Deciding Where and How to Play   177

Chapter 10   Preparing the Organization   197

9

Deciding Where and How to Play

In the public speaking business, it is often said that a good presentation should answer three questions: What? So what? *And now what?* So far in this book, we have addressed the first two questions by introducing the Global Brain and its awesome power to turbocharge innovation, and by describing the four models of network-centric innovation. But we are still left with the third, and perhaps, the most important question—*now what do we do?* How should your company tap into the Global Brain? What model should it use? And how can you prepare your organization to embrace a network-centric innovation strategy? In this chapter, we offer a practical roadmap for companies and managers to identify and pursue opportunities for network-centric innovation that best match the context of the company and its business environment.

In the process of researching this book, we interviewed a senior manager at a large, Midwest-based technology firm who was responsible for leading his company's collaborative innovation initiatives. During our conversation, the manager remarked that in the last two years or so, the company had been dabbling with "open" innovation initiatives. However, he was not satisfied with the progress they had made. He felt that a lot of energy and investment had been expended on these efforts with little to show in terms of tangible outcomes.

The problem was not a lack of commitment from senior management, R&D, or the product development organization. Rather, he felt that the problem lay in the lack of a coherent approach to identify, evaluate, and pursue externally-focused innovation opportunities. Compounding the issue was the fact that the company participates in a wide range of markets and has several thousand products spread across many business units. Faced with a wide array of opportunities, the executive felt that the company was unclear about what opportunities and relationships it should focus on, and how it should pursue promising opportunities.

This concern is echoed by managers in many large companies we have studied. We respond to this concern by offering a three-step approach to addressing the question of where and how a company should tap into the Global Brain through a network-centric innovation strategy:

1. We look at how a company can scope its network-centric innovation initiatives and determine the most appropriate opportunities.

2. We show how the company should prepare itself in terms of organizational capabilities and resources to pursue those specific opportunities.

3. We highlight best practices that it can adopt for implementing its network-centric innovation strategy.

In this chapter, we focus on the first step by providing guidelines for managers to evaluate the different types of opportunities based on industry/market factors and to select the opportunities that best leverage the firm's resources and capabilities as well as align with the firm's overall innovation agenda.

POSITIONING YOUR FIRM IN THE INNOVATION LANDSCAPE

The discussion in the previous four chapters illustrated that different models in the landscape of network-centric innovation have different implications for a participating firm—implications for the nature of the innovation roles, innovation capabilities, innovation outcomes, and value appropriation. If there are "different roles for different folks," how should a company answer the seemingly simple but important question, *"Where does my company fit in the network-centric innovation landscape?"* (see **Figure 9.1**)

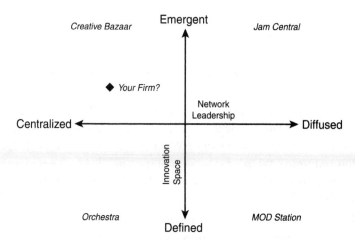

Figure 9.1 Positioning your firm in the network-centric innovation landscape

The first step in answering this question requires analyzing the industry and market characteristics for the firm and identifying the quadrant in the network-centric innovation landscape that is most appropriate for the firm's context. For large multibusiness companies like P&G, DuPont, GE, IBM, and Unilever, this analysis might need to be conducted at the Strategic Business Unit (SBU) level, because the industry and market context is likely to be quite different across the SBUs. For example, at GE, the GE Healthcare business has a very different business context from GE NBC Universal or GE Money.

The second step is to analyze the nature of the innovation contribution that the company can make and the specific role it can play in that part of the network-centric innovation landscape. This analysis has to take into consideration the requirements of the innovation role as well as the unique resources and capabilities that the company can bring to the innovation context.

We start with the first step.

DECIDING ON THE MOST SUITABLE MODEL

The firm's innovation context plays a key role in determining which model of network-centric innovation is most appropriate. Three broad sets of questions frame the context:

- How well defined is the innovation *space*? Are the innovation goals clearly articulated? Does the innovation define a new architecture or extend/enhance an existing architecture? How visible are the market opportunities? How well tied are the innovation goals and the architecture with those market opportunities?

- What is the nature of the *knowledge and capabilities* demanded by the innovation? Do innovation projects involve highly specialized or advanced domain knowledge? What is the extent of knowledge integration required? What are the capabilities needed for participating in the innovation activities? How widely distributed (or available) are these capabilities?

- How well established are the mechanisms for *appropriating value* from the innovation? Will the innovation require establishing radically new value appropriation systems? Does the innovation context allow a mix of "open" and "closed" IP rights systems to coexist? Is it possible to deploy a diverse set of incentives to appeal to different types of contributors?

Table 9.1 captures the important industry and market conditions that reflect the preceding issues and shape the choice of the different network-centric innovation models. Based on these factors, we now describe the typical context that best suits each of the four models.

First, consider a context when there is a clearly defined innovation architecture or technology platform that is well tied to a market opportunity with established mechanisms for value appropriation. As we have seen from the examples of Boeing and Salesforce.com, this context is best suited to the *Orchestra model*, particularly if the knowledge needed for implementing the architecture is highly specialized and held by a few entities or if partners' capabilities are important to enhance the reach and richness of the ecosystem. Further, if the technological or market risk in the innovation project is relatively high, it is important to pool and share risk with a network of partners. Markets that show these characteristics include semiconductors, software, computer hardware, biotechnology, networking equipment, consumer electronics, and so on; in each of these sectors are several examples of the Orchestra model.

Table 9.1 Contingencies for Models of Network-Centric Innovation

Industry/Market Factors	Models of Network-Centric Innovation			
	Orchestra	**Creative Bazaar**	**Jam Central**	**MOD Station**
Innovation goals and architecture	Well-defined innovation goals; clearly specified and modular innovation architecture	Broad innovation goals that can be tied to a specific market space; limited articulation of innovation architecture	Broad innovation goals but not well tied to any particular market space; limited articulation of innovation architecture	Well-defined and relatively modular architecture; innovation opportunities not predictable or well defined
Addressable market for innovation	Clearly defined market opportunity (often significant—greater than $300 million) that is tied to the innovation architecture	Market opportunities are evident but tend to range from small to medium	Market opportunities are not always clearly defined; might involve immature markets that have the potential to grow rapidly	Market opportunities are not always quite evident and tend to be niche
Nature of innovation contributions	Implementing, complementing, or extending the innovation architecture	Mostly stand-alone innovations that meet the broad innovation goals of the firm	Specialized contributions that help define and implement the innovation architecture	Complementing or enhancing the existing innovation architecture; new market opportunities
Nature of technological change	Predictable but potentially major technological changes	Relatively moderate technological changes	Significant and often unpredictable technological changes	Predictable and relatively moderate technological changes
Nature of innovation risk	High development and commercialization risk	Moderate to high development risk; moderate commercialization risks	High development, and commercialization risks	Low development risk; moderate to high commercialization risk

continues

Table 9.1   Continued

Industry/Market Factors	Models of Network-Centric Innovation			
	Orchestra	Creative Bazaar	Jam Central	MOD Station
Nature of innovation knowledge/expertise	Innovation knowledge is complex/diverse and held by a limited number of entities; requires knowledge integration across domains	Innovation knowledge ranges from simple to moderately complex/diverse; some knowledge integration required	Involves integration of complex, new, and diverse knowledge that is, however, widely distributed	Innovation knowledge is somewhat complex/ specialized but widely distributed
Nature of innovation support facilities	Idea development testing requires expensive and sophisticated capabilities	Idea development and testing facilities are more widely available and tend to range from inexpensive to moderately expensive	Idea development and testing facilities can be made widely available although tend to be sophisticated and moderately expensive	Idea development and testing facilities are often widely available and relatively inexpensive
Nature of IP rights management	Highly predictable and manageable IP rights context	IP protection is feasible and predictable but requires more work	Largely unpredictable context; can support mix of open and closed systems	Fairly predictable IP context; supports mix of open and closed systems
Value appropriation systems	Clearly defined mechanisms for value appropriation	Clearly defined and already existing mechanisms for value appropriation	Limited or no existing mechanisms for value appropriation	Mix of existing and new value appropriation mechanisms

In contrast, even if the innovation architecture is clearly defined, if the existing market opportunities have already been exploited and new market opportunities are not very clear, then the context suggests the use of the *MOD Station model* of network-centric innovation. The case of Sun's OpenSPARC Initiative is illustrative of this model. The MOD Station model works particularly well if the innovation knowledge is diffused or widely distributed and the innovation context demands a mix of open and closed IP rights management systems. In such a context, the full or partial unlocking of the innovation architecture to facilitate more "open" and community-based innovation pursuits can uncover new market opportunities for applying or extending the innovation architecture—opportunities that had never been recognized or targeted by the firm that devised the architecture. And as the examples of the computer game industry and the Web-based information services industry suggested, as long as the right mix of incentives (and IP rights systems) are created, such community-led innovation can benefit all the members of the network, including the firm that created the architecture or platform.

In other situations, the innovation architecture or the specific innovation outcomes are not defined but the market opportunities are visible and/or well articulated. If such a context is also marked by innovation expertise and facilities that are not too complex and are rather widely distributed, then the *Creative Bazaar model* becomes relevant. As we saw from the various examples in Chapter 6, "The Creative Bazaar Model," several markets in the consumer products industry (for example, office supplies, home care, and so on) are typical of such innovation contexts. Individual inventors can think of innovative product ideas that align well with the broad market goals and objectives articulated and communicated by large firms. Further, it is important to utilize an existing infrastructure for commercializing the innovation, which can only be provided by a dominant firm in the network.

An additional interesting issue here relates to the nature of the market opportunity. Our research suggests that the typical size of the target market associated with the Creative Bazaar context tends to be relatively modest. Indeed, if the market opportunity is relatively big, then it might pique the interest of a large firm, which would pursue it aggressively. The Creative Bazaar context works well when the market opportunity is diverse and rich in detail—thereby calling for very innovative (even if simple) solutions.

Finally, consider a context where the innovation architecture is not very well defined and neither are the specific market opportunities. Instead, only the broad contours of the innovation domain might be evident. In this context, there is fairly high development risk as well as market risk. Such a context becomes ripe for the *Jam Central model* of network-centric innovation. Examples of such contexts include new and emerging technological areas (for example, biotechnology, nanotechnology, renewable energy, and so on) or previously uncharted areas of existing domains (for example, software, drug discovery, and so on).

In such a context, if the innovation knowledge or expertise is also widely distributed, then it might lead to the formation of a network of innovators who have a shared interest in that innovation domain but do not have any immediate focus on value appropriation. The specific innovation goals and architecture will then emerge from the interactions of these network members, as was the case in the Tropical Disease Initiative discussed in Chapter 7, "The Jam Central Model." The need to continue to attract and maintain the creative energy of the members requires a more "open" governance system, one that ensures every member's ability to voice and influence the innovation proceedings. In addition, the greater the ease with which open IP policies can be deployed in the innovation context, the greater will be the appeal of the community. Further, a combination of factors—including lack of clarity on immediate market potential, longer innovation incubation time, and higher extent of innovation risk—all contribute to corporate entities assuming a sponsoring role rather than a more active role in the innovation process.

The identification of the most appropriate model related to an innovation context is only one part of the solution. The second part is to identify the most appropriate role that the company can play in that innovation context.

DECIDING ON THE MOST SUITABLE INNOVATION ROLE

In earlier chapters, during our discussion of the four models of network-centric innovation, we had identified several innovation roles that firms can play. **Table 9.2** lists these different roles. Firms choosing to play one of these roles should carefully examine the key underlying issues and conditions that would determine the appropriateness of that role or opportunity.

Table 9.2   Roles in Network-Centric Innovation

Model of Network-Centric Innovation	Innovation Roles		
	Architect	*Adapter*	*Agent*
Orchestra model	Integrator Platform leader	Component developer Complementor	
Creative Bazaar model	Innovation portal	Inventor	Idea scout/broker Innovation capitalist
Jam Central model	Innovation steward	Innovator	Innovation sponsor
MOD Station model	Innovation catalyst	Innovator	

PARTICIPATING IN THE ORCHESTRA MODEL

The two types of roles that firms can play in the Orchestra model are the role of the integrator or platform leader and the role of a component developer or complementor.

INTEGRATOR OR PLATFORM LEADER

As our two case studies—Boeing and Salesforce.com—showed, firms wanting to play the role of an architect in the Orchestra model need to own an innovation architecture (or platform) that has significant appeal to a wide range of potential partners who can contribute in developing the innovation components or complementary products and services. In addition to this requirement, two key issues determine whether the firm can play the role of an integrator or platform leader.

The first issue relates to the *addressable market* for the innovation platform or architecture. Is the market opportunity defined by the innovation architecture large or broad enough to support the network? We saw in the case of Boeing that the key initial consideration for the company was the ability to appeal to a large enough market—one that could support and justify the investments made and the risks assumed by Boeing's partners. Similarly, the role of a platform leader will also be more successful if the innovation platform is relevant to diverse market contexts including niche markets. Consider IBM's role as platform leader in its Power architecture network. While the platform's original target market (for example, PCs and Workstations) is considerably large, the ability to find new niche markets is critical to sustain the appeal of the network to existing and new partners. For example, HCL Technologies, an India-based IT firm, recently started innovating on the Power architecture design—specifically, the PowerPC 405 and PowerPC 440 embedded microprocessor cores—to extend its application to wireless and consumer devices areas. Thus, a key consideration for a firm evaluating an opportunity to play the role of architect in an Orchestra model is the size of the addressable market.

The second issue relates to the firm's own *internal resources* and *risk appetite*. Devising an innovation architecture (or platform) and building a network of partners around it takes considerable time and resources. Associated with such an investment is the considerable amount of innovation and market risk. In most cases, the platform will end up in a long and bitter battle of attrition with other platforms (for example, the current battle between the competing Blu-Ray and HD-DVD platforms for high-definition recorded video), and one or more of the platforms might end up getting marginalized (recall the Sony Betamax). Before electing to play the role of an integrator or a platform leader, a firm has to carefully evaluate whether it has the stomach to assume this level of risk. As our earlier example of Salesforce.com showed, a company can also gradually evolve into the role of a platform leader by committing more and more resources to build the network as the firm gains more success in establishing its own core products and technologies. Thus, the key considerations for a firm should be the amount of resources the firm can expend on building the innovation network and the extent of risk it is willing to assume.

COMPONENT DEVELOPER OR COMPLEMENTOR

As an adapter in the Orchestra model—that is, a component developer or a complementor—a firm needs to contribute specialized innovation expertise or capabilities as well as bear its share of the risk associated with the innovation platform or architecture. Two considerations are important in evaluating such an opportunity.

The first issue relates to the *nature of the connection* between the firm's specialized capability (that is, its contribution) and the network (or the innovation platform). On the one hand, the tighter the connection, the more likely that the firm will be a valuable network partner and that it can realize greater returns from its contributions. On the other hand, the tighter the connection, the greater the constraints the network will place on the firm's ability to chart its own goals and strategies. Achieving a balance between these two forces is important. The questions to ask would be, "Can the firm 'specialize' its assets to meet the network's goals without tying its own future with the success of that network?" "Are there opportunities for the firm to deploy the same set of assets to another network?" Or, "Will the opportunity to play the role of an adapter in a network move it away from other networks?" A firm has to consider these important issues before committing to a particular innovation platform or network.

Another issue that can dictate the choice of the adapter role is the *learning potential* associated with that role. By participating in the Orchestra model, a firm can acquire new capabilities or expertise (technological or market related) that might justify the overall risk it assumes in playing that role. For example, in the case of Boeing's partners, some of the Japanese companies, including Kawasaki and Mitsubishi Heavy Industries, have long-term plans of evolving into stand-alone aircraft manufacturers. They firmly believe that their experience and the technological expertise acquired from the 787 development program can help them achieve these future plans. Similarly, firms that develop complementary solutions on an innovation platform (for example, Microsoft's .NET platform or Salesforce.com's AppExchange platform) might discover that the potential to acquire new expertise from other network members would offset some of the risks associated with network failure. Thus, a key consideration in evaluating the adapter role, particularly for smaller firms, should be the potential to acquire additional expertise from their interactions with other network members.

PARTICIPATING IN THE CREATIVE BAZAAR MODEL

We identified three types of roles in the Creative Bazaar model: innovation portal, inventor, and idea scout/innovation capitalist. Given that the role of the inventor is played largely by individuals (customers, amateur inventors, and so on), here we focus on the issues related to the other two roles.

BECOMING AN INNOVATION PORTAL

Firms can play the role of an innovation portal to ensure a rich and continual flow of innovative ideas for their internal product development pipelines.

In evaluating the opportunity to become an innovation portal, the key consideration relates to the range of innovation sourcing mechanisms that the company will have access to in that particular industry/market. Specifically, will the company be able to employ a *balanced portfolio of sourcing mechanisms* that would enable the firm to manage the risks associated with entertaining and playing host to external ideas?

As we discussed in Chapter 6, the sourcing options at the left end of the Creative Bazaar continuum (for example, idea scout, patent broker) are attractive in industries and markets where amateur inventors can work by themselves with limited resources to come up with new product concepts. Thus, companies such as Dial, Staples, Sunbeam, Lifetime Brands, and Church & Dwight (represented by Firm A in **Figure 9.2**) with lots of small and diverse products might favor those mechanisms.

On the other hand, the sourcing options at the right end of the continuum (for example, venture capitalist, external incubator, and so on) are more appropriate in innovation contexts that require considerable domain expertise and significant capital and time for development and market validation. Companies such as DuPont, 3M, and Kodak (represented by Firm B in the figure) who participate in science-based markets might rely more on those mechanisms.

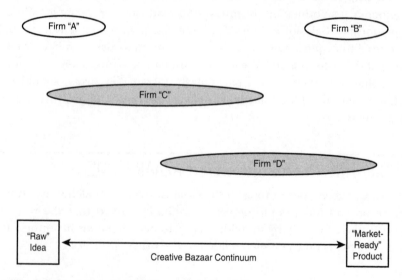

Figure 9.2 Toward a balanced innovation sourcing portfolio

Factors related to a firm's particular market context are likely to imply a bias towards one set of sourcing mechanisms. However, there are downsides associated with relying exclusively on one set of mechanisms—accepting either too many risky ideas or too many expensive ideas. So it is advisable for a firm to balance its innovation sourcing approaches by complementing its favored approach with the other approaches on the continuum. This "move to the middle" might involve working with entities such as the innovation capitalist, who represents a compromise between the traditional two extremes of the continuum. Looking at **Figure 9.2**, Firm C and Firm D have a more balanced innovation sourcing strategy although their market and firm-specific factors might still imply maintaining an overall bias toward the left end and the right end, respectively. Going back to the example of DuPont, while it might find that buying companies is preferable in its traditional mature businesses, alternative approaches—like the use of innovation capitalists—might be used in emerging businesses like bio-based materials or electronics.

Thus, companies planning to play the role of an innovation portal should first evaluate their potential to employ a range of mechanisms so as to minimize the risk of unbalanced sourcing. In short, the greater the range of innovation sourcing options available in the particular industry/market, the better the opportunity for assuming the role of an innovation portal with acceptable risk.

IDEA SCOUTS AND INNOVATION CAPITALISTS

Companies intending to play the role of an agent (product scout, patent broker, innovation capitalist, and so on) in the Creative Bazaar model need to decide the nature of their contribution (or innovation intermediation). In general, the greater the value addition a firm can bring to the innovation sourcing process, the higher the returns it can obtain from the client firm. However, two issues deserve careful consideration: First, what is the uniqueness of the value addition that the firm can bring to innovation sourcing? Second, how important is this value addition in the eyes of the client firm?

Consider the first issue. Does the firm have some unique access to inventor networks that it can leverage? Does the firm have specialized expertise or patented processes to filter innovative ideas or to conduct rapid initial market validation? For example, as we saw earlier, the Big Idea Group (BIG) cultivates its own network of inventors and also conducts unique roadshows that bring together inventors and a panel of experts to seek out good ideas. Or does the firm have unique capabilities to integrate different types of knowledge to advance or transform an innovative idea? Are there unique relationships with large client firms that the firm can bring to the sourcing process? For example, Ignite IP relies on its exclusive network of senior managers in large client firms to become aware of critical trends in technologies and markets. Absent such unique capabilities or relationships, it is unlikely that a firm can be anything more than a broker in the Creative Bazaar model with limited returns.

Typically, entities such as idea scouts and innovation capitalists focus on one or two specific industries or markets where they have deep domain advantage. It is important for such intermediaries to carefully consider the how much value addition the client firm will perceive in the contribution that they make. For example, in certain markets where numerous relatively minor innovative ideas need to be sorted out (for example, home improvement and self-help tools; toys), "idea filtering" might be perceived as valuable; on the other hand, in certain other markets characterized by fuzzy or unpredictable IP rights contexts, validating the IP rights of those ideas might be deemed more valuable. Thus, a firm should carefully consider the relative importance of the different value addition activities in innovation sourcing in a given market and decide the specific role that seems most promising.

PARTICIPATING IN THE JAM CENTRAL MODEL

In the Jam Central model, the most likely role for a firm is that of the innovation sponsor. Given that the ideas emerge from the community, the role of the innovation steward will be carried out by those entities (mostly individuals) that provided the initial spark to the innovation context. Even the role of the innovator will largely be played by individual members of the community. As such, here we limit our focus to the appropriateness of the role of an innovation sponsor.

INNOVATION SPONSOR

Firms don't play the role of an innovation sponsor as an act of altruism or social service. Such decisions are always (and, we believe should rightly be) based on a sound business case.

Consider IBM. It has an important stake in the Open Source Software movement and actively pursues the role of an innovation sponsor in those initiatives.

In an interview with Irving Wladawsky-Berger (IBM's former vice president for technical strategy and innovation), he noted the rigor that IBM brings to this decision:

> IBM takes Linux, Apache, and other such (Open Source) communities very seriously. For us, working with them is a no-nonsense business decision and we make them only after considerable analysis of the technology and market trends, the overall quality and commitment of the community, its licensing and governance, and the quality of its offerings. In our opinion, the key to such open innovation initiatives is the quality of the community, not whether you can have access to the source code of the software. And, if you don't have a good community, then there is nothing in it for us to join. So we ask ourselves all these tough questions abut the community, its goals and objectives, its ways of organization before we make a commitment to support them.[1]

A "business decision" does not mean that a firm should play such a role only if there are direct or visible benefits. In many cases, such direct returns might not exist, at least in the short term. Instead, innovation sponsors need to focus on the indirect, and often long-term benefits that such a role might bring to the firm. For IBM, these benefits might include developing a favorable brand image and gaining influence in the Open Source Software community. In the case of the TDI, large pharmaceutical and biotech companies that are currently exploring a potential sponsoring role with TDI might consider the benefits of being exposed to trends and developments in drug discovery that are outside the scope of its traditional business units.

Another set of issues relate to the innovation outcomes. What are the types of expected innovation outcomes? How promising and significant are these expected outcomes? Do they have the potential to radically change existing markets? What types of IP rights mechanisms are likely to apply to such outputs?

Finally, it is also important to evaluate how the firm's contributions to the innovation community are likely to be perceived. Are the inputs given by the firm as an innovation sponsor likely to be perceived as critical for the overall innovation? And how exactly will it help the community advance its innovation agenda?

The answers to the preceding questions can indicate the long-term success of the community agenda as well as the likely benefits the firm might potentially derive from supporting such an agenda. As such, it is important to give each of these issues careful consideration before committing resources to support the community-led innovation initiative.

PARTICIPATING IN THE MOD STATION MODEL

A firm can play primarily two types of roles in the MOD Station model: an innovation catalyst or an innovator. We start with the role of the innovation catalyst.

INNOVATION CATALYST

As an innovation catalyst, a firm contributes the innovation architecture or platform to initiate community-led innovation activities on it. Earlier, in Chapter 8, "The MOD ("MODification") Station Model," we had identified several incentives for a firm to make such a contribution. However, while the benefits to the firm might be evident, this does not necessarily mean that such a contribution will always spark the creative energy of the community. Indeed, the opportunity to play such a role is critically dependent on the nature of the innovation platform and as such many of the issues revolve around this dependency.

The first issue relates to the innovation potential associated with the platform. Unless the innovation platform is inherently perceived as valuable and also opens up a diverse set of innovative opportunities, it is unlikely that the firm would be able to attract a community of innovators around it. Thus, some of the issues for the firm are—how modular is the innovation platform? Is the modularity of the platform matched with the innovation interest of the community? Are the different innovation opportunities related to the platform visible? Are there specific market opportunities tied to these innovation possibilities?

The second issue relates to the incentives for the community to innovate. Will the firm be able to create a diverse set of incentives to attract and maintain the interest of the innovation community? Can the firm facilitate the application of a mix of IP rights mechanisms (for example, open and closed licensing schemes) that would cater to a wide range of community members—individuals as well as other entities?

Beyond the preceding questions is the issue of the firm's own commitment to the initiative. As the example of Sun and its OpenSPARC initiative indicated, the process of building a community around such innovation architecture can often be slow and calls for continued commitment from the company. Further, the firm's ability to gradually "let go" of control over the innovation platform and actively promote community-led governance will critically shape the continued participation of community members and thereby the success of the initiative. Sun took the step of incorporating lead members of the community into the first governance board that it helped to create. The success of OpenSPARC will be dependent on how well the community governance system works and how well the innovation opportunity offered by OpenSPARC can capture the imagination of the community members.

Thus, overall, a firm should carefully consider how it can open up the innovation platform to the community in a way that benefits everybody, including the firm.

INNOVATOR

Now consider the role of the innovator. Although this role plays out in a community-based innovation forum, as we have seen from the different examples in Chapter 8, there are several ways to appropriate value from such innovation. As such, under certain conditions, it might be appropriate for a firm to play the role of an innovator in the MOD Station model. What are some of these contextual conditions?

First, and perhaps the most important, are the policies related to intellectual property rights. While some of the open licensing policies (for example, GPLv2) might preclude most profit-oriented development activities, other variations of the open licensing schemes might allow certain types of such activities, particularly on derivative products.

Another consideration relates to the overall size and health of the community. The larger and the more active the community, the greater the potential to sustain the platform over the long-term and the more likely there would be market interest for complementary solutions based on the platform. As such, a firm has to take a hard look at the quality of the community that the innovation catalyst has been able to attract around the platform and then decide how worthwhile it would be to play the role of the innovator in that community.

Table 9.3 captures the key issues that we have discussed so far regarding the different roles in the four models of network-centric innovation. As we mentioned earlier, these are only the more important ones; there might be other considerations unique to the firm that it will need to consider in evaluating the different opportunities.

Table 9.3 Considerations for the Roles in Network-Centric Innovation

Role in Network-Centric Innovation	Key Issues for Consideration
Orchestra Model	
Integrator, platform leader	Market positioning of the innovation architecture/platform; risk appetite of the firm
Component developer, complementor	Dependency of the network; opportunity for learning (growth)
Creative Bazaar Model	
Innovation portal	Ability to deploy a balanced portfolio of sourcing mechanisms
Idea scout, innovation capitalist	Uniqueness of value addition; perceived importance of value addition
Jam Central Model	
Innovation sponsor	Quality of community; importance of company's contributions
MOD Station Model	
Innovation catalyst	Ability to "let go" of control over the innovation platform; ability to attract and retain the community
Innovator	Nature of the IP rights policies in the community; overall community health

CREATING A PORTFOLIO OF INNOVATION ROLES AND DECIDING THE "CENTER OF GRAVITY"

Sometimes, not only are there different roles for different folks, there may be different roles applicable within the same firm. Large companies like Unilever, DuPont, and IBM with diverse business units will typically find that there is more than one innovation role they can potentially pursue across their diverse innovation contexts. As such, it is important to think of the portfolio of roles that a large firm should assume as it formulates its network-centric strategy. Consider a few examples.

IBM plays the role of a platform leader in some of its traditional business areas, including systems and servers, semiconductors, and so on. The Power

Architecture discussed earlier is a good example of this. IBM devised and articulated the platform and nurtured a network of partners to expand its reach and potential application areas. Even in many of its software product businesses (for example, middleware software platforms such as WebSphere, operating systems such as AIX, and so on), the company plays the role of a platform leader. On the other hand, more recently, the company has been playing the role of an innovation sponsor in some of the community-led innovation initiatives in the software industry, most particularly, the Linux community. The company has also started playing such a role in innovation communities in other domains—for example, in the biotechnology industry.

Similarly, consider P&G. In the consumer product business, the company follows the Creative Bazaar model and actively plays the role of an innovation portal. P&G partners with a diverse set of innovation agents including product scouts, eR&D marketplaces, and innovation capitalists to seek out innovative ideas that it can then bring inside to commercialize. On the other hand, in some of its other businesses—for example, chemicals, pharmaceuticals, and so on—the company has followed the Orchestra model and played the role of an integrator. Specialized capabilities of partner firms are brought to bear in the development and commercialization of new products.

Sun Microsystems is an example of a firm that participates in both the Orchestra model and the MOD Station model. In much of its server business, Sun is a platform leader, developing and promoting proprietary technology platforms that form the basis for its products such as Sun Fire servers and Sun Ultra workstations. On the other hand, in recent years, the company has contributed some of its proprietary technology platforms to initiate community-led innovation initiatives. We described the OpenSPARC initiative earlier. Other similar initiatives including opening up the Java source code for community-based innovation have further expanded the company's role as an innovation catalyst.

The preceding examples indicate the potential for companies to pursue a portfolio of roles in different parts of the network-centric innovation landscape. The nature of such a portfolio will be shaped by the industry/market characteristics of the different business units of the company. Further, it is also likely that one of those roles within the portfolio will assume dominance depending on the relative size and importance of the different business units. Such a dominant role indicates the location of the "center-of-gravity" of the firm's network-centric innovation initiatives. Going back to the example of IBM, in spite of all the community-led innovation initiatives that the company has joined in recent years, its role as a platform leader is still dominant in its overall collaboration strategy. Similarly, it is evident that for P&G, the center of gravity lies in the Creative Bazaar model.

Why should you be interested in the "center of gravity" of a firm's network-centric innovation strategy? As you will see in the next chapter, the nature of the resources and capabilities that a company needs to muster depends on where its center of gravity falls in the network-centric innovation landscape.

CONCLUSION

In this chapter, we showed how a firm can evaluate the different opportunities to tap into the Global Brain and identify the most appropriate role to play. After the firm has positioned itself in the network-centric innovation landscape, the next set of questions that arises is, "How can I prepare my organization to carry out such a role most effectively?" "What are the capabilities and resources that would be needed?" "What are some of the best practices that my firm should be aware of?" In the next chapter, we explore these issues.

10

Preparing the Organization

Imagine that you are setting out on a trekking expedition to a remote mountainous area. The first step in planning your expedition is to understand the landscape that you will be trekking on, and to plot the best route for your trek. Having done this, you then need to prepare yourself. You need to assemble your team and get them physically as well as mentally prepared for the trip. And you need to gather the supplies and tools that your team will need to survive and succeed. Without careful preparation, undertaking the trek would be dangerous, no matter how well you understand the terrain and the route.

Such is the case in planning your expedition to tap into the power of the Global Brain. In the previous chapter, we focused on understanding the terrain of opportunities, and deciding on a course of action for your organization. After you have identified the opportunities, you need to look inward and ensure that your organization has the capabilities it needs to capitalize on the opportunities.

In this chapter, we offer advice on how to make your organization "innovation ready." We consider two components of a firm's readiness for network-centric innovation initiatives: *organizational readiness* and *operational readiness*.

Organizational readiness refers to the *people* dimension of the capabilities needed for network-centric innovation. Essentially, it is about creating the right environment within the organization to encourage and support participation in network-centric innovation. This includes creating an "open" mindset, getting leadership on board, creating the appropriate organization structure, and communicating the innovation strategy internally and externally. Operational readiness refers to the *process* dimension of the capabilities. This includes designing processes for project selection, partner selection, risk management, integrating internal and external processes, and management of intellectual property rights. Operational readiness also involves creating the tools and technologies to support externally focused innovation and metrics to track your progress and assess your success.

The starting point for readying the organization is to change the mindset of the organization regarding network-centric innovation. This is the most important and the most difficult step in organizational readiness because it goes against the entrenched proprietary mindset that most organizations have regarding innovation. Let us look at the challenges in changing the innovation mindset, and how firms can overcome these challenges.

OPENING YOUR ORGANIZATION'S MIND

As we noted in Chapter 1, "The Power of Network-Centricity," a central challenge for organizations embarking on a network-centric innovation initiative is to create a mindset that encourages looking outward and becoming more accepting of the ideas of outsiders. This is especially challenging when intellectual property and secrecy is at stake. Consider InnoCentive, the much-talked about "innovation marketplace" created as a spin-off from Eli Lilly several years ago. Dr. Alph Bingham, a founder and board member of InnoCentive, recalls the stiff resistance his team faced within Eli Lilly. When they presented the concept internally, the internal R&D and legal teams balked at the heretical notion that Lilly's secret R&D problems would be posted online for the whole world to see. It was a heretical idea for scientists used to the image of "Skunk Works"—the legendary R&D organization within Lockheed where scientists and engineers toiled away in complete secrecy, walled out from the world and even from within the other parts of the organization. But the InnoCentive team persisted, and today, the concept of an open marketplace for innovation seems quite logical.

The responsibility for creating the "open" mindset rests largely with executive management, and it begins with the CEO of the company. In our experience, organizations that have made headway have often been mandated by the CEO to adopt a collaborative and externally focused mindset. It helps if the CEO publicly declares the intent and the goals for the firm to change its innovation strategy. This leaves people with very little choice but to get on board. For example, when P&G's CEO A.G. Lafley proclaimed in 2000 that half of P&G's new products would come *from* its own labs and half would come *through* them, it catalyzed people into action.[1] As Tom Cripe, associate director of P&G's External Business Development (EBD) group told us, "Our senior management has been very focused on this and they repeat it at each and every internal forum, and when they do that, it slowly grows on you, and helps to evolve a culture where people are more receptive to ideas coming from other places."[2]

OVERCOMING THE "WE KNOW EVERYTHING" (WKE) SYNDROME

Malcolm S. Forbes said, "Education's purpose is to replace an empty mind with an open one." So it goes with changing the innovation mindset. There is no greater enemy of learning than our overconfidence that we already know everything. Indeed, we are prisoners of what we know, because we tend to reject other peoples' ideas when we believe we know all we need to know. A lot has been written about the "Not Invented Here" (NIH) syndrome—a culture that rejects ideas, research, and knowledge because it wasn't originated within the organization. We look at this syndrome somewhat differently as the "We Know Everything" (WKE) syndrome, which we define as an organizational mindset that is closed to external ideas and knowledge because of the belief that internal knowledge and expertise is sufficient, and there is no need for importing external expertise.

The WKE syndrome is particularly dangerous for companies with a long and illustrious history of R&D accomplishments, such as Boeing, Kodak, 3M, DuPont, Merck, Motorola, Sony, and IBM. These companies practically invented their industries, and rightfully consider themselves to be the pioneers of their markets. They have also been associated with legendary innovations, and they have within their ranks some of the most talented scientists and engineers. Furthermore, in many of these organizations, the average tenure of researchers and engineers is quite long, and they have a tremendous amount of accumulated knowledge and experience. In such an organization, it is hard to believe that someone outside the organization can tell you something you don't already know!

Consider 3M as an example. It has more than 6,000 scientists and researchers in its R&D setup working in 30 core technology or scientific areas ranging from adhesives, abrasives, and films to fiber optics, imaging, and fuel cells. These scientists work at R&D units at different levels of the organization—in the division labs, in the sector labs, and in the corporate labs. 3M has such deep scientific in-house talent that its scientists and engineers have formed several informal groups or networks based on their specific research areas to share their knowledge and research findings (akin to IEEE-type forums inside the company). 3M has struggled to overcome the WKE syndrome. Explicit acknowledgement from senior management—particularly the CEO or the CTO—that the WKE exists in their organizations can be the most important first step in this regard. In the case of 3M, Jay Ihlenfeld, senior vice president of R&D, played a key role in helping the organization to acknowledge this challenge and to start working on addressing it.[3]

It is also very likely that even the mere admission of such a problem, let alone specific actions to overcome it, is likely to create confusion and resistance within the organization. For example, when Merck's new R&D chief, Peter Kim, acknowledged that the company's internal talent was unlikely to be sufficient to replenish the company's R&D pipeline for the future, he immediately sparked protest within the scientific establishment of the company. Merck R&D veterans such as Emilio Emini (senior vice president of vaccine research), Kathrin Jansen (a research manager who played a key role in the development of the cervical cancer vaccine), and Scott Reines (a top researcher in psychiatric diseases) all left Merck. One of Kim's main jobs was to instill in Merck's R&D setup the notion that it didn't know everything. And, more importantly, there was a need to treat smaller companies looking for potential collaboration with Merck with respect and humility—not as an "arrogant" partner. Specific counseling sessions were conducted—in the words of Dr. Merv Turner, Merck's head of licensing, "We sent our guys to charm school."[4]

Such interventions done by senior management can instill a mindset that acknowledges the limitations of the company's internal knowledge base and is more inviting of external ideas.

THE POWER OF "LETTING GO"

The flip side of the WKE syndrome is the firm's ability to "let go" of its proprietary knowledge and intellectual assets, or cede control over the innovation process in order to advance the overall innovation agenda. This action is particularly challenging for organizations used to controlling every aspect of their innovation activities as well as "hoarding" every single intellectual property asset.

As companies collaborate with external entities (whether other firms or individuals) in innovation initiatives, they have to become comfortable with the notion of loosening control over the innovation process. And they have to become comfortable with the idea that they have to contribute some or all of their "proprietary" knowledge to enhance the innovation effort. Such a need to let go might come as an unpleasant surprise to senior management, too. In Chapter 2, "Understanding Network-Centric Innovation," we described IBM's realization of this need while working on developing the first Olympics Web site (for the Atlanta Olympics). In the words of IBM's Irving Wladawsky-Berger, who led that project in the mid-1990s, such realization can be momentous.

> I remember when we did the Web site for the Atlanta Olympics in '96. My people who did that Web site used Apache instead of IBM's proprietary product. They reported to me at the time and I said, "Well, why are you using Apache?" And they said, "Because it's much better. You want a good Web site or do you want to push your own product?" And, I said, "No, we must have a good Web site, because nobody cares what the stack is. They want the Web site to work well." And this was the first time anybody had put up Olympic results on a Web site. So we really wanted to make sure it worked. And eventually they said, screw it. Let's ditch the IBM product, which has almost no market share and is inferior, and join forces with Apache. At the time, this seemed revolutionary. Now you look at that and you say, it seems to be common sense.

The concept of "letting go" is something that an organization has to get comfortable with over time. In fact, some companies realize that they are letting go of things that they never really *did* control as much as they thought they did. There is an illusion of control that is greater than the reality. However, even if it is an illusion, getting everybody in the organization to acknowledge it is a challenge for senior managers. And, as the example of IBM showed, sometimes it might also percolate from scientists and engineers working on the project up the hierarchy to senior managers.

Preparing the organization to adopt such a mindset requires the senior executives to communicate the benefits of letting go. This process becomes more challenging when the expected returns from letting go are not contemporaneous or even in the same product market or business division. In other words, the payoff from letting go can be distant in both *space* and *time*. Furthermore, often the very act of letting go might in the short term disrupt the firm's existing revenue stream making it even more painful and increasing the resistance within the organization. Thus, the ability of the senior management to see the broader innovation agenda and communicate how "letting go" can actually prove to be beneficial (or even necessary to sustain the growth of the firm) becomes crucial.

An analogy from parenting might help illustrate the challenge and the benefits of letting go. As a parent, you might have the illusion of control over your child's aspirations, careers, and interests, and so letting go can be quite difficult. However, you really don't have as much control over your child as you *think* you do. And the more you let go, the greater the confidence and autonomy you build in your child. Similarly, for an organization, the more it is able to let go of its control or knowledge in an innovation initiative, the more it will likely gain from the participation of collaborators.

STRUCTURING THE ORGANIZATION

After a firm achieves an enlightened innovation mindset, the next aspect of readiness is to create the appropriate structure for the organizational entity that leads network-centric innovation. In this regard, we have encountered two frequent questions, "Do we need to have a dedicated unit to lead our network-centric innovation initiatives?" and "Should we create a new organizational unit or use our R&D unit (or other existing organizational units) to provide this leadership?" Our answer to both of these questions is—it depends!

In some firms, existing organizational units (for example, corporate R&D unit, business development unit, and so on) can evolve or transform to spearhead the network-centric innovation initiatives. In other cases, new units and new positions need to be established to provide the leadership. Three factors shape such decisions:

- Does the company have a *history* of participating in collaborative R&D ventures?

- Is the innovation space the company is mostly focused on for collaboration clearly *defined* or more *diffused* in nature? Further, how *diverse* are the company's innovation partners likely to be?

- Are the initiatives being considered by the company related to its *existing* products and services or to *new/emerging* business areas?

Let us start with the first issue. If a company has a long and considerable collaborative experience (for example, joint ventures in R&D, technology consortiums, and so on), then it is likely that elements of the collaborative spirit as well as associated competencies are present within the organization. If so, there is no need to create new organizational units dedicated to network-centric innovation initiatives. Instead, the firm can rely on transforming one or more existing units that already has the experience to take on the new responsibilities related to leading and coordinating the company's network-centric innovation initiatives.

A good illustration of this collaboration history is P&G's EBD group—a unit with more than 50 people. EBD has shouldered a considerable part of the responsibility for P&G's Connect+Develop initiative right from the early stage in the late 1990s. The EBD group already had considerable experience in interacting with external entities for technology commercialization and licensing deals, and as such, it only needed to evolve further to interact and coordinate with a larger number of external partners (including product scouts, innovation capitalists, and so on). Other business units utilize the services of EBD to seek out external innovation opportunities, negotiate deals, and interact with external partners, and in return, these internal clients contribute to EBD's budget. Thus, in the case of P&G, its prior collaboration experience enabled it to transform existing organizational units such as EBD to assume the responsibility to coordinate the network-centric innovation activities.

On the other hand, if a company's collaborative experience is limited or not widely dispersed across the organization, creating a new unit may be necessary to signal the shift in the company's approach to innovation. This is the approach that Kodak adopted. The company has a 100-year old tradition of being a highly vertically integrated company with abundant internal technological resources. However, as Kodak started undergoing a major transformation from being a chemical/analog company to becoming a digital company, the company realized it couldn't make this shift on its own, and that it needed to be much more aggressive about "going out" to get the breakthrough ideas. So, in recent years, Kodak has created new organizational units and new positions, like the External Alliance Group, to facilitate the development of new partnerships with external innovation networks. The new organizational units are helping Kodak break down the cultural barriers related to externally sourced innovation and establish systems and processes to identify and collaborate with a wide range of external partners, ranging from early stage firms to individual inventors to academic scientists.[5]

The second issue relates to the nature of the innovation space and the diversity of partners. Evidently, if you are participating in the Orchestra model, much of the innovation space is clearly defined and you are likely to interact with a relatively less diverse set of network partners. In this context, the role of a dedicated organizational unit would largely be to establish the standard set of practices that the different parts of the company need to follow. While the unit might assume a strong leadership role in the initial stages, as the processes and practices take root in different parts of the organization, it can step back and pursue a more supportive role.

On the other hand, if the company is participating in the Creative Bazaar model or the Jam Central model, the uncertainties associated with the innovation space and the need to interact with a much more diverse set of partners demand a very different role for the organizational unit responsible for network-centric innovation activities. First, as companies like IBM and Sun have realized, partnership with innovation communities and other such entities often involve spontaneous or unplanned interactions between a company's employees and such external partners. A dedicated organizational unit can help to increase the coherence of these interactions and to facilitate the interactions in such a way that they advance the company's innovation agenda. More specifically, to ensure that value generated through these interactions are captured and do not "fall through the cracks." The more diverse the set of innovation partners, the more diverse the set of innovation capabilities needed. So another role for the organizational unit is to seek out and assemble capabilities from different players. In sum, in a diffused innovation space and with a diverse partner network, the dedicated organizational unit acts less as a process enforcer and more as a *clearinghouse for best practices and skills.*

The final issue to consider in defining the appropriate structure is whether the innovation initiative relates to the company's existing markets (products/services) or does it take the firm into very new arenas? If the firm is staying close to existing markets, then it is likely that the company will have to create strong linkages between the organizational unit spearheading network-centric innovation activities and the R&D units within individual business divisions associated with those existing markets/products. For example, 3M has focused on using its corporate R&D unit to lead its network-centric innovation activities. However, given that many of these initiatives relate to existing products and markets, the early focus has been on bringing together the divisional R&D units to develop a coherent plan for network-centric innovation.

On the other hand, if the initiatives relate to emerging or new business areas, a very different structure might be needed. For example, in the case of DuPont, the bio-based materials area is one market where the company intends to actively pursue network-centric innovation approach. Thus, it has created new positions to coordinate external innovation sourcing activities in the bio-based materials business area. These new structural arrangements are not yet tied to the R&D units in other business areas. However, it is expected that as DuPont's innovation strategy expands to other corners of the organization, eventually those linkages would also be established.

Overall, we believe that dedicated units are likely to be helpful to spearhead and provide coherence to a company's network-centric innovation activities. However, the extent of influence and control such organizational units should exercise depends on the nature of the firm's portfolio of network-centric innovation initiatives.

LEADING AND RELATING WITH PARTNERS

When participating in network-centric innovation, companies might often need to lead their networks and at the very least, relate well to other network partners. In the four models of network-centric innovation that we discussed in this book, the nature of such leadership and relational capabilities needed are quite different.

Earlier, we discussed how, in the Orchestra model, a company such as Boeing has to exercise leadership in ways that bring coherence to the goals and activities of the network members and instill a sense of fairness and predictability in the processes related to value creation and value appropriation.

In our discussion with managers in such companies, one leadership theme has come again and again to the forefront: the need to project an image of *decisiveness* without implying a "high-handed" approach to decision making. Such decisiveness can relate to one or more of the following issues: who gets to play, what is the architecture that will guide the play, and how will the play proceed?

Indeed, most of the companies that play the role of an adapter (complementor, innovator) in the Orchestra model seek decisiveness from the network leader. Decisiveness helps them evaluate the opportunity to participate in the network with much more clarity. And it helps them plan their contributions to the network in ways that lend stability to their own goals and strategies.

Even in the case of the Creative Bazaar model, although the company playing the role of the innovation portal might not interact directly with all the network partners, its ability to create a level playing field for all participants is a critical element of leadership. The leadership role includes bringing more *transparency* to the innovation process—for example, making explicit what the company is looking for, how it would evaluate the innovative product ideas, and how it would go about bringing such ideas to the market. While companies such as Kraft have put out calls on their Web sites for customer participation in innovation, the emphasis should be on informing the inventor community about how that process of such innovation sourcing will unfold.

In the two community-led models—Jam Central and MOD Station—while a company might not play a direct leadership role, it can still provide considerable support to the community innovation goals and thereby offer an element of more indirect leadership. In this case, leadership is more like *good citizenship*. After the leader gains the trust of the community and is accepted into the fold, the community members expect it to contribute towards the innovation agenda. In some cases, employees of the company might play leadership roles in the community based on their own individual expertise and capabilities—for example, some of IBM's employees play such roles in the Linux community. In some other cases, contributions might take the form of harnessing the company's expertise in innovation management for the benefit of the community-led project. For example, some of the large pharmaceutical companies such as Pfizer and Eli Lilly have started making such contributions to the community-led innovation projects in the biomedical industry.

Turning to relational capabilities, two important themes run through the different models of network-centric innovation.

The first theme relates to the potential *asymmetry in power and resources* between the larger and the smaller participants or network members in all four models of network-centric innovation. It is obvious in the cases of both the Orchestra and the Creative Bazaar models. It is even evident in the community-led projects, too, as members range from individuals to large companies to non-profit entities. As such, an important relational capability is the ability to interact with a diverse set of partners with a varying extent of resources and influence on the innovation process.

As one manager of a large consumer products firm put it, "the first competence that we have focused on developing here is to be able to interact with our smaller partners without making them feel overwhelmed. We don't want to be perceived as the 800-pound gorilla trying to steal their ideas—rather we want to come across as the senior partner who has the responsibility to look out for the welfare of all of our partners, including the smaller firms. And, we spend considerable effort in educating our managers as to what this means with regard to their day-to-day interactions with our partners."

Another theme relates to the ability to *build trust* through more open communication and interactions. Again, trust is equally important in the Orchestra model as in the Jam Central model although the mechanisms to build such trust among network partners might vary. When Dial, Inc. acquires the help of national inventor associations to communicate to individual inventors, it is focusing on building such trust with its potential contributors. Similarly, when Boeing builds an extensive IT-based virtual collaboration system to enhance information sharing among its partners, it is focusing on facilitating trust-based interactions in the network.

Or as P&G has discovered in playing the role of the innovation portal, trust builds with each additional interaction with an external partner. The company calls this the *Weed's law*[6]—"The second deal with a partner takes half the time as the first one did. And, the next deal takes half of that time, and so on...." As we discussed in Chapter 5, "The Orchestra Model," cultivating relationships with a selected set of innovation capitalists and other intermediaries helps P&G to use the mutual understanding and trust developed through repeated interactions to accelerate the overall innovation process. Thus, the ability to identify appropriate mechanisms to build such trust in different contexts can critically shape the success of a firm in network-centric innovation.

MANAGING DEPENDENCIES BY STAYING FLEXIBLE

By definition, network-centric innovation creates dependencies between the firm and its collaborators—dependencies on innovation plans of other partner companies and dependencies on the capabilities of external inventors and other such entities. For example, a company that develops a software application to run on Salesforce.com's AppExchange platform is joined at the hip with the platform and its future. Similarly, when an innovation capitalist such as Evergreen IP decides to focus on a particular market (say, toys) and cater to the innovation needs of a selected set of large client firms, it is in effect creating a dependency that links its portfolio of projects with the market needs of its clients. Even in the Jam Central model, when companies commit to a particular community-led project and start contributing resources and expertise to move the innovation forward, they create dependencies that might be less explicit, but no less relevant. So it is important for a firm to acknowledge such dependencies and create sufficient flexibility in its strategy to manage the associated risks.

One dimension of flexibility relates to the innovation assets that the company contributes to the innovation effort. The ability to identify *alternate deployment opportunities* for such assets can enable the company to reduce or manage the dependencies on the network-centric innovation project. Recall Boeing's 787 development project. Many of the new technologies being developed by the Japanese firms also involve deeper expertise that those companies could apply to other projects—particularly, their own independent initiatives in aircraft manufacturing.

Another approach to bring flexibility to the innovation strategy is to participate in more than one innovation network, if possible. Hedging one's bets might allow a company to balance the associated risks and manage the technological and market dependencies. For example, some of the companies building applications on Salesforce.com's AppExchange platform have incorporated standards and architecture that enable them to port add-on solutions to other customer-relationship management (CRM) solutions and thereby reduce their risk. The objective of such an approach is to *manage the "distance"* or separation between the company's own innovation goals and the goals of the network-centric innovation projects it participates in.

We now turn to the second half of preparing the organization—operational readiness for network-centric innovation. We start with the processes that are needed to support the innovation effort.

PROCESSES TO SUPPORT NETWORK-CENTRIC INNOVATION

When most companies decide to look outside for innovative ideas, more than likely such initiatives would start out in an ad-hoc fashion. However, as more and more resources get committed to such initiatives, the need for clearly defined processes soon becomes apparent. Unless basic processes are established to guide and manage the company's participation in external innovation initiatives, the organization's ability to derive returns from such activities can be seriously hampered.

Our discussions with managers in companies such as 3M, DuPont, Unilever, P&G, and Kodak lead us to conclude that establishing processes early in the evolution of the firm's network-centric innovation initiatives is critically important, as this helps bring discipline to the innovation activities. Although the specifics of the different processes and their implementation depend on the particular organizational context, we point to some generic processes that are needed to support network-centric innovation (NCI).

The most important process is the *selection of business areas* within the company that would be most appropriate for pursuing network-centric innovation initiatives. How should the company decide its nature and level of involvement? Who should make such decisions? What criteria should be considered in making such a decision?

Another focus for NCI processes should be the *selection of external innovation networks and network partners*. It is critical that a company has a coherent set of policies for selecting its partners (whether it is an individual firm or an innovation community) that it could implement organization-wide. Large companies may already have established processes for selecting partners for joint ventures and technology alliances. For example, 3M has a steering committee that evaluates all potential candidate projects for external collaboration and selects the most suitable based on a set of criteria, including the ability to define parameters for success and relevance to business. As the diversity of partners increases, such processes might need to be modified to include a host of other factors that might not have been of importance in one-on-one partnerships. Typically, such processes should consider factors such as the company's prior relationships, complementarity of technology/expertise, and so on.

Third, processes also need to be established to *identify and manage the risks* associated with participating in network-centric innovation projects. Participating in community-led innovation projects poses different types of risks than participating in innovation networks that the company leads. For example, in entertaining ideas from amateur inventors and customers, there are IP-related risks and companies need to institute processes to mitigate these risks. On the other hand, when participating in an open project such as Linux or TDI, a company might allow its employees to make intellectual contributions. Different types of risks are associated with this scenario. Thus the nature of the risk varies with the type of innovation project. Some of these risks are likely to be those that the company has not faced before. Also, many of the relationships the company creates as it pursues its network-centric innovation agenda might require careful consideration of the legal implications. It is a good idea to institute processes to vet the different projects for the legal issues involved.

In addition to the preceding areas, processes might also be established to manage other aspects of a company's participation including sharing knowledge with external partners, coordinating innovation activities with external partners, and managing relationships with a diverse set of network partners.

The overall objective of the process infrastructure should be to enable the company to use a uniform yardstick to monitor and measure performance in the NCI activities across the different business units of the organization and to ensure a level of repeatability in such performance.

DEPLOYING TOOLS AND TECHNOLOGIES

Over the past few years, a wide range of tools and technologies to support collaborative innovation have been created. Some of these tools facilitate communication and knowledge sharing among network members while some other tools enable coordination and management of collaborative innovation processes.

As we saw earlier in the book in the case of Boeing and its development of the 787, the use of appropriate information technology (IT) tools can significantly enhance the quality of collaboration among partner firms and lead to more effective participation in such external innovation projects. Similarly, in the TDI project, the Web-based infrastructure provided by the non-profit organization TSL was instrumental in facilitating the collaboration among the scientists and other participants of the network.

IT-based tools can be used in four areas of network-centric innovation:[7]

- They can be used as *process management* mechanisms to instill structured product development processes and to bring a level of rigor and stability to the innovation activities. Although some of the tools might implement generic and industry-specific process models (for example, the Capability Maturity model in the software industry or the Stage Gate model in product development), several proprietary process models also exist (for example, PACE). These tools and technologies enable network members to integrate their innovation processes without losing control over them.

- They facilitate basic *project management* functions—scheduling, coordinating, and managing resources related to a complex project, whether it is an Orchestra model project like the Boeing 787 or a Jam Central project like TDI. Some of these tools provide a virtual "command center" or "war room" with access to all project information through a common interface.

- They support *information sharing* among the different network members. They utilize different data and information standards (for example, ISO-STEP) to handle different types of information (including graphics, audio, video, and so on). Some of the tools also offer more versatile facilities capable of combining structured and unstructured information in real-time.

- They provide *communication support* ranging from facilities for a community of innovators to come together to highly secure forums for a defined set of partner firms to interact and share documents.

Although these tools and technologies can be implemented separately, there are some comprehensive tools that include most of the preceding functionalities. For example, Product Lifecycle Management (PLM) tools provide a wide range of features and functionalities to support network-centric innovation projects, particularly in the Orchestra and the Creative Bazaar models. In particular, functionalities related to project resource management, product platform management, product data management, and collaboration management assume considerable significance in the network-centric innovation project context.

For example, in the aerospace and defense industry, Northrop Gunman uses PLM solutions to support its collaborative development of the U.S. Navy's next-generation destroyer. The project, a good example of the Orchestra model, involves multiple partners and the company utilizes PLM solutions from Dassault Systems (a leading PLM solutions provider) to support its collaborative design and development activities.[8] Similarly, Herman Miller (the office furniture manufacturer) has implemented PLM solutions to support collaborative design activities between the company and its partners (including customers and dealers).[9]

Although PLM and other such tools might vary in their features and functionalities, the key issue here is how well those features support the network members to achieve the overall innovation goals. The more integrated the tools are with the underlying innovation processes in the network and the capabilities of the network members, the greater the potential returns from such tools. Thus, the bottom line for companies is to use these technologies to devise an integrated innovation environment that embraces the network members and brings coherence to their activities and contributions.

MEASURING "SUCCESS"

An important element of operational readiness is the ability to evaluate the company's performance and returns from network-centric innovation. This ability demands the creation of an appropriate portfolio of *innovation metrics*.

As the old adage goes, "Be careful about what you measure." Measuring the wrong thing could lead a company down the wrong path. For example, counting the number of partners might give a false sense of the intensity of the collaborative activity of the company. Similarly, counting the number of patents produced through collaboration might again give a wrong picture of innovation success because patents don't "pay the bills." Thus, identifying the right set of innovation metrics is of utmost importance.

Network-centric innovation metrics differ in nature and focus. Some metrics are more generic and apply to all models of network-centric innovation, while others are specific to the model the company participates in and the role it assumes. While some metrics are defined at the level of the innovation network, others focus on the company and reflect the impact of the company's participation on its internal activities and outcomes.

Table 10.1 provides an inventory of the metrics that fall into each of these categories. Note that this list of metrics is only meant to be representative, and not exhaustive.

Table 10.1　Metrics for Network-Centric Innovation (NCI)

Nature/Focus of the Innovation Metric	Network-Related	Company-Related
General	Capabilities and reputation of the partner firms	Diffusion of NCI-related culture within organizational units
	Extent of trust and commitment among partner firms	Maturity of NCI-related processes and systems
	Quality of value appropriation mechanisms in the network	Perception of the company among network partners
	Nature of IP rights mechanisms deployed	Awareness of NCI opportunities among divisional managers
		Extent of coherence in firm's NCI initiatives
Model-specific Orchestra model	Extent of investments made/risk assumed by partner firms	Market reach of the product/platforms
	Uniqueness of partner contributions	Time to market
	Clarity of product/platform architecture	Extent of risk assumed by the company

Nature/Focus of the Innovation Metric	Network-Related	Company-Related
Creative Bazaar model	Size and geographic scope of inventor network	Number of ideas sourced from inventor network
	Nature of ties with intermediaries (innovation capitalist)	Number of new products generated from external ideas
	Extent of idea transformation (and risk assumed) by partners	Cost of innovation sourcing
Jam Central model	Number of members in the innovation community	Company's image in the innovation community
	Turnover in innovation community membership	Extent of company's influence on innovation outcomes
	Quality of innovation infrastructure	Extent of "learning" achieved
MOD Station model	Intensity of activity in the innovation community	Reach to new or emerging markets
	Diversity of community membership	Increase in product/platform lifecycle
	Community involvement in network governance	Quality of relationship with community members

The first set of metrics relates to the overall network. These metrics allow a company to evaluate whether it is partnering with the "right" network and might also indicate when the company might have to rethink its collaboration strategy. For example, for a company such as Dial, Staples, or P&G that plays the role of an innovation portal in the Creative Bazaar model, a valuable metric would be the reach and geographic scope of its network—the number of inventors and intermediaries that the company has been able to reach out to. Similarly, for a company playing the role of innovation sponsor in the Jam Central model, a useful measure would relate to the stability of the innovation community—the number of members in the community and the average turnover in membership. Such measures indicate the *overall quality of the network* and inform on the current and future innovation potential of the network, and thus could help a company to continuously evaluate whether it is partnering with the right set of external entities.

The second set of metrics, which relates to the impact of the collaboration on the company, indicates how well the company is fairing or gaining from its participation in the innovation project. Going back to the Creative Bazaar example, the number of external ideas entering a company's product development pipeline or the number of new products that can be traced back to such external sources indicates the clear and the most direct impact of the company's participation in the network. Similarly, a company playing the role of innovation catalyst might consider the number of new markets that it has been able to expand as an indication of the impact of its participation in the network.

Some of the company-specific measures could be more generic and relate to the internal innovation infrastructure or capabilities. For example, an audit of the company's internal innovation processes—process maturity—might indicate its overall preparedness to identify and exploit different types of network-centric innovation opportunities. Similarly, perceptual measures can also be used to understand the company's overall performance. For example, measures that capture the company's image among network partners could prove to be very useful in evaluating and building relational and leadership competencies. Similarly, internal measures that reflect the extent of managers' awareness of network-centric innovation opportunities might indicate the cultural and behavioral issues that might impact the company's performance in network-centric innovation.

As **Table 10.1** shows, a company can utilize a range of measures. Given that each measure provides a unique view or perspective of success in network-centric innovation, it is imperative that a company adopt a portfolio of such measures. Most importantly, the selection of the metrics should reflect the company's desired focus in participating in network-centric innovation.

CONCLUSION

In this chapter, we considered many of the issues that companies have to carefully address to prepare their organization to navigate the network-centric innovation landscape. **Table 10.2** captures these different issues.

Table 10.2   Dimensions of Network-Centric Innovation Readiness

Dimension of Readiness	Questions to Consider
Organizational Readiness	
Culture and Mindset	Does the company suffer from the WKE syndrome? If so, what steps has the senior management taken to address it? Is the company capable of "letting go" its intellectual assets and control to advance the overall innovation agenda?
Structural Arrangements	How will the company ensure coherence to the NCI activities across the organization? Is there any one unit that will have the responsibility to provide such internal leadership to the NCI activities?
Leadership and Relational Capabilities	Is the company capable of providing leadership to the network partners, if required? How well-developed is the company's relational capabilities? What mechanisms have been instituted within the firm to build and instill the appropriate set of relational capabilities?
Dependencies and Flexibility	What is the nature of the linkages between the company's innovation goals and the goals of the innovation network it participates in? Is the company aware of the nature of dependencies it has with the NCI initiative? What proactive measures has the company taken to manage such dependencies and introduce flexibility to its innovation strategy?
Operational Readiness	
Processes for NCI	Has the company implemented repeatable and measurable processes related to its various NCI activities? Are these processes adopted widely within the different parts of the organization? Is there any one unit or person responsible for maintaining these processes?

continues

Table 10.2 Continued

Dimension of Readiness	Questions to Consider
Tools and Technologies	Has the company identified and implemented the appropriate set of tools and technologies to support its NCI activities? How well integrated are these tools and technologies with the NCI processes? How readily can the company integrate these tools and technologies with those of its partner firms?
Metrics for NCI	Has the company identified a portfolio of innovation metrics appropriate to the nature of its NCI activities? Does the portfolio of metrics give a well-rounded perspective of the company's performance in NCI initiatives? Have specific organizational units or roles been established to collect the data related to these metrics?

As we noted in the beginning of this chapter, our task here has been to identify the important dimensions of such network-centric innovation readiness. As each individual company charts its own path in the network-centric innovation landscape, it will need to acquire the particular set of resources and capabilities that would enable it follow that unique path. With this focus on organizational preparedness, we come to the end of our journey that we started in Chapter 3, "The Four Models of Network-Centric Innovation," by describing the landscape of network-centric innovation.

In the next chapter, we broaden our horizon and consider the global context for network-centric innovation—specifically, the opportunities and potential for companies in emerging economies like India, China, Russia and Brazil, to participate in network-centric innovation and how large companies can leverage talent in emerging economies for innovation.

Globalization and Network-Centric Innovation

Chapter 11   Globalizing Network-Centric Innovation:
The Dragon and the Tiger   219

Chapter 12   Concluding Thoughts & Actions for
"Monday" Morning ...   237

11

Globalizing Network-Centric Innovation: The Dragon and the Tiger

Perhaps no company has played a more important role in making the world a smaller place than the Boeing Company. Ever since the launch of the Boeing 707 long-haul commercial aircraft in 1958, followed by the legendary Boeing 747 in 1970, Boeing has enabled business travelers to crisscross the globe to conduct global business. Boeing has customers in 145 countries, and despite the recent gains made by Airbus, over 75% of the commercial aircraft in service today were manufactured by Boeing.

Paradoxically, while Boeing aircraft fly around the world, until recently, they were designed very close to Seattle. With the exception of a few selected Japanese and European partners, Boeing did much of the design and engineering for its aircraft in-house. Emerging economies hardly showed up on Boeing's radar as sources of engineering and research talent. But this situation began to change when the airline industry went into a tailspin following the events of September 11, 2001. Boeing's sales crashed, and it was forced to cut costs. To reduce development costs, Boeing began to move some low-level engineering tasks like validation, verification, and testing to low-cost geographic areas like India.

With the 787 Dreamliner project, Boeing has made dramatic strides in taking its innovation process global and tapping into talent from emerging economies. Boeing is now involving Indian IT firms in end-to-end system design work—from systems requirements definition, design, testing, certification, and support. In a landmark agreement signed in early 2005 with Boeing, HCL Technologies, an Indian IT and engineering services company, was selected to provide diverse technologies for the various 787 avionics systems including the Airborne Collision Avoidance system, display systems, crew alerting systems, proximity warning systems, ground-based software tools, and the auxiliary power unit. Boeing has also partnered with the Indian Institute of Science, Bangalore, to conduct research in aerospace materials, structures, and manufacturing technologies. These partnerships are not about cost-cutting and they do not involve low-skilled jobs. They are partnerships to drive innovation, and they demand very highly skilled engineers and aerospace scientists.

So far in this book, we have focused on the search for creativity outside the boundaries of the firm. But, as the Boeing example suggests, the Global Brain also transcends the boundaries of geography. In particular, there is vast untapped brain power in the emerging BRIC economies of Brazil, Russia, India, and China. As recently as a decade or so ago, geographical barriers prevented firms operating in the United States and Western Europe from reaching out to the global talent pool in countries such as India, China, and Russia. In recent years, advances in Internet and communications technologies have dramatically changed this picture. The Global Brain can now be accessed effortlessly over a wire halfway across the world.

In the words of Tom Friedman, the best-selling author and the leading chronicler of globalization, we now live in a "flat world"—an interconnected world where the competitive playing field is being leveled with the advances of information technology, bringing emerging economies like India and China onto the world stage.[1] Although one can get carried away by the breathless hype of journalists and analysts about the rise of emerging economies, there is no doubt that network-centric innovation is rapidly becoming a global phenomenon. More importantly, companies in the emerging economies have the potential to play important roles in such global network-centric innovation initiatives.

What are the trends driving the globalization of innovation? What types of partners can firms tap into as they seek to globalize their innovation efforts? What are the opportunities for companies in countries such as India and China to participate in the various forms of global network-centric innovation? How should companies prepare for such global innovation opportunities? These are the questions that we consider in this chapter.

THE DRAGON AND THE TIGER: RISE OF CHINA AND INDIA

Almost 40% of the world's population lives in China and India. This fact has two important implications for global commerce. On the demand side, these countries are swiftly becoming the most important markets in the world for a wide range of products and services. On the supply side, these countries have already become the most important source for technical and scientific talent. Let's look at these trends in turn.

CONSUMERISM IN THE EMERGING ECONOMIES: THE MASS CLASS

An important hallmark of any rapidly developing economy is its prodigious appetite for consumer products and services. Consumerism has taken on new dimensions in most of the emerging economies, particularly in India and China. Indeed, it has led to the emergence of a new class of consumer that has been termed the *MASS class*: "the hundreds of millions of global consumers who are now unified in their quest for the best deals on offer on a global scale in virtually each B2C category."[2] How big is this MASS class? Consider some statistics.

It is projected that by 2015 more than 800 million people in the BRIC countries will have an annual income that is above $3,000 and by 2025, approximately 200 million will have an annual income above $15,000. Such projections imply a massive surge in demand for all types of consumer products—basic goods such as refrigerators, air conditioners, cell phones, and TV sets as well as higher-priced branded and luxury products ranging from Mercedes cars to Armani clothes and gold jewelry.

This consumer demand is already evident. In 2006, India's middle-income group was pegged at approximately 260 million, representing about 25% of the overall population. This number is expected to grow to 628 million by 2015. This middle class is largely responsible for the current $450 billion Indian consumer goods market (approximately 65% of the total GDP).

An important part of the Indian consumer class is the young and educated population—people less than 30 years of age and working in knowledge-intensive sectors such as information technology (IT) and business process outsourcing (BPO). These young and educated workers earning an average of $600 a month—a relatively high income in India—might form the driving force of consumerism in India. With around 2 million of these people spending more than a billion and half dollars every month, the demand for offerings ranging from designer jeans and cosmetics to computers and cars have increased exponentially.

This surging demand for consumer products in the emerging economies has created important market opportunities for foreign companies. One company that understands the implications of the expanding consumerism of the BRIC countries is Ikea, the Swedish furniture giant. The company has opened mega stores in countries such as China and Russia. In China itself, the company expects to have a total of 10 new stores by 2010—in Beijing, Guangdong, and Shanghai's Pudong New District.

In many of these emerging economies, people are also hungry for information, creating new opportunities for Western media companies, too. For example, the Iowa-based media conglomerate Meredith Corp. launched an India edition of its best-selling women's magazine, *Better Homes and Gardens*, in early 2007. Similarly, Conde Nast Publications Inc., the New York-based media giant, has decided to publish an Indian edition of *Vogue* magazine.

The emergence of the MASS class thus implies new market opportunities for multinational consumer companies, such as Ikea, P&G, and J&J—also calling for the creation of new innovative offerings tailored to these markets. However, this demand for innovation—driven by the consumerism of the BRIC countries—also has a flip side. The rapidly expanding base of quality- and trend-conscious consumers in India, China, and Russia also presents another opportunity for companies, one that is directly related to network-centric innovation. Specifically, the emerging MASS class represents a large and growing pool of innovators whose creativity and talent is waiting to be tapped.

DEEP TECHNOLOGICAL AND SCIENTIFIC TALENT

The emerging economies, particularly in India, China, and Russia, have also become a deep reservoir of technological and scientific expertise in fields such as computer science, mathematics, biotechnology, medicine, and environmental science.

Many of the Western economies are facing the effects of an older and shrinking workforce—a rapidly depleting pool of scientists and technologists. On the other hand, in countries such as India and China, the number of graduates in technical and engineering programs continues to expand exponentially.

Consider some numbers to put things in perspective. India has 270 universities and several world-class engineering and research institutions. In 2005, India produced 220,000 engineers with four-year degrees, and 195,000 engineers with three-year diplomas. In China, the annual output of engineering institutions is close to 640,000 graduates (of which approximately 350,000 are from bachelor-level degree programs and the remainder from associate-equivalent programs). By comparison, U.S. institutions graduate only about 70,000 engineering students annually and European Union institutions together graduate approximately 100,000 students.[3,4]

It is, thus, now widely acknowledged that the balance of the global labor supply has shifted to the emerging economies. In the future, this shift is likely to become even more skewed. For example, it has been projected that 97% of the 438 million people to be added to the global workforce by 2050 will come from developing countries.[5] Consequently, the competition for such global talent has become more intense—as Western multinationals as well as indigenous companies in these emerging economies try to tap into these new sources of talent.

However, it is not just the run-of-the-mill engineering or scientific talent that these countries now possess. They are also becoming the source of more specialized technological and scientific expertise. For example, Russia has an abundance of rocket scientists who are capable of doing very high-end mathematics with wide ranging applications—in financial and securities industry, software industry, and biotechnology. Russia is becoming a rich source of talent in a niche area—complex mathematics and computing. Similarly, with a rapidly growing talent base for R&D in microprocessors, India has evolved into a global center for high-end microprocessor design.

The importance of this combination of both general and niche technological and scientific talent for Western multinationals is perhaps quite evident. For example, India is already home to R&D centers of more than 125 Fortune 500 companies. However, this vast talent base also poses important opportunities for companies in these very same countries—opportunities for assuming important roles in global network-centric innovation initiatives.

NON-PROFIT AND NON-GOVERNMENTAL ORGANIZATIONS

A third trend evident in the BRIC countries is the rapid emergence of a new type of player capable of participating in the global innovation initiatives—non-profit and non-governmental organizations.

The market openness and the embracing of global capitalism in the BRIC countries has also been accompanied by the birth of a host of non-profit and non-governmental organizations (NGOs) to champion the interests of varied stakeholders in the society. Many of the NGOs were established over the years to protest skewed regional development plans or corporate policies that negatively impact certain sections of the society and to promote sustainable development policies and initiatives. For example, NGOs' efforts have focused on liability in the case of oil spills, child labor, violation of human rights in certain industries, food quality standards, and so on.

Over the last several years, however, many of these same NGOs have evolved and adopted a more open agenda that includes partnership with corporate entities to promote or advance mutually beneficial social and economic goals.[6]

For example, consider the initiatives pursued by Hewlett Packard's Emerging Market Solutions (EMS) unit.[7] The EMS team launched HP's i-community (inclusion community) program to develop and introduce IT solutions that are particularly relevant for emerging markets and directly support social and economic development. In India, the company partnered with NGOs to support the operation of a community information center (CIC) in the remote town of Kuppam in the state of Tamil Nadu. Similarly, in South Africa, the company partnered with the International Computer Driving License (ICDL) Foundation, an NGO, to establish a training and testing center for Open Source Software at the Mogalakwena HP i-community.

Similarly, Microsoft's partnership with the Indian NGO Pratham to diffuse computer technology in Indian villages, Nestlé's partnership with NGOs in Peru to distribute nutritionally fortified food products to the poor, and ABN AMRO's partnership with NGO Accion International to pursue microfinance business in Latin America all indicate how the convergence of the goals and objectives of corporate organizations and NGOs can lead to unique opportunities for value creation in the emerging economies. As the number and the diversity of the NGOs in the emerging economies increase, companies are likely to find a wider range of such partnership opportunities—partnerships that extend to network-centric innovation initiatives, too.

EMERGING ECONOMIES AND NETWORK-CENTRIC INNOVATION OPPORTUNITIES

These trends evident in the emerging economies tell us about the valuable roles companies in these countries can play in network-centric innovation. Let us explore some of these opportunities in more detail by going through the four models of network-centric innovation.

OPPORTUNITIES RELATED TO THE ORCHESTRA MODEL

As we discussed in Chapter 5, "The Orchestra Model," companies can either play a leading role (for example, platform leader) or an adaptor role in the Orchestra model. Given the highly specialized expertise and competencies evident in the companies in the emerging economies, we believe the *adapter* role (complementor, innovator) promises the best opportunity for these companies to participate in network-centric innovation.

Companies can leverage their capabilities in niche technology areas to make unique value contributions as a *complementor* to a platform-based global innovation network. HCL Technologies, a leading India-based IT services company, provides a good illustration of this role.

HCL Technologies is part of HCL Enterprise, a $2.7 billion global technology behemoth founded in 1976 as one of India's first IT garage startups. The company has a wide range of offerings, much of it relating to software-led IT solutions, business process outsourcing, and infrastructure management. A key part of its business focuses on R&D services, particularly in the semiconductors and the telecom sectors.

Over the years, the company has acquired considerable expertise on VLSI and hardware design by working on system design solutions for vertical industries such as consumer electronics and telecom. Drawing on its unique internal expertise, the company recently decided to focus on building add-on and complementary solutions for IBM's Power Architecture. In 2005, the company opened a Power Architecture Design Center (the first such outside IBM's own walls) that offers System-on-Chip (SoC) solutions on the Power platform for a wide range of original equipment manufacturers (OEMs). To do this, the company sublicenses IBM's PowerPC 405 and PowerPC 440 embedded microprocessor cores, and then builds on them to create innovative offerings tailored for specific markets. Thus, in this initiative, HCL's focus is to play the role of a complementor—by bringing its unique technological expertise in semiconductor design to expand the reach of IBM's Power Architecture to areas such as consumer devices and wireless networking. Such an approach that involves channeling specialized expertise to advance the innovation agenda of a platform leader is one that would be of particular appeal to companies in the emerging economies.

Similarly, many companies in countries such as India, Russia, and China have expertise in niche areas that can be effectively deployed to play the role of an *innovator* in the Orchestra-Integrator model of network-centric innovation. For example, in the beginning of this chapter, we described how HCL Technologies plays such a role as an innovator in Boeing's 787 Dreamliner project by contributing software technology components.

Wipro, an Indian technology services conglomerate, offers another example of the innovator role. The company has set up a 10,000-strong Product Engineering Solutions (PES) group that offers high-end R&D services in niche areas to clients in a wide range of industries—from semiconductor and consumer electronics to automotive and medical devices. Much of its offerings relate to playing the role of an innovator by putting to use its extended engineering capabilities. For example, recently a U.S.-based gaming device vendor wanted to develop a high-performance accelerator chip as part of its next-generation product. Instead of establishing an in-house hardware team, the company tapped into Wipro's deep expertise in VLSI design and its EagleWision design methodology that aims to reduce iterations in the design of silicon chips. The client firm integrated Wipro's capabilities with its own proprietary architecture to define the SoC, design it, and test it. Wipro's engineers were able to produce a zero-defect chip sample in just 15 months, thereby helping the client firm to reduce the cycle time by four to five months.[8]

Still another example of such an adapter role is provided by the pharmaceutical industry. Clinical trials—testing new medications for safety and efficacy in human patients to gain the required approvals from government agencies—form an important, expensive, and time-consuming phase in the development of new drugs. The potential to leverage specialized capabilities and expertise resident in countries such as India in clinical trials have attracted a host of large pharma companies. For example, Wyeth Pharmaceuticals Inc. has partnered with Accenture's Life Sciences Center in Bangalore to enhance its clinical trials.[9] A comprehensive team of India-based Accenture life sciences experts—medical doctors, PhDs, pharmacists, statisticians, and so on—work on the design, development, execution, and the reporting of clinical trials for clients like Wyeth. Similarly, SIRO Clinpham is an Indian CRO (contract research organization), established in 1996, that offers a full-suite of specialist services in clinical trials to cater to global biotechnology and pharmaceutical companies.[10] It leverages its strong capabilities in clinical trials to plug into the drug development projects of large pharma companies and help them accelerate the development process as well as reduce the development costs. In the case of Wyeth, its partnership with Accenture helped the company reduce the average time to prepare clinical trial reports from six months to a few weeks—each day saved translates into a savings of about $1 million in development cost.

OPPORTUNITIES RELATED TO THE CREATIVE BAZAAR MODEL

Rapidly increasing consumerism in the emerging economies holds two implications for companies—one very obvious and the other less obvious. First, it is very evident that the MASS class is driving the demand for innovative products and services; that is, innovative offerings that are tailored to fit the needs of the emerging markets. Second, the increasing number of knowledgeable and articulate customers in these markets also indicates the considerable potential for companies to source innovative ideas from these very same markets. This second implication might be less obvious today, but may have far-reaching significance in the future. Cost-effective innovations created in emerging economies might find a home in the markets of the developed nations. Let us examine this implication in more detail and understand the opportunities that this presents to companies.

The MASS class in countries such as India and China has attracted a horde of Western companies to these markets. However, some of the early initiatives of these firms ended up as failures that on further analysis indicate a lack of understanding of the market needs. For example, consider Kellogg's first foray into the Indian market in 1995 with its Corn Flakes product. Despite a well-known brand name and a reasonably priced product, the results were quite disappointing. Sales were less than 20% of the initial target. What went wrong? The company overlooked a simple fact. Indians prefer hot milk in their cereal and a product made for cold milk was not very appealing. It was only when it realized this and revamped its product that Kellogg found success in the Indian market.

These and other such examples (for example, McDonald's introduction of "Maharaja Mac," and so on) indicate the need for companies—both foreign and domestic—to carefully understand the unique needs of these emerging markets and to innovate before trying to push products and brands that have found success elsewhere. These examples also indicate the critical importance of the vast and diverse set of customer innovators in these markets whose ideas and insights can be tapped to create the new offerings. Further, ideas sourced from such customers (and amateur inventors) might even have wider appeal to other markets.

This opportunity has important implications for large companies that might play the role of an *innovation portal*. For example, in India, companies such as

Hindustan Lever Limited (a Unilever subsidiary in India), the Tata Group, and Reliance Industries with long-term presence and well-developed brand image in the local markets are particularly well suited to pursue such opportunities. These companies have the capabilities and the infrastructure to seek out innovative ideas and technologies from independent inventors and commercialize them for local as well as global markets.

However, as we saw in Chapter 6, "The Creative Bazaar Model," to be an effective innovation portal, large companies need the help of smaller companies that can play the role of innovation intermediaries. Intermediaries such as *idea brokers* and *innovation capitalists* can source innovative ideas from inventor networks, mediate the interactions with large companies, and add value to the innovation process. Unlike the North American context, in the emerging economies very few such entities exist, and as such, we believe this presents a promising opportunity for small companies to play a role in network-centric innovation.

Consider Ideawicket, a New Delhi-based innovation intermediary launched in early 2007. The young company focuses on playing the role of an idea broker— it allows independent inventors to post their innovative ideas on its Web portal and then provides companies (subscribers) access to those ideas. As the inventor networks established by companies such as Ideawicket expand, the opportunities for companies to tap into such consumer creativity in the emerging economies will also grow.

Small firms that already play complementary activities in this space—market research firms, innovation consulting firms, and so on—might also be uniquely positioned to assume such intermediary roles given their knowledge of the customers in these countries. They would need to develop deeper relationships with customer networks and with amateur inventors, and as we described in detail in Chapter 6, they can gain several insights from the experience of U.S.-based innovation intermediaries such as BIG, Evergreen IP, and Ignite IP.

The promise of sourcing innovation extends beyond the consumer product sector to technology-based products, too. For example, consider the software industry in Russia. With so many small software startups and highly sophisticated talent, there are bound to be a number of innovative product and technology ideas that have not progressed due to lack of commercialization expertise and resources. Innovation intermediaries that are able to seek out such ideas and bring them to the attention of global software vendors might be able to pursue a very useful and profitable business in IP placement. Such an opportunity is not, however, limited to the software industry. Technology-based industries ranging from environmental management, energy, and telecom to medical devices and aerospace are also prime contexts for launching such IP placement businesses.

OPPORTUNITIES RELATED TO THE JAM CENTRAL MODEL

As we noted previously, one of the hallmarks of the emerging economies is the large number of technologists and scientists in varied fields. This vast scientific resource presents numerous opportunities for community-led innovation initiatives that are focused on solving problems unique to the emerging economies. In facilitating and supporting such community-led innovation initiatives, companies as well as non-profit organizations can play a very valuable role as innovation sponsors (for example, by providing access to varied resources including computing capacity, knowledge bases, innovation tools, infrastructure, and so on).

Many of the issues that countries such as India and China face relate to providing better infrastructure to their vast population—from drinking water to health care and education. Most such issues demand unique solutions— solutions that leverage local resources and capabilities in a cost-effective manner.

Many NGOs and other such agencies are involved in addressing these challenges. However, as these entities have realized, the critical factor in addressing such challenges is not just the availability of financial or technological resources but the ingenuity and innovativeness that can be harnessed from the "community" in order to come up with novel solutions. Thus, the key task is to fashion the right environment for the community to come together and contribute toward such innovative solutions.

C.K. Prahalad's recent work focused on the partnerships between corporate organizations and NGOs in emerging economies to develop new businesses aimed at the markets at the "bottom of the pyramid."[11] We believe NGOs and companies can extend such partnerships to network-centric innovation initiatives by sponsoring and supporting such community innovation initiatives that might have both social and economic goals.

In assuming such a role as innovation sponsor, both NGOs as well as corporate entities would need to bring unique capabilities to advance the community-based innovation agenda. NGOs can bring their extensive reach into the community that faces the particular issue and is likely to benefit from the innovation. They can also bring significant credibility to the innovation initiative, thereby appealing to and attracting the community members who are likely to contribute to the innovation. On the other hand, corporate organizations can bring particular expertise and technologies to organize and facilitate the community interactions. They can also bring capabilities that would support the development and the implementation of the innovation.

Recall the Tropical Disease Initiative (TDI) discussed in Chapter 7, "The Jam Central Model." One of the project ideas in the TDI relates to a disease called Chagas—a human tropical parasitic disease that plagues South America. Because it is a highly localized disease and one that doesn't have the same visibility as, say, malaria, it doesn't attract the attention and focus of researchers worldwide. This is a situation where NGOs and corporate organizations could step in to help sponsor or support the innovation activities. For example, NGOs in countries affected by this disease (for example, Venezuela) would be well positioned to reach out to the affected communities and help close the gap between the researchers participating in the TDI and these communities. Pharmaceutical companies, on the other hand, can sponsor or champion such research initiatives by providing access to related proprietary databases or making available particular research tools or technologies.

With a diverse set of issues and challenges being taken up by such community-led innovation initiatives in the emerging economies, the opportunities for companies and NGOs to assume the role of innovation sponsor and partner with one another are also likely to be equally diverse.

OPPORTUNITIES RELATED TO THE MOD STATION MODEL

Finally, technology and innovation platforms that have been "opened" up for community-based initiatives also present unique opportunities to small companies in the emerging economies to participate as *innovators* in the MOD Station model of network-centric innovation.

Many small companies in these countries possess valuable expertise in one or more niche areas that are related to such technology platforms and can contribute to the innovation initiatives. For example, as you saw in Chapter 8, "The MOD ("MODification") Station Model," some of the innovator participants in Sun's OpenSPARC initiative are small companies based in Europe.

Similarly, consider SugarCRM—the California-based company that offers commercial and open source solutions in the customer relationship management area. Apart from the commercial (proprietary) version of its flagship CRM solution, the company also offers an open source version (Sugar OpenSource) that depends on the contributions of the global software development community. The Sugar CRM community has grown to more than 7,000 external contributors, many of them in the emerging economies. Community members can contribute to the core open source product itself or they can contribute to the add-on modules and other extensions to the open source product. Such add-on modules and extensions enhance the reach and capabilities of the core product—for example, porting the product to other platforms and languages. Small firms (as well as individuals) in the emerging economies have been instrumental in making translation of the Sugar CRM open source product into more than 40 different languages around the world, thereby facilitating easier use of the product in countries such as India, China, Russia, and Korea. In many cases, these contributors have not only gained visibility but also attracted additional consulting and service projects from companies using the SugarCRM solutions.

Such examples indicate the potential for technology firms in countries such as India and China to plug into such global "open" innovation networks and garner global visibility and exposure that might in turn lead to other innovation opportunities with more direct economic returns.

GLOBAL INNOVATION NETWORKS WITH "CHINDIA" AS A HUB

In discussing globalization of network-centric innovation, our primary focus has been on understanding the specific roles and network-centric innovation opportunities for companies in the emerging economies, such as India and China. However, there is something deeper and broader at work. We are witnessing a global restructuring of research and development activities in corporations, resulting in the creation of global innovation networks. No longer is R&D geographically confined to Redmond (in the case of Microsoft), Tokyo (in the case of Sony), or Munich (in the case of Siemens). Global corporations are creating "centers of excellence" within specific geographies that take advantage of innovation-related capabilities that can be sourced locally and be relevant to local markets. These geographically distributed centers of excellence, created in collaboration with a network of local partners, can then be stitched together to create a global network of innovation.

The computer industry offers an excellent example of these global networks in action. In the laptop computer market, name-brand manufacturers such as HP, IBM, and Apple have for some time relied on global innovation networks to design (yes, design!), develop, and manufacture their products. The case of Quanta Computer illustrates how such networks evolve and operate.

Quanta Computer is a Taipei-based company, established in 1988, that specializes in the design and development of laptop/notebook computers.[12] The company has a 3,500-strong in-house design and engineering team that churns out fully functioning prototypes of new laptop/notebook computer models. The objective is not to design the next radical product. Instead, the focus is on designing and developing the *next version* of the laptop or the notebook computer. Client firms, which include large U.S. computer vendors, chose their models from these prototypes designed by Quanta. After the model is picked by a client firm, Quanta will also manage the manufacturing and logistics activities. The company doesn't do the manufacturing itself. Instead, it parcels out the job to a network of manufacturers, most of them based in China. By leveraging its design capabilities and by establishing and coordinating such a global innovation network, Quanta has been able to become the world's largest original design manufacturer (ODM) for notebook computers.

Increasingly this model is emerging in other industries, too—notably, in consumer electronics, pharmaceuticals, and the automotive industry. OfficeMax, the third-largest office products retailer in the United States with annual sales of $9 billion, is a good illustration of a global innovation network in action.[13] OfficeMax has embarked on an aggressive private label strategy in an effort to differentiate itself from competitors like Staples and Office Depot. Private label products command much higher margins than national brands, because the retailer does not have to pay the brand premium for national brands. Traditionally, private label products are sold primarily on price and are labeled with the retailer's brand. OfficeMax was no exception. Most of its private label products were imitations of national brands, most were sourced from overseas suppliers who serve the entire industry, and almost all of them were labeled with the OfficeMax store name. But OfficeMax wanted to do something different. It decided to create a new brand from the ground up, and to control the entire process from inception through design and production. The way OfficeMax went about this process illustrates the power of global innovation networks.

There were three actors in the project to create OfficeMax's first design-based private label brand, TUL—a selection of new premium Modernist design–inspired pens and dry-erase markers. OfficeMax provided the expertise in merchandising and retailing. The second actor was Gravity Tank, a Chicago-based design consulting firm that OfficeMax hired to provide the expertise in customer insights, industrial design, and brand identity. Gravity Tank conducted ethnographic research observing a variety of external office workers, talking with office managers who bought stationery supplies in bulk, and speaking to store clerks and customers alike. This research led to the insight of creating a line of writing instruments that would serve the goal of "everyday premium"—instruments that would be an expression of personality and would create the personal attachment that people felt towards very expensive fountain pens to the lower-end roller ball pens. The third set of actors was the Chinese companies who were experts at low-cost high-quality manufacturing and logistics. OfficeMax and Gravity Tank communicated the unique design and identity of the TUL line to the suppliers, who would otherwise have created look-alike pens with identical parts that they sell to all retailers, with the only difference being the retailer's logo emblazoned on the side.

A combination of the retailing skills of OfficeMax, the design skills of Gravity Tank and the manufacturing skills of Chinese suppliers allowed OfficeMax to create a proprietary brand that has become a strong differentiator for them, because it is designed and developed by the retailer, and is available exclusively at OfficeMax stores. This example shows the power of network-centric innovation in the global context. As the OfficeMax case shows, globalizing network-centric innovation not only takes advantage of the network partners' differential innovation capabilities and talent (as in traditional NCI), but also of their lower cost structure due to the geographic location. In effect, the model illustrates the potential for "global resource arbitrage" in network-centric innovation. The benefits of resource arbitrage can either be millions of dollars in product development savings and/or weeks and months shaved from the product development time.

As the quality, diversity, and the sophistication of R&D services available from India and China rapidly increase, we are likely to see more and more global network-centric innovation initiatives centered on service offerings. For example, by the end of 2007, fully 31% of global R&D staff will be in India and China.[14] Similarly, according to a recent study by Booz Allen Hamilton and NASSCOM (India's software industry association), India could capture as much as 25% to 30% of the world's engineering services market, which would mean $50 billion in services related to engineering, design, and R&D.[15] And China is not far behind.

All of these examples point to the incorporation of India-China (or "Chindia"[16]) as an important hub in global innovation networks, as well as an increasing effort to integrate the complementary R&D and engineering services from these two countries to create innovative offerings rapidly and cost effectively for the global market.

PREPARING FOR THESE GLOBAL OPPORTUNITIES

Many of the trends and the related opportunities that we have discussed till now are unfolding right now in these economies. The interesting question then is, how should companies prepare for such global innovation opportunities?

In Chapter 9, "Deciding Where and How to Play," and Chapter 10, "Preparing the Organization," we discussed in detail the various issues related to organizational preparedness for network-centric innovation. All these issues assume relevance in the globalization context, too.

Companies first need to carefully examine and decide what specific innovation role they can play in such global networks given their unique resources and capabilities. We highlighted some of the more relevant roles for companies situated in the emerging economies. Managers need to examine the appropriateness of such roles and understand the underlying issues and challenges. For example, as we discussed in Chapter 9, companies that are exploring the potential to play adaptor roles need to examine two key issues. One is determining the *nature of the connection* between a company's specialized capability (that is, its contribution) and the network (or the innovation platform). The second consideration in evaluating the adapter role should be the potential to acquire additional expertise from their interactions with other network members—in other words, what is the learning opportunity? This issue is particularly important for companies in the emerging economies as participation in global network-centric innovation initiatives might pave the way for the acquisition of new capabilities and diversification of offerings.

Plugging into the global network-centric innovation initiatives requires more than just technical or engineering expertise. It also requires organizational and management capabilities that enable the company to operate effectively in the network and to appropriate the value generated. In Chapter 10, we discussed the related issues ranging from organizational culture and structure to innovation processes and technologies/tools. These issues assume relevance here, too.

For example, consider relational skills. Many of the companies in the emerging economies possess limited collaborative experience, particularly with regard to participating in large innovation networks that cross national boundaries. Mismanaging the challenges related to regional cultural issues could impede a company's success in participating in a network-centric innovation initiative. Thus, companies need to invest considerable time and resources to develop appropriate relationship management capabilities.

Similarly, many of the smaller companies might also lack formal internal innovation management systems and processes and might be faced with steep learning curves associated with participation in large-scale collaborative technology development projects. As we discussed in earlier chapters, harmonization of the innovation processes across the network members is important and assumes greater significance when such networks are global in scope. All of these issues indicate the need to carefully identify the requisite capabilities appropriate to the role (described in detail in Chapter 10) and to develop them.

CONCLUSION

Much has been written in recent years about the burgeoning impact of countries such as India and China on the world economy. For example, a 2004 Goldman Sachs report[17] projected that the BRIC economies' share of world growth would rise from 20% in 2003 to more than 40% in 2025. The same report also projected that their total weight in the world economy (expressed as a share of the global market capitalization) would rise from approximately 10% in 2004 to more than 20% in 2025. Such predictions help to underline the path of rapid growth and development that these countries are on. However, what is perhaps even more evident right now is the impact of these countries on global innovation.

In this chapter, we outlined the different ways in which global network-centric innovation initiatives could incorporate the capabilities and expertise resident in the emerging economies. The specific implementation of these different innovation roles might evolve over the years as companies experiment with different business models. However, one fact remains certain—emerging economies, led by India and China, will become central players in creating global networks of innovation in coming years.

12

Concluding Thoughts and Actions for "Monday" Morning...

We started this book by outlining the innovation crisis that many companies are facing as a result of declining R&D productivity on the one hand and the quickening pace of competition on the other hand. Companies such as Dell, Kraft, and Merck are grappling with the innovation crisis. While these high-profile companies have gotten a lot of press because they have fallen on hard times, the innovation crisis is not limited to a few large companies. Indeed, companies large and small across a wide range of industries are facing similar problems.

Is your company facing an innovation crisis? Ask yourself the following questions:

■ Have you seen a steep increase in new product development costs in recent years?

■ Are you seeing a decline in the productivity of R&D dollars spent by your company?

■ Are you faced with shrinking life cycles for your products?

■ Are your products getting commoditized faster than in the past?

■ Is your commercialization cost for new offerings at least twice that of the best-in-class competitor?

- Is your concept-to-commercialization time at least twice as long as the best-in-class competitor?

- Are you faced with unfamiliar competitors from China and India who have significantly lower development and manufacturing costs than your company?

- Are you finding it more difficult and more expensive to hire high-quality engineering and scientific talent?

- Are you finding that, even with a bigger number of projects in your pipeline, you are not able to deliver enough "hit" products to the market?

- Overall, are you finding that your innovation process is not up to meeting investor growth expectations?

If you answered "yes" to a majority of these questions, welcome to the innovation crisis. You are joining the ranks of companies like Motorola, which has seen the price of its wildly popular Razr phone plummet from a high of $500 when the phone was introduced in November 2004, to $200 in mid-2005, and finally to less than $50 by the end of 2006. In the last quarter of 2006, Motorola sold 48% more Razr phones than in the year-ago quarter, but its revenues still fell. To stem the erosion, Motorola introduced a follow-up product called the Krzr, but this was seen as an incremental product that got commoditized even faster. The result—the very future of Motorola is at stake. Remember the Red Queen effect that we described in Chapter 1, "The Power of Network-Centricity"? This is an example of the Red Queen effect in action.

Or perhaps your company is like General Motors, which offers the lowest-priced car in the United States, the $10,560 Chevrolet Aveo, while an Indian auto company, Tata Motors, is working on a car that it aims to sell for $2,500. The "people's car," being developed with the ingenuity of Indian automotive engineers and the dramatically lower development costs in India, might rival the Ford Model T or the Volkswagen Beetle as a breakthrough in affordability and be responsible for bringing millions of new customers into the automobile market.[1] Although the tiny and underpowered Tata car might never be sold in the United States, Tata Motors will certainly learn valuable lessons it can put to use in creating cheaper cars targeted at Western markets. This is the face of global competition.

The multiple dimensions of the innovation crisis—cost, time to market, quality, creativity—combine to create a multiplier effect that can jeopardize your company's future. To secure its future, you need to look outside your firm for ideas, technologies, and products. You need to harness the power of the Global

Brain to improve the reach, increase the speed, and reduce the cost of your innovation process. You need to choose and implement network-centric innovation models and roles that are most appropriate for your company.

The core argument of our book is that tapping into the Global Brain is no longer a matter of choice. It is more a question of *how*, rather than whether, a company should pursue a network-centric innovation strategy. This sense of crisis is what has stoked executive management's interest in network-centric innovation initiatives, evidenced in the urgent call for action issued by several high-profile CEOs.

The CEO is who should begin the journey towards network-centric innovation, so it is fitting that we conclude the book by focusing in this chapter on the role of the CEO in communicating a sense of crisis to the organization and evangelizing or building the faith in network-centric innovation initiatives.

We take a step back by reflecting on some of the core themes and practices that underlie network-centric innovation—themes and practices that reflect the insights and the wisdom distilled from experiences of the firms and the managers that we have interacted with while researching this book. Some of these experiences were successes whereas others ended in failure. As such, they capture practices that can significantly advance a company's innovation initiative as well as those that might remove potential barriers to success.

EVANGELIZE AND "BUILD THE FAITH"

A theme that has surfaced repeatedly in our discussions with managers across companies and industries is the central role of the CEO in "building the faith" in the organization about looking outside the organization for ideas and partnering with external actors and communities to further the firm's innovation agenda.

In many large companies, this has taken the form of the CEO setting out explicit goals related to network-centric innovation. Companies such as DuPont, P&G, Staples, and IBM come to mind. In some of these cases, the CEO's goals have gotten wider visibility in the business community.

However, as the phrase *build the faith* indicates, the CEO's role goes beyond just setting goals related to how much innovation should be sourced from outside or how much new revenue should be generated from network-centric innovation initiatives. CEOs need to champion a new set of beliefs that might initially be perceived as heretical and generate stiff internal resistance. Often, internal resistance comes from senior managers—people who have the power and the motive to sabotage the initiatives.

Overcoming this internal resistance is what Sam Palmisano, the CEO of IBM, had to do when its "Global Innovation Outlook" (GIO) was conceived in early 2004. The idea that IBM would open its technology and business forecasting processes to a broad set of clients and partners seemed heretical and attracted plenty of resistance when it was first proposed. David Yaun, the vice president for corporate communication at IBM, recalls initial response ranged from comments that ridiculed the value of the idea to suggestions that the team behind the GIO would damage IBM's credibility and brand image.[2] Some managers felt that "We already do this," while others opined, "What you're doing is very dangerous. I won't stand for it." One executive "forbid" the team from contacting "*my* clients" and a senior researcher was even more caustic, noting that, "My job is to prevent you from embarrassing our chairman."

Palmisano played a crucial role in "pushing" the organization to accept these initiatives. He strongly endorsed the initiative and gave the GIO team their marching orders. He pushed them to slash the proposed time for implementing the GIO initiative from 18 months to 5 months, and suggested to the team that, if at any time they felt comfortable with their progress, then their approach was wrong—in other words, they would be playing it too safe. To overcome internal objections, he steered away from a mandate. Instead, he gave the team flexible funding, freedom to experiment (and fail), and most important, constituted an executive sponsor board (including some of the original skeptics) to steer the initiative—in effect, giving them a personal stake in its success. This approach signaled the seriousness of the initiative in the chairman's perspective, and went a long way in shaping the thinking of the organization in the right direction. The IBM experience illustrates how a CEO has to be the "sword and the shield" for opening up the company's innovation efforts and shifting to a more network-centric approach.

Another dimension of building the faith is providing the *right perspective* for the organization to view external innovation opportunities. The evangelization efforts initiated by the CEO's office should also incorporate a broad outline of questions that managers need to consider in embarking on network-centric innovation initiatives. For example, what are the broad parameters on which the organization is committing itself to explore network-centric innovation initiatives? Are there certain models of network-centric innovation that the organization will not pursue? Is the organization going to partner with non-traditional partners (for example, non-profit organizations, individual inventors, and so on)? How much control and influence is the organization willing to "let go" of in these initiatives? Will this approach be broadly applied or largely limited to those business divisions in new or emerging markets?

Addressing such questions early helps managers evaluate the extent of organizational commitment on network-centric innovation as well as understand the "hows" and the "whys" that underlie such commitment. As one manager put it to us, "Goals are important. However, we have lot of 'goals' floating around in our company at any one time. So one more set of goals is not going to be very useful. What we need is a framework or a mental model for us to approach this issue uniformly. And I believe that it is the job of the CEO to provide this framework."

In short, public announcements of organizational aspirations regarding network-centric innovation is only one part (perhaps the more visible part), but the more important task for the CEO is to set out the broad approach in a way that really helps build the faith of the organization in external innovation initiatives.

"ENGAGE" THE ENTIRE ORGANIZATION

As we have seen in exploring the four models of network-centric innovation, the opportunities for leading or participating in network-centric innovation can emanate from different types of external entities—individual inventors, innovation capitalists and other such intermediaries, customers, technology partners, suppliers, non-profit organizations, and so on. Further, these different external entities typically come into contact with different parts of the organization— marketing, R&D, business development, procurement and so on. As such, it is important to "engage" the entire organization in the effort to identify and evaluate the different network-centric innovation opportunities, even if there is one unit assigned with the responsibility to coordinate the different initiatives.

The first step in engaging the organization is to get the message about network-centric innovation out to every corner of the organization. Although this step can partly be accomplished by the CEO's evangelization efforts, these efforts need to be supplemented with a more extensive information campaign. For example, in the case of 3M, this job has largely been the responsibility of its corporate R&D unit. As Robert Finnochiaro, 3M's corporate technical director told us, "Our task in the last couple of years has been to complement the work done by our senior management and to get everybody in the organization, particularly all of our business divisions and their local R&D units, on the same page."

Another approach to drive broader engagement is to deploy the network-based strategy inside your organization first. When IBM sought to promote its Innovation Jam initiative—an "online brainstorming session" to mine new and innovative business ideas and opportunities—it conducted the first Jam experiment in 2003 by involving its own employees. The objective of this "Values Jam" was to identify the core values of the organization and to develop a consensus around the core values. After the first Jam was deemed successful, IBM refocused the Jam on innovation, calling it the Innovation Jam, and expanded the participants to include its ecosystem partners—customers, suppliers, and so on. The objective of the second Innovation Jam, conducted in 2006, was to identify emerging technology trends in the key markets that mattered to IBM. In the next round, IBM expanded the boundaries further by focusing the Innovation Jam on specific industries and audiences. For example, in March 2007, it conducted an Innovation Jam focused on the automotive industry called the Automotive Supplier Jam. This initiative brought together individuals from supplier organizations as well as from OEMs, government, academia, industry associations, and others affiliated with the automotive supplier segment. More than 2,000 people from 150 organizations and 17 countries participated in the Automotive Supplier Jam on topics like program lifecycle profitability, creating an innovative culture, and embracing green technologies.

IBM's approach is reminiscent of the old adage, "Charity begins at home." In broadening the engagement with network-centric innovation, starting from the inside is best by "opening up inside" before "opening up outside." This inside-to-outside approach allows the diffusion of the values associated with network-centric innovation broadly and deeply across the organization.

Getting buy-in from the entire organization requires not just getting the message out, but more importantly, building the "capability" for the managers in the different functional units and/or business divisions to recognize promising network-centric innovation opportunities and to "connect with" and share information with other organizational units that can act on those opportunities. If such a capability is created, then wherever such opportunities might arise—whether it is the marketing function or the global procurement unit—the organization will be able to identify, evaluate, and pursue them without skipping a beat. Ideally, every manager and every function should become a "personal portal" into the external world, constantly scanning the environment for external innovation opportunities.

Thus, in "building the faith" and "engaging the organization," the key question to ask is, *"Is your organization wired for network-centric innovation?"*

EXPERIMENT! EXPERIMENT!—AROUND VALUE CREATION AND VALUE CAPTURE

An important theme that we have gleaned from our discussions with managers is the need for continued experimentation—around value creation as well as value capture. As we suggested in our examination of the network-centric innovation landscape, several parts of this terrain are still not well populated and many of the innovation roles are new and ill-defined. This being the case, you are not likely to find explicit guidelines on how to pursue network-centric innovation initiatives. Therefore, you have to be willing to experiment and to make mistakes.

Consider the Creative Bazaar model. Companies such as P&G, Dial, and Staples have all experimented with different approaches to connect with individual inventors. For example, whereas Dial launched a company-hosted competition to directly connect with individual inventors, Staples used an intermediary to do the same, and P&G opted to deal mostly with value-adding innovation capitalists. In each case, the companies didn't have a clear understanding of how everything would work out and were essentially experimenting with the different approaches. As their initiatives progressed, they learned what worked and what didn't and they adapted their strategies appropriately.

In the pharmaceutical industry, companies such as Merck and Pfizer are realizing the importance of experimentation in their innovation models and processes. As we described in Chapter 7, "The Jam Central Model," alternate modes of drug discovery have led to new contexts for such experimentation for pharma and biotech companies—contexts that involve non-traditional partners (for example, non-profits such as The Synaptic Leap) and innovation outcomes that lack clarity on value appropriation and sharing. Despite the nature of such unpaved roads and the associated uncertainties, pharma companies are forging ahead by pursuing different network-centric innovation initiatives and addressing the issues as and when they come by.

The same experimentation mindset was visible in many of the other companies and industries we studied. In many cases, not only were the approaches not clear to the companies themselves, but they were also facing a number of questions from their network partners, too. For example, when Sun launched its OpenSPARC initiative, it faced a barrage of questions from the community members regarding innovation goals and processes, IP rights management, value capture, and so on. As Dave Weaver of Sun puts it: "To be very frank, we hadn't thought about many of these issues the members were raising (in the community) and so it was a lot of learning for us—first to understand the issues and then to come up with answers that would be acceptable to all."

Experimentation does not mean pursuing roles that don't make business sense for the company. On the other hand, it indicates the willingness to pursue those roles that make good business sense but whose details are not very clear at the outset. It implies the need to keep an open mind regarding the initiative so as to continuously adapt and evolve to get the processes and the governance right.

The key message for senior managers: *Promote experimentation and reward reasoned failure!*

LOOK BEYOND THE IDEA—ESCAPING THE VALLEY OF DEATH!

One issue that came up repeatedly in our discussions with managers is the need to have end-to-end capabilities to really benefit from network-centric innovation.

Much of the excitement about externally focused attention has been focused on getting new *ideas* to feed the fuzzy front-end of the innovation funnel. But you cannot eat ideas for lunch! Ideas that cannot be converted into commercialized products and services are of little use. When the innovative ideas are brought in from outside (whether from amateur inventors or customers or partners), they need to be shepherded through the development and commercialization process in order for the company to benefit from those ideas. Executives point to the "valley of death" that separates ideation from commercialization, where ideas get "lost in transition" because the commercialization resources aren't aligned with the ideation and discovery initiatives. We find that this is a common problem when sourcing innovative ideas from the outside, owing to the fact that often no natural home exists in a business unit for externally sourced innovation.

Crossing the "valley of death" requires two things: a set of structured, formal processes that integrate external and internal activities and a committed project champion.[3]

As we emphasized in Chapter 9, "Deciding Where and How to Play," preparing the organization for network-centric innovation involves paying close attention to processes for integrating internal and external innovation activities—for example, processes that bridge the gap between ideation and execution. Many of the companies that we studied did not have clearly defined processes to ensure that the product vision developed around the externally sourced idea is communicated well to and acted upon effectively by the people responsible for development and commercialization. Such processes should specify how the project will evolve and become part of the company's regularly funded development and commercial activities—that is, how the project will attract resources from established budgets, what decision processes and criteria will be used for project approval and evaluation, and so on. As the managers we talked with noted, lack of such process could lead to poor transitioning from ideation to execution, with major implications on the innovation success itself.

Creating clear organizational responsibilities for commercialization of externally sourced innovation in collaboration with business units is also important. Assigning informal champions for each project is one way to go, as companies such as Dial, Unilever, and so on have found. Such "champions" serve as the driving force in getting the project across the valley of death by owning the "business case" associated with the idea, by networking and connecting people across the ideation-execution divide, and negotiating to acquire appropriate organizational resources and capabilities.

Thus, before launching network-centric innovation initiatives, taking a step back to re-examine or re-evaluate your back-end product development processes and capabilities is a good idea. Do you need to revamp them to adapt to the new approaches that you are adopting? Do you need to invest in new back-end capabilities? Do you need to create new organizational roles? And remember, depending on the model of network-centric innovation and the role that your company plays in it, the nature of these back-end processes and capabilities might vary.

MANAGE THE NETWORK "PUSHES" AND "PULLS"

Organizations embarking on network-centric innovation initiatives have to acknowledge one important factor—dependencies! We talked about this earlier in Chapter 10, "Preparing the Organization." However, it is worth repeating the important role that dependencies play in such initiatives.

An organization's ability to manage the "pushes" and the "pulls" experienced in its interactions with the network members can become very important in ensuring long-term success. Managing these network forces might consume significant organizational resources. Decisions and actions undertaken by partners might disrupt or force changes in internal R&D plans. They might create new centers of resistances within different parts of the organization toward network-centric innovation itself. Particularly, if dependencies exist between a firm's externally oriented projects and its other internal innovation projects.

Such dependencies can exist in the different models of network-centric innovation that we discussed. For example, in the Orchestra model, smaller companies that partner with platform leaders such as Microsoft, Intel, and Salesforce.com often feel pulled in different directions when the market positioning and standards of the complementary technology they possess start diverging from those of the platform as the platform evolves. Similarly, as some of Boeing's Japanese partners discovered over time, their own internal plans (for example, pursuing long-term plans to be standalone aircraft manufacturers) might at times be in conflict with the decisions made by the larger partner.

In some instances, the larger firm might need to take care of such dependencies. For example, as IBM started collaborating with Open Source Software communities, it soon discovered that what happens in the Open Source arena has important implications on its other products/services. Some of these could be decisions to abandon internal innovation efforts in certain areas—for example, not pursuing the development of proprietary solutions that compete with the Apache HTTP stack. Some of them could be redefining goals and strategies—for example, modifying/adapting developing plans so as to leverage the evolution of the Linux platform.

The key message here is *not to lose awareness of the nature of dependencies* that your firm will be getting into when deciding to pursue network-centric innovation initiatives. Such awareness can serve as a trigger to reexamine periodically the company's internal innovation goals and decisions and its participation in the network-centric innovation initiative. This is important to make sure that disruptive forces that originate in external networks do not derail your company's innovation agenda.

WEAR MORE THAN ONE "HAT"—BUT, CAREFULLY!

In Chapter 9, we discussed how some of the large companies have started playing more than one role in network-centric innovation. For example, IBM has become both a platform leader (in its Power technology) and an innovation sponsor in some of the Open Source Software communities. Similarly, Sun has started focusing on playing the role of an innovation catalyst in the OpenSPARC initiative, in addition to being the platform leader in its core server business.

When firms wear multiple "hats" in network-centric innovation, they can take a more balanced approach to external innovation activities. For example, a company can take a lead role in certain initiatives and at the same time play a more supportive role in some other initiatives. The diversity of roles can reduce the overall risk involved in externally oriented innovation. It also facilitates the acquisition of knowledge or "learning" from a more diverse set of partners as well as a more diverse set of innovation activities.

However, a multiplicity of roles imposes additional costs for the company. For example, as we discussed in Chapter 9, "Deciding Where and How to Play," different roles call for different types of resources and capabilities. As companies pursue a portfolio of innovation roles, the diversity of competencies and infrastructure that might need to be established to support those roles will increase. While for many of the large companies such as P&G, DuPont, 3M, and IBM, the resource implications might not be too critical, for smaller companies these issues might be of particular significance.

Thus, the attraction of a "multi-player" strategy has to be tempered with the likely demand for additional organizational resources and capabilities.

REALLOCATE (NOT DECREASE) YOUR INNOVATION DOLLARS!

Innovation networks and communities indicate the considerable potential that exists outside of a firm to enhance its rate and quality of innovation. When companies consider this potential, there is a tendency to assume that they can reduce their investment in internal R&D. A key message from companies that have been successful in pursuing network-centric innovation is, *reallocate— not decrease—your company's innovation investments.*

In the short term, companies might be able to substitute internal resources with external resources and maintain their innovation agenda with lower levels of R&D investments. But it is not likely to work in the long term. Remember, your ability to derive returns from network-centric innovation is going to depend on the innovation assets and capabilities that you bring to the network. The greater the value of such internal assets, the greater the returns from participating in the network.

Thus, participation in network-centric innovation doesn't imply making lower investments in the company's innovation pursuits. However, it might lead to different choices for those investments. For example, some companies might invest more in downstream processes and capabilities whereas others might invest more in upstream capabilities. Reallocation of investment priorities should reflect the role(s) the company has decided to pursue in network-centric innovation.

Decreasing the company's innovation budget only lowers the overall capability of the company to participate in network-centric innovation and limits its ability to exploit the potential of external networks and communities.

DON'T FORGET TO MAKE MONEY

The flip side of the efforts to encourage and build the organization's faith in network-centric innovation is the responsibility for the senior management to let the company know that at the end, *the innovation initiatives have to contribute to organizational growth*—whether in the short term or in the long term.

As our examples of companies such as IBM and Sun showed, even partnering with innovation communities such as open source communities should be based on sound business logic. Many external innovation opportunities might look tempting, especially for managers who want to demonstrate their commitment to the CEO's call for action on network-centric innovation. In such a context, underlining the need for not abandoning the rigor with which decisions are made to pursue external innovation opportunities is equally important.

As one mid-level manager in a large consumer product company told us, once there is significant buzz in the organization about partnering with external inventor networks and communities, there is a tendency for the network-centric innovation initiative to *become an end* in itself. This becomes more evident when metrics such as "number of ideas sourced from outside" and "number of external partners" gain higher visibility than those that reflect the real impact of network-centric innovation initiatives on firm growth or revenues.

Senior managers can again take a very key role in emphasizing the need to link all network-centric innovation activities with the company's overall growth objectives. Thus, when Sun opens up its SPARC architecture and pursues the OpenSPARC initiative, it keeps its focus on the new markets that are likely to open up for its core products and services as a result of the innovation activities of the OpenSPARC community, even if it is in the longer term.

The lesson for senior managers is to make sure that the excitement regarding network-centric innovation opportunities is grounded in the company's revenue and profit goals.

ACTIONS FOR "MONDAY" MORNING

We started our journey by exploring the power of the Global Brain and by painting a picture of the landscape of network-centric innovation. Our journey has also taken us into a more detailed analysis of the varied opportunities and the resources and capabilities that companies need to develop to take advantage of such opportunities. Our primary objective in this book has been to prepare you, the reader, to be able to position your company as a player in the rich and diverse landscape of network-centric innovation.

Now that you have gained a deep understanding of network-centric innovation, it is time to chart your company's own path in this initiative. We have a simple mantra for this: Think BIG, Start SMALL, Scale FAST.

Dial Inc. provides a good case study of how this mantra can play out.

THINK BIG!

It is important that you consider the entire canvas of network-centric innovation and apply a wider perspective before starting to tunnel down to specific opportunities. Thinking big means ensuring that you are able to develop a coherent story that connects all of your innovation initiatives—even if some of these initiatives emerge or evolve over time. This is where the CEO's role in providing the "perspective" becomes important.

When Dial first started thinking of exploring external innovation sources—that is, going beyond its traditional sources such as suppliers and partnering with independent inventors—the company didn't focus on one specific initiative. Instead, its approach was to "think big" and focus on the value such external sourcing can bring to the organization in the long term. The CEO and executive management communicated to the organization their strong commitment to network-centric innovation by establishing an independent organizational unit—the Technology Acquisition group—to orchestrate such efforts. The message was clear—the company is building the foundation for the various network-centric innovation initiatives that are likely to evolve over time.

START SMALL!

After you have developed a broad perspective for your company to view network-centric innovation opportunities, it is also equally important to start with an initiative that has manageable scope and whose returns (or results) will be clearly evident. For example, do you have a particular product market or customer segment where you can launch your first network-centric innovation initiative? Or can you isolate the initiative to a particular geographical location or business division?

Creating a "clean room" for your network-centric innovation strategy so as to evaluate and learn from your first initiative is a good idea. Such an approach can also help you earn a quick "win" that can then be used to propel other initiatives.

In the case of Dial, the "clean room" was a simple Web-based initiative called Quest for the Best that the company launched to start connecting with independent inventors. The initiative didn't involve extensive investments in infrastructure or involve a large number of organizational members. While it was a relatively small program, it was very innovative. Dial was the first consumer product company to establish such a program that involved interacting directly with independent inventors and inventor associations. The results from this program were very positive (several ideas entered the company's development pipeline), and the program served as a "proof of concept" for the company's broader network-centric innovation strategy.

SCALE FAST!

When you have found success in that first initiative, don't forget to celebrate the win. However, more importantly, don't also forget to take things to the next level by "scaling fast."

Set a more ambitious set of objectives for the initiative, engage the different parts of the organization, and invest extensively in developing the organizational capabilities that would help you achieve those objectives. Your ability to rapidly engage the entire organization in the initiative will help it to take root within the company and attract more organizational resources and creative talent. It will also help generate more initiatives from the different parts of the organization.

Going back to Dial's example, the scaling of the initiative occurred right after the first inventor competition. Dial formalized the initiative and called it "Partners in Innovation." The interactions with independent inventors were made to be on a continuous basis and expanded to cover all parts of the company's product portfolio.

The company also rapidly scaled the program to be global in nature by establishing linkages with the R&D group of its parent company, the Henkel group. With this expanded reach, the entire Henkel Group of companies became potential customers for ideas sourced from U.S.-based inventors by Dial's technology acquisition group. The company followed this with a global competition, called the Henkel Innovation Trophy, which Dial's technology acquisition group is driving on behalf of all Henkel companies. This time, the focus for external sourcing is not just U.S.-based inventors but independent inventors anywhere in the world, and the target for placing the innovative ideas is not just Dial but the entire Henkel group. Truly global scaling!

Thus the moral of the story here is—"think big" and make sure the right perspective is adopted, "start small" to get that quick result, and "scale fast" to rapidly engage and involve the entire organization.

We hope that, as you put down this book, you can begin taking the first steps in applying the ideas and concepts that we have talked about. This is the REAL journey—the journey to pursue organic growth by harnessing the creative power of the Global Brain. Good luck on this journey!

References

INTRODUCTION

1. "Expanding the Innovation Horizon," IBM Global CEO Study 2006 (http://www-1.ibm.com/services/uk/bcs/html/bcs_landing_ceostudy.html); accessed on August 15, 2006.

2. For example, see Nambisan, S. "Designing Virtual Customer Environments for New Product Development: Toward a Theory," *Academy of Management Review* (2002), 27(3), 392–413; Nambisan, S. and R. Baron. "Interactions in Virtual Customer Environments: Implications for Product Support and Customer Relationship Management," Journal of Interactive Marketing, (2007), 21(2), 42–62.

3. See Sawhney, M. and E. Prandelli, "Communities of Creation: Managing Distributed Innovation in Turbulent Markets," *California Management Review* (2000) 24–54.

4. Sawhney, M., E. Prandelli, and G. Verona, "The Power of Innomediation," *MIT Sloan Management Review* (2003), 44(2), 77–82.

5. Management Tools and Trends Survey, Bain & Co., 2005.

CHAPTER ONE

1. "World's Best Innovators Are 'Six Times More Successful' in Getting Better Products to Market Faster, UGS Chairman, CEO and President Tony Affuso Tells Fellow Automotive Industry Leaders" (http://www.prnewswire.com/cgi-bin/stories.pl?ACCT=104&STORY=/www/story/10-12-2005/0004166925&EDATE=); accessed on August 15, 2006.

2. The blueprint for such large corporate R&D labs focused on basic scientific research can be traced back to a report titled, "Science, The Endless Frontier" written by Vannevar Bush, science advisor to President Franklin Roosevelt, in the final year of WWII. For an interesting discussion of how corporations have started shifting their focus from "research" to "development" and its implications for their internal "temples of innovation," see "Out of the Dusty Labs," *The Economist* (March 3, 2007), 74–76.

3. Source: FactStat MergerStat (http://www.mergerstat.com/new/indexnew.asp).

4. "World Class Transactions: Insights into Creating Shareholder Value through Mergers and Acquisitions," *KPMG*, 2001; "Why Mergers Fail," Matthias M. Bekier, Anna J. Bogardus, and Timothy Oldham, *McKinsey Quarterly*, 2001, No. 4; "There's No Magic in Mergers," David Henry, *Business Week* (October 14, 2002) pp. 60.

5. As reported in IBM Global CEO Study 2006; Bain & Co., CEO Survey 2005.

6. "Sony's Revitalization in the Changing CE World," Howard Stringer's remarks, CEATEC, Tokyo, October 4, 2005 (http://www.sony.com/SCA/speeches/ 051004_stringer.shtml); accessed on August 15, 2006.

7. Quote from Chapter 2 of *Through the Looking Glass* by Lewis Carroll, The MILENNIUM FULCRUM Edition © 1991.

8. Kraft R&D figures sourced from the presentation made by Jean Spence, executive vice president, Kraft on May 10, 2005, as part of Kraft Investor Day (http://media. corporate-ir.net/media_files/nys/kft/presentations/kft_050510e.pdf); Also see "At Kraft, A Fresh Big Cheese," Adrienne Carter, *BusinessWeek*, June 26, 2006 (http://www.businessweek.com/investor/content/jun2006/pi20060626_973843.htm).

9. The term is taken from the Red Queen's race in Lewis Carroll's *Through the Looking Glass*. The Red Queen effect was originally proposed by the University of Chicago paleontologist, Leigh Van Valen, in 1973 to explain the constant evolutionary arms race between competing species.

10. Dave Bayless is a principal and co-founder of Evergreen IP. To get more details on Dave's simulation, view his videoblog at http://www.evergreenip.com/ presentations/redqueen/redqueen.html; accessed on July 5, 2007.

11. "Kraft Looks Outside the Box for Inspiration," *The Wall Street Journal*, June 2, 2006.

12. "Research Stirs Up Merck, Seeks Outside Aid," *The Wall Street Journal*, June 7, 2006.

13. Source: Authors' interview with Tom Cripe on March 30, 2006.

14. "Innovate America," National Innovation Initiative Report, Council on Competitiveness, Dec. 2004.

15. "IBM GIO 2.0 Report" 2006 (http://domino.research.ibm.com/comm/www_innovate.nsf/pages/world.gio.html#).

16. David J. Farber; K. Larson "The Architecture of a Distributed Computer System—An Informal Description," Technical Report Number 11 (Sept. 1970), University of California, Irvine.

17. Foster, Ian; Carl Kesselman. *The Grid: Blueprint for a New Computing Infrastructure*. Morgan Kaufmann Publishers. ISBN 1-55860-475-8.

18. Exhibit A for this is perhaps project SETI—the Search for Extraterrestrial Intelligence. The general objective of SETI is to detect the existence of "intelligent" transmissions from distant planets. This is not a trivial task and requires significant computing power to analyze the vast amount of telescopic data gathered. The SETI@Home, launched by U.C.–Berkeley in May 1999, involves utilizing the power of home computers linked to the Internet to analyze such radio telescopic data and contribute toward the SETI goals. Any individual can participate in this project by downloading and running the SETI@Home software package, which then runs signal analysis on a "work unit" of data recorded from the central 2.5 MHz wide band of the SERENDIP IV instrument. The analysis results are automatically reported back to UC–Berkeley. More than 5.4 million computer users in more than 225 countries have signed up for SETI@Home and have collectively contributed more than 24 billion hours of computer processing time (current statistics on SETI retrieved from http://seticlassic.ssl.berkeley.edu/totals.html on July 5, 2007).

19. Network-Centric Warfare (NCW) is also called Network-Centric Operations (NCO) in some military quarters. In the U.K., it is referred to as Network Enabled Capability. Vice Admiral Arthur Cebrowski of the U.S. Navy is often referred to as the "Godfather" of the network-centric warfare concept. Other notable contributors to the development of this concept include Dr. David S. Alberts, who proposed the universal command and communications theory by integrating the concepts of information superiority and network-centric warfare, and John J. Garstka of the Office of Force Transformation in the United States Department of Defense (U.S. DoD).

20. "Network Centric Warfare," DoD Report to U.S. Congress, July 27, 2001 (report available at http://www.dod.mil/nii/NCW/).

21. See *Network Centric Warfare* David Albert, John Garstka, and Frederick Stein, CCRP, 2nd Edition, 1999.

22. "The Future of Supply Chain Management: Network-centric Operations and the Supply Chain," Terry Tucker, *Supply & Demand Chain Executive* 2004 (http://sdcexec.com/article_arch.asp?article_id=7285).

23. For a detailed description of Cisco's experience and the concept of NVO, see *Net Ready* by Amir Hartman and John Sifonis, McGraw Hill, 1999.

24. "The Networked Virtual Organization: A Business Model for Today's Uncertain Environment" John Sifonis, *iQ Magazine*, March/April 2003.

25. Several Web sites and blogs exist on the topic of network-centric advocacy. One of the better ones is http://www.network-centricadvocacy.net/.

26. "Network-Centric Advocacy," Marty Kearns, retrieved on August 20, 2006 from http://activist.blogs.com/networkcentricadvocacypaper.pdf.

27. Wheeler, David A. "More Than a Gigabuck: Estimating GNU/Linux's Size" (July 29, 2002): (http://www.dwheeler.com/sloc/redhat71-v1/redhat71sloc.html), retrieved on August 16, 2006.

28. "Internet Encyclopedias Go Head to Head," *Nature*, 438 (December 15, 2005): 900–901.

29. "Online Newspaper Shakes Up Korean Politics," Howard French, *The New York Times*, March 6, 2003.

30. Sawhney M., E. Prandelli, and G. Verona. "The Power of Innomediation," *MIT Sloan Management Review* (2003), 44(2), 77–82.

31. Huston, L. and N. Sakkab. "Connect and Develop: Inside P&G's New Model for Innovation," *Harvard Business Review* (March 2006).

32. IBM Global CEO Study 2006.

33. *Let Go to Grow*, Linda Sanford and Dave Taylor, Prentice Hall, 2005.

CHAPTER TWO

1. See http://www.ornl.gov/sci/techresources/Human_Genome/home.shtml.

2. See "Communities of Creation: Managing Distributed Innovation in Turbulent Markets," M. Sawhney and E. Prandelli, *California Management Review* (Summer 2000): 4294, 24–54.

3. See the "Coase's Penguin, or, Linux and the Nature of the Firm," Y. Benkler, *Yale Law Journal*, 112 (Winter 2002–2003). Also see *The Wealth of Networks*, Yochai Benkler, MIT Press (2006).

4. Visit http://wearesmarter.org for more details on this project.

5. A more formal definition of the Open Source has been offered by the Open Source Initiative (see http://www.opensource.org/docs/definition_plain.php).

6. Sawhney & Prandelli, 2000, pp. 28.

7. The term *Open Source* has been attributed to Christine Peterson of the Foresight Institute. For more information on the story behind it, visit "History of the OSI" at http://www.opensource.org/docs/history.php.

8. Visit http://www.opensource.org/.

9. Source: http://www.Sourceforge.net (as of September 2006).

10. For an extensive list of these Open Source applications, visit http://en.wikipedia.org/wiki/Open_source.

11. The definition comes from James Moore's 1996 book, *The Death of Competition: Leadership and Strategy in the Age of Business Ecosystems,* Harper Business. His earlier related HBR article was "Predators and Prey: A New Ecology of Competition," *Harvard Business Review* (1993).

12. See "Constellation Strategy: Managing Alliance Groups," by Gomes-Casseres, Benjamin, *Ivey Business Journal* (May 2003). Also see Gomes-Casseres, B., "Competitive Advantage in Alliance Constellations," *Strategic Organization*, Vol 1 (3) (August 2003): pp. 327–335.

13. Gomes-Casseres, B., "Group Versus Group: How Alliance Networks Compete," *Harvard Business Review* (July–August 1994): pp. 62–74.

14. For an excellent review of this strategy, see Gawer and Cusumano's book, *Platform Leadership,* HBS Press (2003).

15. See O'Reilly's article at http://tim.oreilly.com/articles/paradigmshift_0504.html.

16. For a discussion of the era of ferment and technology cycles, see "Technological Discontinues and Dominant Designs: A Cyclical Model of Technological Change," P. Anderson and M. Tushman, *Administrative Science Quarterly* (1990): 35, 604–633.

17. Authors' interview with Irving Wladawsky-Berger on April 7, 2006.

18. See http://www.infoworld.com/article/05/12/14/HNnovellibm_1.html; also see Yochai Benkler's book, *The Wealth of Networks,* where on pp. 47, he gives a graph of IBM's revenue growth from open source–related services.

19. Sawhney, M., Verona, G., and E. Prandelli, "Collaborating to Create: The Internet as a Platform for Customer Engagement in Product Innovation," *Journal of Interactive Marketing* (2005): 4–17.

20. "Staples Turns to Inventors for New Product Ideas," William Bulkeley, *The Wall Street Journal* (July 13, 2006; B1).

21. Interview with Jevin Eagle, senior vice president, Staples Brands (June 2006).

22. Authors' interview with Dr. Robert Finocchiaro, technical director, 3M (on July 26, 2006).

CHAPTER THREE

1. Visit the project Web site at http://www.aswarmofangels.com/.

2. See the Wikipedia entry on Current TV for more details: http://en.wikipedia.org/wiki/Current_TV.

3. "Uncle Al Wants You," *East Bay Express* (Jan. 26, 2005). http://www.eastbayexpress.com/issues/2005-01-26/news/feature.html.

4. Visit http://www.current.tv/.

5. "Hack This Film," Jason Silverman, *Wired* (January 2006): http://www.wired.com/wired/archive/14.01/play.html?pg=2.

6. See the article "MOD Films" on the Creative Commons Web site: http://creativecommons.org/video/mod-films.

7. http://modfilms.com/.

8. Morley, E. and A. Silver, "A Film Director's Approach to Managing Creativity," *Harvard Business Review* (March–April 1977): 59–70.

9. For a more recent article on business lessons from Hollywood, see "Hollywood: A Business Model for the Future?" Charles Grantham, SIGCPR Conference (2000) ACM.

10. http://www.echochamberproject.com/.

11. This is definitely a very limited and brief conceptualization of the core/periphery network. For more rigorous definition and discussion of the implications, see "Models of Core/Periphery Structure," S. Borgatti and M. Everett, *Social Networks* 1999, 21, 375–395.

12. As noted in, "Measure for Measure: Exploring the Mysteries of Conducting," Justin Davidson, *The New Yorker* (Aug. 21, 2006): pp. 60–69.

13. "Orchestra: A Users Manual" by Andrew Hugill, http://www.mti.dmu.ac.uk/~ahugill/manual/. Also see the Wikipedia entry for Orchestra: http://en.wikipedia.org/wiki/Orchestra.

14. See "Call and Response in Music" at http://en.wikipedia.org/wiki/Call_and_response_%28music%29.

15. See the entry for *jam* in the Online Etymology Dictionary at http://www.etymonline.com/index.php?search=jam&searchmode=none.

16. Mod (or, to use its full name, Modernism or sometimes Modism)—a lifestyle-based movement—reached its peak in the early to mid-1960s. People who followed this

lifestyle were known as Mods, and were mainly found in Southern England. Consider, for example, the TV series, *The Mod Squad,* which appeared in the late '60s. The 1979 film *Quadrophenia,* based on the 1973 album of the same name by The Who, celebrated the Mod movement and partly inspired a Mod revival in the U.K. during the late 1970s. For more on this movement, read *Mod, a Very British Phenomenon* by Terry Rawlings, (2000) Omnibus Press.

CHAPTER FOUR

1. See "The Keystone Advantage" M. Iansiti and R Levien, *Harvard Business School Press* (2004): pp. 94.

2. See "The Power of Innomediation" Sawhney, M., E. Prandelli, and G. Verona. *MIT Sloan Management Review* (Winter 2003): 77–82.

3. For these and other examples regarding IDEO's role as technology broker, see Andrew Hargadon's book, *How Breakthroughs Happen,* HBS Press (2003).

4. See "A General Theory of Network Governance: Exchange Conditions and Social Mechanisms," Candace Jones, William Hesterly, and Stephen Borgatti, *Academy of Management Review* 22(4) (1997): 911–945. In addition to this, there is a significant amount of research done in the management area on the broad topic of network governance.

5. Davenport, T.H., & Prusak, L. *Information Ecology: Mastering the Information and Knowledge Environment* (1997): New York: Oxford University Press. Also see M. Alavi. "Managing Organizational Knowledge" in *Framing the Domains of IT Management* (2000): Pinnaflex Educational Resources, Cincinnati, OH.

6. For more details on Intel's compliance workshop, see *Platform Leadership* by A. Gawer and M. Cusumano, HBS Press (2002): pp. 57–60.

7. See Inkpen, Andrew. "Learning, knowledge management and strategic alliances: So many studies, so many unanswered questions." In Cooperative Strategies and Alliances, Contractor FJ, Lorange P (eds). 2002. Pergamon: London; 267-289.

8. For a more detailed description of IP and its history, see "Intellectual Property— The Ground Rules" by James Conley and David Orozco, Kellogg School of Management Technical Note 7-305-501 (August 2005).

9. See *The Economics and Management of Intellectual Property* by Ove Grandstrand, Edward Elgar Publishing, MA (2000).

10. For more on Clark Foams and the surfboard industry, read "Black Monday: Will Surfing Ever Be the Same?" *The New Yorker* (August 21, 2006): 36–43.

11. http://creativecommons.org/.

CHAPTER FIVE

1. The base plane (787-8) can carry 200 passengers on routes up to 8,300 nautical miles while the larger version (787-9) can carry 250 passengers on routes up to 8,500 nautical miles. A shorter-range version (787-3) with carrying capacity of up to 300 seats will be optimized for routes of around 3,500 nautical miles.

2. The first order for the 787 was placed by All Nippon Airways—for 50 787s. The order, valued at around $6 billion, is the single largest launch order ever in Boeing's 88-year history. As of October 2006, 29 customers have placed orders for a total of 420 airplanes (of which 377 are firm orders worth around $52 billion).

3. Boeing and its partners conducted extensive research for two years prior to the official project launch in 2004 to investigate potential materials and to demonstrate the effectiveness of composite manufacturing technology. The new materials and design is also supposed to allow the quietest takeoffs and landings in its class, thereby providing an added environmental benefit.

4. Both engines are designed to provide the 55,000 to 80,500 pounds of required thrust. The improved engine design would itself contribute around 8% of the increased efficiency gains attributed to the 787.

5. "Boeing, Boeing, Gone?" by William Sweetman, *Popular Science* (June 2004): pp. 97.

6. "A Smart Bet," *Boeing Frontiers* (June 2003).

7. "Sharing the Dream," *Boeing Frontiers* (August 2006).

8. As quoted in "Boeing's Diffusion of Commercial Aircraft Design and Manufacturing Technology to Japan," by David Pritchard and Alan MacPherson, SUNY Buffalo, (March 2005): www.custac.buffalo.edu/docs/OccasionalPaper30.pdf.

9. Source: "Customers Get an Update from Boeing," Yvonne Leach, *Boeing Frontiers* (February 2005).

10. "Just Plane Genius," *BusinessWeek* (April 17, 2006).

11. "Firm, Toned, and Taut," Lori Gunter, *Boeing Frontiers* (November 2005).

12. See Dominic Gates "Boeing 787: Parts from around the world will be swiftly integrated," *The Seattle Times*, September 11, 2005.

13. Pritchard & MacPherson (2005).

14. Fingleton, E. "Boeing, Boeing, Gone: Outsourced to Death," *American Conservative* (January 24, 2005).

15. E-mail interview with Scott Strode, vice president of airplane development and production, Boeing (March 2007).

16. Boeing's slogan for the 2016 vision is "People working together as a global enterprise for aerospace leadership." Boeing explicitly acknowledges in this vision its role as large-scale systems integrator as a core competence. See www.boeing.com/vision.

17. Ibid.

18. "Boeing: New Jet, New Way of Doing Business," *CIO Insight* (March 6, 2006).

19. "The Evolution of Creation," Debby Arkell, *Boeing Frontiers* (March 2005).

20. "Boeing's Diffusion of Commercial Aircraft Design and Manufacturing Technology to Japan," David Pritchard and Alan MacPherson, State University of New York, Buffalo (March 2005).

21. "Sharing the Dream," *Boeing Frontiers* (August 2006).

22. "Wings Around the World," Adam Morgan, *Boeing Frontiers* (March 2006).

23. "The Evolution of Creation," Debby Arkell, *Boeing Frontiers* (March 2005).

24. "Outsourcing U.S. Commercial Aircraft Technology and Innovation," David Pritchard and Alan MacPherson, State University of New York, Buffalo (April 2004).

25. "Wayward Airbus," *BusinessWeek* (October 23, 2006).

26. EADS (2003 European Aeronatuci Defence and Space Company) EADS N.V. Financial Year 2002: www.financial.eads.net/docredozuk4.pdf.

27. CIO insight article.

28. Gartner report, 2006.

29. "Salesforce.com's New Gamble," CNET (July 26, 2005).

30. "Salesforce.com Buys into Google AdWords," CNET (August 21, 2006).

31. Author's interview with Adam Gross, vice president of developer marketing, Salesforce.com (November 2006).

32. "Envox Phonelink Now Available on Salesforce.com's AppExchange," *CRM Today* (October 11, 2006).

33. Author's interview with Adam Gross, vice president of developer marketing, Salesforce.com (November 2006).

34. "Salesforce.com Strives for the On-Demand Apex," Dan Farber, *ZDnet* (October 8, 2006).

35. "Salesforce.com Cooks Up On-Demand Programming Language," Stacey Cowley, CRN (October 9 2006): http://www.crn.com/sections/breakingnews/breakingnews.jhtml?articleId=193105561&cid=CRNBreakingNews.

36. "Salesforce Strives for the On-Demand Apex," *ZDNet* (October 9, 2006).

37. "Salesforce.com Launches AppExchange Incubator," *CRM Today* (October 10, 2006): http://www.crm2day.com/news/crm/120085.php.

38. For a detailed case study of Intel and Microsoft's platform strategies, see *Platform Leadership* by Annabelle Gawer and Michael Cusumano, HBS Press (2003).

CHAPTER SIX

1. See the P&G Connect+Develop Web site: http://pg.t2h.yet2.com/t2h/page/homepage.

2. See the P&G Web site: http://submitmyideatopg.com/submitmyidea/.

3. See "The Power of Innomediation," Sawhney, M., E. Prandelli, and G. Verona. *MIT Sloan Management Review* (Winter 2003); and "Connect and Develop," Huston, L and N. Sakkab. *Harvard Business Review* (March 2006).

4. Authors' interview with Debra Park, Dial Corporation on March 24, 2006.

5. "Inventing Better Outlet for Inventors," Scott Kirsner, *Boston Globe* (October 17, 2005).

6. See http://ww2.wpp.com/Press/2006/20060906_1.html.

7. Visit PDG at http://www.pdgevaluations.com/index.php.

8. Intellectual Ventures: http://www.intellectualventures.com/default.aspx.

9. "IV Moves from Myth to Reality," Victoria Slind-Flor, *Intellectual Asset Management* (August/September 2006), Issues 19, 29–34.

10. Ibid.

11. Interview with Stephan J Mallenbaum, Jones Day, NY (March 6, 2006).

12. Interview with John Funk on March 1, 2006.

13. Interview with David Duncan in June 2006.

CHAPTER SEVEN

1. Source: November 2005 Netcraft Web Server Survey.

2. Touiller, O., Olliaro PL. "Drug Development Output from 1975 to 1996: What Proportions for Tropical Diseases?" *International Journal of Infectious Diseases* (1999) 3: 61–63.

3. WHO World Health Report, 2004.

4. "Can Open Source R&D Reinvigorate Drug Research?" Bernard Munos, *Nature Reviews Drug Discovery* (September 5, 2006): 723–729.

5. Ibid.

6. William Jorgensen, "The Many Roles of Computation in Drug Discovery," *Science* (2004): 1813:1818.

7. Visit www.openscience.org.

8. Authors' interview with Andrej Sali, Stephen Maurer, and Arti Rai in November/December 2006.

9. Visit http://thesynapticleap.org.

10. Author's interview with Ginger Taylor on November 15, 2006.

11. Source: International HapMap site at http://www.hapmap.org/.

12. "Open and Collaborative Research: A New Model for Biomedicine," Arti Rai, *Intellectual Property Rights in Frontier Industries: Biotech and Software* (AEI-Brookings Press, 2005): http://eprints.law.duke.edu/archive/000000882/.

13. *Copyleft* is a general method for making a program or other work free, and requiring all modified and extended versions of the program to be free as well. See http://www.gnu.org/copyleft/.

14. "Avatar-Based Marketing," Paul Hemp, *Harvard Business Review* (June 2006).

15. Visit http://www.myvirtualband.com/.

16. Visit http://bioitalliance.org/.

17. "Redmond Forms Biotech Alliance," *Red Herring* (April 4, 2006).

CHAPTER EIGHT

1. http://steampowered.com/status/game_stats.html.

2. Zvi Rosen, "Mod, Man, and Law: A Reexamination of the Law of Computer Game Modifications," *Chicago-Kent Journal of Intellectual Property* (2005).

3. http://www.opensparc.net/opensparc-charter.html.

4. Authors' interview with David Weaver, Architecture Technologies Group, Sun Microsystems, in December 2006.

5. http://www.opensparc.net/opensparc-guiding-principles.html.

6. http://www.opensparc.net/ca_policy.html.

7. http://www.opensolaris.org/os/.

8. "Enterprise Open Source" by Simon Phipps (November 2006): Line56.com (http://www.line56.com/articles/default.asp?ArticleID=8034).

9. Visit Mappr at http://mappr.com/.

10. Visit the ProgrammableWeb (http://programmableweb.com/mashups) for a listing of all mashups.

11. "Mix, Match, and Mutate," *Business Week* (July 25, 2005): http://www.businessweek.com/magazine/content/05_30/b3944108_mz063.htm.

CHAPTER NINE

1. Authors' interview with Irving Wladawsky-Berger on April 7, 2006.

CHAPTER TEN

1. "Connect and Develop: P&G's New Innovation Model" by Larry Huston and Nabil Sakkab, *Harvard Business Review* (March 2006): 84(3).

2. Authors' interview with Tom Cripe, March 3, 2006.

3. Based on authors' interview with Dr. Robert Finnocchiaro, 3M, on July 26, 2006.

4. "Research Stirs up Merck, Seeks Outside Aid," *The Wall Street Journal* (June 7, 2006).

5. Authors' interview with Kodak executives—Gary Einhaus (Director of Research Labs); Kim Pugliese, (Head of External Alliance Group), and Richard Marken (Director of External Relations)—in June 2006.

6. Weed's law is attributed to Jeff Weedman, vice president of EBD at P&G.

7. Nambisan, S. "Information Systems as a Reference Discipline for New Product Development," *MIS Quarterly,* 27(1), 1–18.

8. "Northrop Gunman CIO Talks Collaborative CAD and Data Management," Manufacturing Business Technology (February 2005): 23(20), pp. 38.

9. Also see "Building Collaborative Innovation Capability," by Morgan Swink, *Research Technology Management* (March 2006): 49(2), pp. 37–47.

CHAPTER ELEVEN

1. See *The World is Flat: A Brief History of the Twenty-first Century,* Thomas L. Friedman (2005).

2. http://www.trendwatching.com/trends/MASS_CLASS.htm.

3. Source: www.nasscom.in.

4. http://www.nationalacademies.org/.

5. "The Rise of the Multi-Polar World," Accenture Report (2007): (http://www.accenture.com/Global/Research_and_Insights/Policy_And_Corporate_Affairs/ExecutiveSummary.htm).

6. See Jeb Brugmann and C.K. Prahalad. "Co-creating business's new social compact," *Harvard Business Review* (February 2007): 80–90.

7. http://government.hp.com/content_detail.asp?contentid=363&agencyid=0&mtxs=home-pub&mtxb=B1&mtxl=L1.

8. "Wipro Plugs R&D Service into Innovation Networks," Navi Radjou, *Forrester Research* (July 2005). Also visit http://www.wipro.com/pes/index.htm.

9. "How Accenture One-Upped Bangalore," *Business Week* (April 23, 2007).

10. http://www.siroindia.com/.

11. For example, Jeb Brugmann and C.K. Prahalad. "Co-creating Business's New Social Compact," *Harvard Business Review* (February 2007): 80–90. Also see C. K. Prahalad's book, *The Fortune at the Bottom of the Pyramid,* Wharton Publishing (2005).

12. "Innovation Ships Out," *CIO Magazine* (January 15, 2005).

13. "The Revenge of the Generic," *Business Week* (December 27, 2006) and personal interview with Michael Winnick, co-founder of Gravity Tank.

14. "Innovation: Is Global the Way Forward?" Insead & Booz Allen Hamilton Study, 2006.

15. Source: NASSCOM (www.nasscom.in).

16. One of India's leading economists, Jairam Ramesh, coined the term "Chindia" and wrote a book on the potential cooperation between India and China. See *Making Sense of Chindia: Reflections on China and India,* India Research Press, New Delhi (2005). *Business Week* later made this term more popular globally by launching a special issue on this topic (issue dated August 22, 2005).

17. "The BRICs Dream," Goldman Sachs Report 2006; http://www2.goldmansachs.com/insight/research/reports/report32.html.

CHAPTER TWELVE

1. "The Incredible Story of Tata Motors and the Rs. 1-Lakh Car," Robyn Meredith, *Forbes* (March 30, 2007).

2. Based on a presentation made by David Yaun at the Kellogg Innovation Network meeting, Almaden, CA (March 2007).

3. Also see, "Moving Technologies from Lab to Market," Stephen Markham, *Research-Technology Management* (Nov/Dec 2002): 31–42.

INDEX

A

Accenture's Life Sciences Center, 226
ActiMates Interactive Barney, 19
Active World, 147
activities
  adapters, 71
  agents, 72-73
  architects, 69
adapters, 71
addressable market, 185
advocacy, 22-23
agents, 72-73
Airborne Collision Avoidance
    system, 220
Airbus A380 mega jumbo, 97
AIX, IBM as platform leader, 195
Alenia Aeronautica, 90
alliance constellation, 34
alternate deployment
    opportunities, 207
Amylin Pharmaceuticals, 155
Annual Academy of Management
    Meeting, 3
Apache development, 139-141
Apache Software Foundation
    (ASF), 140
Apex, 102
AppExchange, 43
AppExchange Central Business
    Incubator, 108-109
AppExchange forum, 100-101
  AppExchange network, 103-104
  governance of AppExchange,
    105-106
  on-demand technology platform,
    102-103

Applied Biosystems, 155
appropriability regime, 80
architects, 69-70
architecture of participation, 38
ASF (Apache Software
    Foundation), 140
Automotive Supplier Jam (IBM), 242
awareness, 37

B

balanced approach to innovative
    activities, 246-247
balanced portfolio of sourcing
    mechanisms, 188
Bayless, Dave, 15
Benioff, Marc, 101
Benkler, Yochai, 31
Benoiff, Marc, 42
Big Idea Group (BIG), 121-124
Bingham, Dr. Alph, 198
BioIT Alliance, 155
biomedical research, 145-146
Blair, Michael, 89
Boeing 787 Dreamliner project
  globalization of innovation, 219
  Orchestra-Integrator model of
    network-centric innovation,
    87-98
book publishing, as commons-based
    peer production model, 31
BPO (business process
    outsourcing), 221
Bradley, Jean-Claude, 144
Broomall, Vern, 92

building faith in organization, 239-241
business ecosystems, 34-35
business process outsourcing (BPO), 221
Bye, Kent, 55

C

CA (Contributor Agreement), 168
CATIA (V5), 93
Center for Research in Innovation and
    Technology, 3
centers of excellence, 231-233
centralization, 58
certification, 105
challenges to innovation, 26-27
China, 221-224
CIC (community information center), 224
Cisco, 4, 22
citizen journalism, 25
Clark Foams, 80
Clark, Gordon "Grubby," 80
co-marketing, Salesforce.com, 107
Coase, Ronald, 30
Collaborative Drug Discovery, 155
collaborative experience (P&G), 203
Collaborative Molecular Environment, 155
collaborative projects, 67
collective sanctions (governance
    mechanism), 77
Collins, Mike, 121
commons-based peer production model, 31
communication support, IT tools, 211
communities of creation, 1
community information center (CIC), 224
companion planting, 70
company context, 47
competencies, ICs (innovation capitalists),
    127-133
complementors, 186-187
compliance workshops (Intel), 78
component developers, 186-187
computational drug discovery, 142
computer gaming industry, MOD Station
    model, 158-162
computing, network-centric, 20-21
conceptualization, 89
Conde Nast Publications Inc., 222
Connect+Develop initiative (P&G), 27, 114
ConnectNY network, 19
Consumerism, MASS class, 221-222
contextualization challenges (innovation
    opportunities), 27
continuum of centralization, 58

continuum of innovation sourcing
    mechanisms (Creative Bazaar
    model), 114-136
contract research organizations (CROs), 226
Contributor Agreement (CA), 168
conversions, MOD Station model, 158-159
copyrights, 80, 160
core (networks), 58
Council of Competitiveness, National
    Innovation Initiative report, 18
Counter Strike, 65, 159
Creative Bazaar model, 62-63, 113-114
    continuum of innovation sourcing
        mechanisms, 114-136
    globalization opportunities, 227-229
    idea scouts, BIG (Big Idea Group), 121-124
    roles in network-centric innovation,
        187-190
Creative Commons Attribution License, 167
Creative Commons initiative, 81
Cripe, Tom, 17, 135, 199
crisis in innovation, 14, 237-239
    limits of internally focused innovation,
        15-17
    opportunities to overcome, 17-19
    power of network-centricity, 19-26
    "Red Queen" effect, 14-15
CRM (Customer Relationship Management)
    market, 42, 101
CROs (contract research organizations), 226
crowd sourcing, 1
cultural challenges (innovation
    opportunities), 26-27
Current TV, 53
customer communities, Ducati Motor, 39-40
customer partners, Boeing, 89
Customer Relationship Management (CRM)
    market, 42, 101

D

Dassault Systems, 93, 211
decentralized nature of decision making, 153
Dell Inc., 12, 15
DELMIA, 93
dependencies, 245-246
dependency management, 207-208
detailed design phase, development of the
    Boeing 787, 90-91
DEV (Deutscher Erfinderverband), 120
Develop and Refine competency
    (innovation capitalists), 131
developer networks, 42-43

development
  Apache, 139-141
  Boeing 787, 89
Dial, 4
  Partners in Innovation initiative,
    117-121, 250
  Quest for the Best, 250
  Technology Acquisition group, 249
dimensions of network-centric innovation,
  56-59
direct-to-consumer business model, 15
distributed innovation, 3
Dreamliner (787) project
  globalization of innovation, 219
  Orchestra-Integrator model of
    network-centric innovation, 87-98
Ducati Motor
  as customer community example, 39-40
  knowledge management, 77-78
Duncan, David, 136
DuPont, 4

E

Eagle, Jevin, 41
EagleWision design methodology
  (Wipro), 226
eBay, 77
EBD (External Business Development)
  group (P&G), 17
Echo Chamber Project, 55
EIP (Evergreen IP), 124-125
electronic R&D marketplaces (3M), 44
ElekSen, 72
ElekTex, 72
Elements, MOD Station model, 171-173
emergent nature of the innovation goals, 152
emerging economies, 224
  consumerism and the MASS class, 221-222
  opportunities related to
    Creative Bazaar model, 227-229
    Jam Central model, 229-230
    MOD Station model, 230-231
    Orchestra model, 225-227
Emini, Emilio, 200
EMS (Emerging Market Solutions), 224
engagement of the entire organization,
  241-242
ENOVIA, 93
enterprise, network-centric, 22
Enterprise Edition (Java EE), 169
enterprise information systems, 21
envision and direct innovation
  (architects), 69

Eureka Ranch, 4, 130
Evergreen IP (EIP), 4, 124-125
execution challenges (innovation
  opportunities), 27
experimentation, 243-244
External Alliance Group (Kodak), 203
External Business Development (EBD)
  group (P&G), 17, 135
external incubators, 115
external innovation networks, 209
Extra Fox, 54

F

Finnochiaro, Robert, 241
firm-centric innovation, 4
first-person shooter (FPS) games, 159
Fisher Price, 19
formal mechanisms
  AppExchange governance, 105-106
  innovation networks, 76
forms, network-centric innovation, 38, 44
  customer communities, 39-40
  developer networks, 42-43
  electronic R&D marketplaces, 44
  implications for organizational
    capabilities, 46
  implications for range of innovation, 45-46
  implications for risks and returns, 46-47
  inventor networks, 41
  OSS communities, 39
FPS (first-person shooter) games, 159
Friedman, Tom, 220
Fuji Heavy Industries, 90
Funk, John, 135

G

gated network approach (governance
  mechanism), 76
General Public License (GPL), 81
Gentoo Linux, 166
geographically distributed centers of
  excellence, 231-233
Geospiza, 155
Gillette, Walter, 89, 93
GIO (Global Innovation Outlook) (IBM), 18
Global Collaboration Environment
  (Boeing), 93
Global Innovation Outlook (GIO) (IBM), 18
global partners, Boeing, 88, 93-94
globalization of innovation, 15, 219-220
  China and India, 221-223
  emerging economies, 224-231

geographically distributed centers of excellence, 231-233
preparing for opportunities, 234-235
GNU General Public License (GPL), 81, 161
goals, network-centric innovation, 36
Goodrich, 90
governance, 75-77
  AppExchange (Salesforce.com), 105-106
  OpenSPARC Initiative, 166-167
GPL (General Public License), 81, 161
granularity of innovation tasks, 38
Gravity Tank, 232
grid computing, 20-21
Gross, Adam, 102
growth, quest for profitable growth, 12-14

H

Half-Life, MOD Station model, 65, 159-160
Hanson, Matt, 52
Haplotype Mapping (HapMap), 146
hard synergies, M&A deals, 13
HCL Technologies, 225
Henkel Innovation Trophy, 120
Henkel KGaA, 117
Hewlett Packard, 155, 224
HGP (Human Genome project), 29, 146
hierarchy-based production, 30
Hindustan Lever, 228
history, network-centric innovation
  business ecosystems, 34-35
  modes of production, 30-32
  Open Source concept, 33-35
Homeworld 2, 160
Human Genome project (HGP), 29, 146

I

i-community (Hewlett Packard), 224
IBM, 4
  GIO (Global Innovation Outlook), 18
  Innovation Jam initiative, 242
  leveraging innovation networks, 27
  as OSS community example, 39
  portfolio of innovation roles, 194
  Power Architecture, 225
  Power chip innovation alliance, 59
ICDL (International Computer Driving License) Foundation, 224
ICs (innovation capitalists)
  Creative Bazaar model, 116-117, 124-136
  Evergreen IP (EIP), 124-125
  IgniteIP (IIP), 125
idea hunts, 122-124

idea scouts, 72, 121-124, 189-190
IdeaExchange, 106-107
ideation to commercialization, 244-245
Ideawicket, 228
identification of risks, 209
IDEO, 72
IgniteIP (IIP), 4, 125
Ikea, 222
incentives for modding, 160-162
inclusion community, 224
independent software developers (ISV), 103
India, 221
  consumerism and the MASS class, 221-222
  emergence of NGOs, 223-224
  technological and scientific expertise, 222-223
INdTV, 53
informal mechanisms
  AppExchange governance, 105-106
  innovation networks, 76
information sharing, IT tools, 210
information technology (IT) tools, 210-211
infrastructure, OpenSPARC Initiative, 166-167
infrastructure services (adapters), 71
InnoCentive, 4, 25, 44, 198
innovation, 1. *See also* network-centric innovation
  challenges, 26-27
  crisis, 14-26, 237-239
  distributed innovation, 3
  firm-centric, 4
innovation capitalists (ICs). *See* ICs (innovation capitalists)
innovation catalysts, 160
  MOD Station model, 173-174, 192-193
  OpenSPARC Initiative, 164
Innovation Jam initiative (IBM), 242
innovation metrics, 211-214
innovation networks, 1
innovation portals
  as Creative Bazaar model innovation role, 187-189
  Dial, 119
innovation sponsors
  as Jam Central model innovation role, 190-192
  TDI-TSL network, 144
innovation steward, TDI-TSL network, 143
innovation transformation (agents), 73
innovators
  as MOD Station model innovation role, 193
  OpenSPARC Initiative, 164
  TDI-TSL network, 144

Intacct Corp., 71
Integrators, as Orchestra model innovation
    role, 185-186
Intel, 78
intellectual property. *See* IP rights
    management
Intellectual Ventures LLC (IV), 123
Interknowlogy, 155
internal evangelism, 134
internal incubators, 115
internal resources, 186
internally focused innovation, limits of, 15-17
International Computer Driving License
    (ICDL) Foundation, 224
International HapMap project, 146
InventionQuest (Staples Inc.), 41
inventor networks, Staples Inc., 41
inventors, partnerships, 117-121
IP rights management, 79-82
    computer games, 160-161
    innovation capitalists, 132
    OpenSPARC Initiative, 167-169
    TDI network, 145
ISV (independent software developers), 103
IT (information technology) tools, 210-211

J–K

Jailbreak, 160
Jam Central model, 64-65, 139-141
    biomedical research, open databases
        approach, 145-146
    elements of, 151-154
    globalization opportunities, 229-230
    large companies, 154-156
    roles in network-centric innovation,
        190-192
    Second Life (virtual reality world), 146-150
    Tropical Disease Initiative, 141-145
Jansen, Kathrin, 200
Java EE (Enterprise Edition), 169
Java ME (Micro Edition), 169
Java SE (Standard Edition), 169
joint development phase, development of
    the Boeing 787, 89-90
Joy, Bill, 17
Jung, Edward, 123

Kawasaki Heavy Industries, 90
Kellogg Innovation Network (KIN), 3
Kellogg's, 227
Kieden, 109
Kim, Peter, 17, 200
KIN (Kellogg Innovation Network), 3

knowledge management, 77-79
knowledge transfer (agents), 72
knowledge-based tasks, R&D process, 142
knowledge-management mechanisms, 85
Kodak, 203
Kraft, 16

L–M

Lafley, A.G, 199
leadership
    organizational readiness for
        network-centric innovation, 205-207
    structure of network leadership, 57-59
learning potential, adapter role, 187
Lenovo, 15
licensing scheme (GPL), 81
Linden Lab, 149
linking members (agents), 72
Linux, 24
Logitech, 72

M&A (mergers and acquisitions) deals, 13
management
    dependencies, 207-208
    intellectual property rights, 132
    networks, 74-82
    risks, support processes, 209
mantra for innovation, 249-250
Mappr, 170
Market competency (innovation capitalists),
    132-133
market-based production, 30
market-ready products, 114
Mashup movement, 170-171
MASS class, consumerism, 221-222
Maurer, Stephen, 141
mechanisms, sourcing innovation, 114
mediation, agents, 72-73
Merck, 17
Meredith Corp., 222
mergers and acquisitions (M&A) deals, 13
Merwin, 130
Metaverse (virtual reality world), 146
metrics (innovation metrics), 211-214
Micro Edition (JAVA ME), 169
Microsoft
    ActiMates Interactive Barney, 19
    BioIT Alliance, 155
Miller, David, 166
mindset challenges (innovation
    opportunities), 26-27
Mitsubishi Heavy Industries, 90
MOD Films, 53

MOD Station model, 65-66, 157-158
    computer gaming industry, 158-162
    elements, 171-173
    globalization opportunities, 230-231
    innovation catalysts, 173-174
    Mashup movement, 170-171
    OpenSPARC Initiative, 162-169
    roles in network-centric innovation,
        192-193
modders, 160
models, network-centric innovation, 59,
    193-194
    choosing most appropriate model, 179-184
    Creative Bazaar model, 62-63, 113-136,
        187-190, 227-229
    Jam Central model, 64-65, 139-156,
        190-192, 229-230
    Mod Station model, 65-66, 157-174,
        192-193, 230-231
    Orchestra model, 60-62, 85-111, 185-187,
        225-227
modes of production, 30-32
MODification (MOD) Station model. See
    MOD Station model
modularity of the innovation system, 38
Moore, James, 34
Morley, Eileen, 54
Mulally, Alan, 87
MVB (MyVirtualBand.com), 150-151
Myhrvold, Nathan, 123

N

National Innovation Initiative report
    (Council of Competitiveness), 18
nature of the collaboration
    infrastructure, 153
The Nature of the Firm, 30
NCA (network-centric advocacy), 22-23
NCE (network-centric enterprise), 22
NCI (network-centric innovation). See
    network-centric innovation
NCO (network-centric operations), 21-22
NCW (network-centric warfare), 21
network governance, 75-77
network management, 74
    IP rights management, 79-82
    knowledge management, 77-79
    network governance, 75-77
network partners, Boeing, 91
network-centric advocacy (NCA), 22-23
network-centric enterprise (NCE), 22

network-centric innovation (NCI), 4, 23-26,
    29-30, 51-54, 67-68
    balanced approach to innovative
        activities, 246-247
    building faith in organization, 239-241
    company context considerations, 47
    contribution to organizational growth, 248
    dependencies, 245-246
    engagement of the entire organization,
        241-242
    experimentation, 243-244
    forms, 38
        customer communities, 39-40
        developer networks, 42-43
        electronic R&D marketplaces, 44
        implications for organizational
            capabilities, 46
        implications for range of innovation,
            45-46
        implications for risks and returns,
            46-47
        inventor networks, 41
        OSS communities, 39
    globalization, 219-220
        China and India, 221-224
        emerging economies, 224-231
        geographically distributed centers of
            excellence, 231-233
        preparing for opportunities, 234-235
    historical and philosophical roots of, 30-35
    ideation to commercialization, 244-245
    implications for innovation roles, 73-74
    landscape of, 55-59
    mantra for innovation, 249-250
    members, 68-73
    models, 59
        Creative Bazaar model, 62-63,
            113-136, 187-190, 227-229
        Jam Central model, 64-65, 139-156,
            190-192, 229-230
        Mod Station model, 65-66, 157-174,
            192-193, 230-231
        Orchestra model, 60-62, 85-111,
            185-187, 225-227
    network management, 74-82
    organizational and operational readiness,
        197-198
        innovation metrics, 211-214
        leadership and relational capabilities,
            205-207
        letting go of innovation process,
            200-202
        management of dependencies, 207-208
        structure of the organization, 202-205

support processes, 208-209
tools and technologies, 210-211
We Know Everything (WKE)
    syndrome, 199-200
positioning firm in innovation
    landscape, 178
    analysis of industry and market
        characteristics, 179-184
    portfolio of roles, 194-196
    requirements of innovation role, 179,
        184-194
principles of, 35-38
reallocation of innovation investments,
    247-248
network-centric operations (NCO), 21-22
network-centric warfare (NCW), 21
Networked Virtual Organization (NVO)
    (Cisco), 22
NGOs (non-profit and non-governmental
    organizations)
    emergence of in BRIC countries, 223-224
    globalization of innovation, 229-230
NIH (Not Invented Here) syndrome, 199
NineSigma, 44
Northrop Gunman, PLM tools, 211
Not Invented Here (NIH) syndrome, 199
NVO (Networked Virtual Organization)
    (Cisco), 22

O

O'Reilly, Tim, 38
objectives
    AppExchange, 104
    network-centric innovation, 36
ODMs (original design manufacturers), 232
OEMs (original equipment
    manufacturers), 225
OfficeMax, 232-233
OhmyNews, 25
on-demand software, 101
on-demand technology platform, 102-103
open databases approach, 145-146
open market innovation, 1
Open Source concept, 25
    filmmaking, 33
    hardware, 33
    intelligence (OSINT), 33
    network-centric innovation, 33-35
    open source curriculum, 33
Open Source Development Lab (OSDL), 155
Open Source Software (OSS) movement, 4,
    24, 33, 39
OpenJava initiative, 169
OpenSolaris project, 169

OpenSPARC Initiative, 162-164
    combining with other Sun initiatives, 169
    community governance and
        infrastructure, 166-167
    community members, 164-166
    IP rights management and value
        appropriation, 167-169
operational readiness, 197-198
    innovation metrics, 211-214
    support processes, 208-209
    tools and technologies, 210-211
operations, network-centric, 21-22
Orchestra model, 60-62, 85-86
    globalization opportunities, 225-227
    Orchestra-Integrator model, 86-98
    Orchestra-Platform model, 86, 100-111
    roles in network-centric innovation,
        185-187
Orchestra-Integrator model, 86-88
    comparisons with A380 and
        Boeing 777 projects, 98
    strategy, 88-96
Orchestra-Platform model, 86
    critical elements, 109-111
    Salesforce.com and AppExchange forum,
        100-101
        AppExchange network, 103-104
        governance of AppExchange, 105-106
        on-demand technology platform,
            102-103
    Salesforce.com initiatives, 106
        AppExchange Central Business
            Incubator, 108-109
        co-marketing and value
            appropriation, 107
        IdeaExchange, 106-107
        partner alliances, 107-108
organizational capabilities, implications of
    network-centric innovation, 46
organizational engagement, 241-242
organizational growth, 248
organizational readiness, 197-198
    leadership and relational capabilities,
        205-207
    letting go of innovation process, 200-202
    management of dependencies, 207-208
    structure of the organization, 202-205
    We Know Everything (WKE) syndrome,
        199-200
original design manufacturers (ODMs), 232
original equipment manufacturers
    (OEMs), 225
OSDL (Open Source Development Lab), 155
Osher, John, 116

OSINT (open source intelligence), 33
OSS (Open Source Software) movement, 4, 24, 33, 39

P

P&G (Proctor & Gamble), 4
  Connect+Develop initiative, 27, 114
  EBD group, collaboration history, 203
  External Business Development group, 135
  innovation initiatives, 17
  leveraging innovation networks, 27
  portfolio of innovation roles, 195
  SpinBrush product, 115
Park, Debra, 117
partial conversions, 65, 158
partner alliances, Salesforce.com, 107-108
Partners in Innovation (Dial), 117-121, 250
partnerships
  Dial Corporation, 117-121
  innovation capitalists, 124-127, 133-136
patented technology, computer games, 160
patents, 80
PC Pack (ActiMates Interactive Barney), 20
PDG (Product Development Group) LLC, 122
Perens, Bruce, 33
periphery (networks), 58
PES (Product Engineering Solutions), Wipro, 226
philosophical roots, network-centric innovation
  business ecosystems, 34-35
  modes of production, 30-32
  Open Source concept, 33-35
Pickering, Thomas, 88-91
platform leaders, 185-186
platform monitoring, 105
PLM (Product Lifecycle Management) tools, 211
PlugFests (Intel), 78
portfolio of roles, 194-196
positioning firm in innovation landscape, 178
  analysis of industry and market characteristics, 179-184
  portfolio of roles, 194-196
  requirements of innovation role, 179-194
    Creative Bazaar model, 187-190
    Jam Central model, 190-192
    MOD Station model, 192-193
    Orchestra model, 185-187
Power Architecture (IBM), 195, 225
Power Architecture Design Center (HCL Technologies), 225
Power chip innovation alliance (IBM), 59

principles, network-centric innovation, 35
  architecture of participation, 38
  creation of social knowledge, 37
  shared awareness and world view, 37
  shared goals and objectives, 36
process management mechanisms, 210
Proctor & Gamble. See P&G (Proctor & Gamble)
Product Development Group (PDG) LLC, 122
Product Engineering Solutions (PES), Wipro, 226
Product Lifecycle Management (PLM) tools, 211
profitable growth, 12-14
project management, IT tools, 210

Q–R

QPong, 160
Quake, 159
quality rating, 105
Quanta Computer, 232
Quest for the Best contest (Dial), 118, 250

R&D process, drug discovery, 142
Rai, Arti, 141
RAMP (Research Accelerator for Multiple Processors), 166
Raven Software, 161
raw ideas, 114
Raymond, Eric, 33
reach of the mechanism, sourcing innovation, 114
reallocation of innovation investments, 247-248
Red Hat Linux, 24
"Red Queen" effect, 14-15
Reduced Instruction Set Architecture (RISC), 162
Reines, Scott, 200
relational capabilities
  innovation capitalists, 132
  organizational readiness for network-centric innovation, 205-207
Reliance Industries, 228
reports, National Innovation Initiative (Council of Competitiveness), 18
reputational systems (governance mechanism), 77
Research Accelerator for Multiple Processors (RAMP), 166
reverse flow model, 134
RISC (Reduced Instruction Set Architecture), 162

risk
identification and management, 209
innovation architecture, 186
mitigation, 114
risks and returns, implications of
network-centric innovation, 46-47
roadshows (BIG), 121
roles, network-centric innovation, 184-194
Creative Bazaar model, 187-190
Jam Central model, 190-192
MOD Station model, 192-193
Orchestra model, 185-187
portfolio of roles, 194-196
rule-based tasks, R&D process, 142

S

Salesforce.com
AppExchange forum, 100-106
as developer network example, 42-43
initiatives as platform leader, 106-109
Sali, Andrej, 141
Samsung, commoditization, 15
Sanctuary, 54
Sanger Institute, 69
Sargent, Ron, 41
SBU (Strategic Business Unit) level, 179
Scalable Processor Architecture. *See* SPARC
architecture
Schistosomiasis project, 144
Science Commons initiative, 81
scientific expertise, emerging economies of
India and China, 222-223
Scripps Research Institute, 155
Second Life (SL). *See* SL (Second Life)
Seek and Evaluate competency (innovation
capitalists), 128-130
787 Boeing Dreamliner project
globalization of innovation, 219
Orchestra-Integrator model of
network-centric innovation, 87-98
Shaffer, Steve, 92, 94
shared awareness, 37
shared goals, 36
shared world view, 134
Silver, Andrew, 54
Simply RISC, 165
SIRO Clinpham, 226
SL (Second Life), 146-147
behavioral norms, 149-150
network and players, 148-149
Smith, Dan, 95
sniff test, 129
Snow Crash, 146
SNP consortium, 146

SOC (System On a Chip) design, 163, 225
social knowledge, 37
social mechanisms, 76
soft synergies, M&A deals, 13
software as service, 101
software development, 142
Solaris OS, 169
space, innovation space, 180
SPARC architecture, OpenSPARC Initiative,
162-164
combining with other Sun initiatives, 169
community governance and
infrastructure, 166-167
community members, 164-166
IP rights management and value
appropriation, 167-169
SPARCstation1, 162
specialized knowledge (adapters), 71
SpinBrush product (P&G), 115
Staples Inc., 4, 41
Star Alliance, 34
Stephenson, Neal, 146
Stonecipher, Harry, 87
Strategic Business Unit (SBU) level, 179
Strategies, Boeing's network-centric
innovation, 88-96
Streiff, Christian, 99
Strode, Scott, 92
structure
innovation space, 56-57
network leadership, 57-59
organization, 202-205
Submit & Win sweepstakes (Dial), 118
SugarCRM, 230
Sun Microsystems Inc., 155
OpenSPARC Initiative, 162-169
portfolio of innovation roles, 195
support processes, 208-209
A Swarm of Angels, 52
The Synaptic Leap (TSL), 144
System On a Chip (SOC) design, 163, 225

T

Taiwan Semiconductor Manufacturing
Company (TSMC), 71
Tata, 15
Taylor, Ginger, 143
TDI (Tropical Disease Initiative), 141-144
TDI-TSL network, 144-145
Team Fortress, 159
Team Reaction, 160
technological expertise, emerging
economies of India and China,
222-223

technologies, operational readiness for
network-centric innovation, 210-211
Technology Acquisition group (Dial),
117, 249
technology brokers, 72
tending the innovation network
(architects), 70
3M, 4, 44, 199
time to market, 114
Todd, Mathew, 144
tools, operational readiness for
network-centric innovation, 210-211
total conversions, 65, 159
Toyota, 22
trade secrets, 80, 160
trademarks, 80, 160
transaction costs, 30
trigger and catalyze innovation
(architects), 69
Tropical Disease Initiative (TDI), 33,
141-144
trust-based environment, Boeing, 94-96
TSL (The Synaptic Leap), 144
TSMC (Taiwan Semiconductor
Manufacturing Company), 71
Turner, Dr. Merv, 200
TV Pack (ActiMates Interactive Barney), 20

U–V

U.K.-based Wellcome Trust, 69
Ubuntu Linux, 166
UIA (United Inventor Association), 119
UltraSPARC T1, 163
Unilever, 4
United Inventor Association (UIA), 119

value appropriation, 180
OpenSPARC Initiative, 167-169
Salesforce.com, 107
value capture, 243-244

value chain, ICs (innovation capitalists), 127
Develop and Refine competency, 131
Market competency, 132-133
Seek and Evaluate competency, 128-130
value creation, 243-244
value nets, 21
value networks, 21
Valve Corporation, *Half Life,* 65, 159
Vendlink LLP, 19
venture capitalists, 115
Viewer Created Content (Current TV), 53
VizX Labs, 155
Vought Aircraft Industries, 90

W–Z

Walmart, 22
Warfare, network-centric, 21
The Watch, 54
We Are Smarter Than Me, 31
We Know Everything (WKE) syndrome,
199-200
Weaver, David, 166
web-delivered software, 101
WebSphere, IBM as platform leader, 195
Weed's law, 207
Wellcome Trust, 69
Wikipedia, 24
Williams, Brandon, 133
Williamson, Oliver, 30
Wipro, 226
WKE (We Know Everything) syndrome,
199-200
Wladawsky-Berger, Irving, 39, 191, 201
world view, 37
Worldcraft, 160
Wyeth Pharmaceuticals Inc., 226

Ⓤ Wharton School Publishing

In the face of accelerating turbulence and change, business leaders and policy makers need new ways of thinking to sustain performance and growth.

Wharton School Publishing offers a trusted source for stimulating ideas from thought leaders who provide new mental models to address changes in strategy, management, and finance. We seek out authors from diverse disciplines with a profound understanding of change and its implications. We offer books and tools that help executives respond to the challenge of change.

Every book and management tool we publish meets quality standards set by The Wharton School of the University of Pennsylvania. Each title is reviewed by the Wharton School Publishing Editorial Board before being given Wharton's seal of approval. This ensures that Wharton publications are timely, relevant, important, conceptually sound or empirically based, and implementable.

To fit our readers' learning preferences, Wharton publications are available in multiple formats, including books, audio, and electronic.

To find out more about our books and management tools, visit us at whartonsp.com and Wharton's executive education site, exceed.wharton.upenn.edu.

In five days, even Darwin would be shocked at how you've changed.

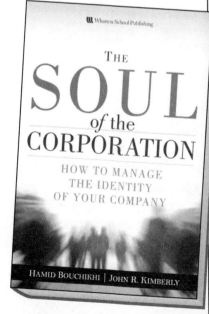